D0847570

ONE
WOMAN'S
ARMY

☆　☆　☆　☆　☆　　☆　☆　☆　☆

ONE WOMAN'S ARMY

☆ ☆ ☆ ☆ ☆ ☆ ☆ ☆ ☆ ☆ ☆

A BLACK OFFICER REMEMBERS THE WAC

Charity Adams Earley

TEXAS A&M UNIVERSITY PRESS

COLLEGE STATION

The paper used in this book meets the minimum requirements of the
American National Standard for Permanence of Paper for Printed
Library Materials, Z39.48-1984. Binding materials have been
chosen for durability.

Library of Congress Cataloging-in-Publication Data
Earley, Charity Adams, 1918–
    One woman's Army : a Black officer remem-
bers the WAC / by Charity Adams Earley. — 1st ed.
       p.   cm. — (Texas A&M University mili-
tary history series ; no. 12)
    Includes index.
    ISBN 0-89096-375-4 (alk. paper) :
    1. Earley, Charity Adams, 1918– . 2. World
War, 1939–1945 — Personal narratives, American.
3. United States. Army. Women's Army Corps —
Biography. 4. Women soldiers — United States
— Biography. 5. Afro-American soldiers —
Biography. I. Title. II. Series: Texas A & M
University military history series ; 12.
D811.E23 1989
940.54′03 — dc19
[B]   88-20181
                                        CIP

Contents

☆ ☆ ☆ ☆ ☆ ☆ ☆ ☆ ☆ ☆ ☆ ☆

Illustrations

☆   ☆   ☆   ☆   ☆   ☆   ☆   ☆   ☆   ☆   ☆   ☆

Preface

The future of women in the military seems assured. There will be for some time debate about whether and where women can serve in combat, but other areas of duty are well defined and relatively unrestricted.

What may be lost in time is the story of how it happened. The barriers of sex and race were, and sometimes still are, very difficult to overcome, the second even more than the first. During World War II women in the service were often subjected to ridicule and disrespect even as they performed more than satisfactorily. In the midst of doubts we adjusted to regimentation and learned self-discipline.

Each year the number of people who shared the stress of these accomplishments lessens. In another generation young black women who join the military will have scant record of their predecessors who fought on the two fronts of discrimination — segregation and reluctant acceptance by males.

The laws of the land have moved toward desegregation; only attitudinal changes and opportunity will assure integration. Some areas of our society have moved faster than others.

"Negro" was the accepted racial designation during World War II, although the term "colored" was also commonly used. "Black," now generally accepted, was a derogatory and inflammatory applicative before the 1960s. In this book I have tried to use the terminology of the times in which the events took place.

This is a tribute to all women who served in the Allied cause during World War II. It is my thanks for all the heartaches, hard work, and companionship we shared and for the lasting friendships we still hold dear.

I am deeply grateful to my husband for his encouragement, patience, and suggestions as I wrote this account. My special thanks go to my friends, David and Doris Ponitz, who believed in my ability to record my memories.

Glossary

OF ABBREVIATIONS AND SPECIAL TERMS

AGCT	Army General Classification Test	OCS	Officer Candidate School
AGD	Adjutant Generals Department	pinks	Color of dress uniform skirt (or pants)
AOS	Advanced Officers School	PK	Preacher's Kid
ASR	Army Status Report	POW	Prisoner of War
ATC	Air Transport Command	PR	Public Relations
C&R	Command and Reconnaissance	PT	Physical Training
		PTO	Pacific Theater of Operations
CO	Commanding Officer		
Com Z	Communications Zone	R&R	Rest and Recreation
CQ	Charge of Quarters	SHAEF	Supreme Headquarters American Expeditionary Forces
EFS	Extended Field Service		
ETO	European Theater of Operations		
		TC	Training Center
GI	Government Issue	TD	Temporary Duty
IOS	Intermediate Officers School	T/O	Table of Organization
		USO	United Service Organizations
MAT	Military Air Transport		
MP	Military Police	WAAC	Women's Army Auxiliary Corps
NCO	Noncommissioned Officer		
OC	Officer Candidate	WAC	Women's Army Corps

ONE
WOMAN'S
ARMY

Before

Even before my schooling began I had witnessed one of the most visible evidences of southern bigotry. From the second-story porch of our downtown parsonage my brother and I, seated on our father's lap, watched one of the largest Ku Klux Klan parades ever held.

When we started school, my brother and I lost our closest friends. Mitchell and Zena, the children of our Greek neighbors, had played with Avery (my brother) and me for the two years we had lived in the parsonage. From the day that Mitchell, the older child in his family, and I, the older child in my family then, finished the first day in separate schools, the four of us were no longer allowed to play together. Just as I had not understood about the KKK parade, I did not understand this event. Parental explanations did not satisfy; later in adulthood I recognized their refusal to teach hatred.

There are four children in my family (I am the oldest, followed by a brother, a sister, and a brother), and we were expected to perform well. My mother had been a teacher before marriage and never lost the knack; my father was a minister and educator, called to and trained for both. In our family, as in most Negro families, there was a special kind of closeness that fostered feelings of self-worth, personal dignity, intellectual ambition, and the value of sharing. In the early days my father's pay was often "in kind," mostly food and sometimes clothing, but even with a pauper's purse my mother had a philanthropist's heart. She shared with others whatever was in the family coffers; it was a way of life.

By the time I finished high school I had attended three different schools in the segregated Columbia, South Carolina, school system. The first school, Old Howard, was about a mile away from our house and was directly across the street from the city jail. Most of my schoolmates had to walk much farther than I. When my father's assignment changed, we moved out of the parsonage and into a house he had purchased earlier. My walk to the same school was now about three miles. These walks to and from school were socially important for the large number of us who walked together to the other side of the city; friendships, some of them lifelong, were established on these walks, as well as childhood memories.

Waverly School, the second school I attended, was less than a block from our house. When we moved into the neighborhood, the school was for white students, but after more and more Negro families moved in, Waverly School was made a "colored" school. I missed the long walks with my friends. Now other students had the long distances to cover.

We were always encouraged to bring our friends home, and in bad weather our house was a waiting place. September through November was the hurricane season, and frequently we were released from school early after a hurricane warning. Annie Mae Franklin and her brother Roosevelt lived farther from school than any other student—more than five miles, and they were among my closest friends. Whenever we had a hurricane warning, Annie Mae and Franklin stayed overnight at our house. Sometimes, depending on how early the warning was given, other students also spent the night. My mother always had the makings of a few pallets.

At the beginning of my last year in elementary school the class was tested and, based on our academic records and scores on these tests, about twelve of us were promoted, to be sent to the freshman year of high school a year early. I never made it. I stopped by home on my way to Booker T. Washington High School to share the good news with my parents. I expected praise, but they would have none of it. I was already two years ahead, having begun my schooling in the second grade. They feared that I would miss too much by skipping a grade at this point and sent me back to elementary school. I was hurt and embarrassed until I found out that only two sets of parents had permitted the promotion. Of these two advanced students, one graduated with the rest of us and the other finished high school a year later.

High school provided new experiences and opportunities. Now the walks to and from school were much longer. In the case of students in my neighborhood, we had to walk through a small shopping area in which most of the customers were white. As long as we kept walking, everything was all right, but occasionally very strong derogatory remarks were directed at us.

There had always been definite time frames our parents set for our arrival from school, but now the schedule was more relaxed. In spite of the flexible schedule, one thing did not change. My father had church members and associates all over the city, and our actions could be observed wherever we were. If we misbehaved in any way, talked too loudly, talked back to an adult, went in stores that were inappropriate, put on makeup, or if we girls got too familiar with the boys, our mother always seemed to have been informed by the time we arrived home. If we were punished at school, however minor the infraction, there was a second round of punishment at home. My brother and I belonged to the great fraternity of PKs, preachers' kids, and we were not expected to behave like other children.

As we grew older there came a gradual awareness of a black social order and a white social order, each interdependent but separate and unequal. Each side knew the rules even though the white order, having made the rules, included members who changed the rules at will. In general, children in their early years were protected by their parents from the harshness of the system.

Time was the best informer: on public transportation Negroes seated from the rear; eating places, depending on the ownership, served either Negroes or whites; certain stores and shops refused service to Negroes whereas others were willing to sell goods to Negroes provided goods were not tried on or tested. Negroes could buy anything they wanted if they showed the potential for paying the price and did not expect to be addressed as "Mr.," "Mrs.," or "Miss." It was puzzling that if they addressed us by anything other than our first names, whites were happy to address Negroes as "Doctor," "Professor," "Reverend," and "Attorney" even though these titles implied years of academic achievement.

For example: after I started teaching, my father secured a health insurance policy for me and paid the premiums for the first six months. As the time approached for the next premium due date, a company agent showed up at our house. It was June, and the whole family was sitting on the front porch when this white man came toward us and said, "I want to speak to Edna."

We waited for my father to react.

"There's a Miss Edna Adams here."

"I can't call her 'Miss,'" said the agent, "because I have to call colored people by their first name."

"Then you have to cancel this policy and never set foot on this property again."

Certain forms of address left over from slavery were perpetuated. Negro adults were addressed as "Uncle" and "Auntie" and, frequently, senior citizens as "Grandpa" or "Grannie." One day a white man about the age of my father drove onto our street with a vegetable wagon. He announced his wares in a loud voice. When my father approached the wagon, the vendor said to him, "Good morning, Uncle, how are things with you?"

Daddy looked over the fresh produce as he replied, "Fine. And how is your mother, my sister?"

The vendor was suddenly in a hurry and had no more time for our neighborhood.

Then there were the signs designating racial use. "Colored" and "white" entrances, "colored" and "white" elevators in a few cities, "colored" and "white" service areas in stand-up eating counters, "colored" and "white" restrooms. There were a few places that separated people by race and sex: the signs read "white gentlemen," "colored men," "white ladies," and "colored women." My friends and I had a favorite spot in a dime-store type of variety store. It was the only one in our city that had water fountains marked "colored" and "white." We knew that the water came from one pipe. We would go in the store loudly declaring our intention to have some regular milk and some chocolate milk. Even the white citizens shopping in the store laughed watching our performances.

As each of us reached the appropriate age, we were read to, taught to read, and read along with routinely. The house was filled with books, new and used, from the great books to modern novels. In addition, Avery and I read our fair share of "junk." Every week during the summer we spent a portion of our small earned allowances for reading material: we read all of the Horatio Alger books as well as regular issues of paperbacks featuring the likes of Doc Savage and The Shadow. Each week we would "go to town" and purchase two new Alger novels. After we returned home, we would sit on the front porch swing, going back and forth in rhythm, and read. We always finished about the same time, and without a word or a loss of rhythm, we exchanged books. Before we moved, we each had read both books. We whipped through these books so rapidly that our father began to question whether we were reading with understanding. For two or three weeks he actually read our books and questioned us about the content. There was only one plot — poor boy makes good through hard work and lots of lucky happenings — so that except for the minor details about which we were questioned, Daddy would never have known whether we read the books.

My father was a scholar; when he was well into retirement he could, and would, read Greek and Hebrew, as had been required in his seminary training, and he purchased newspapers in those languages at the newsstands. He was also very knowledgeable about all of our school subjects. His education had not come easy, and perhaps that is why his retention level was so high. There was no high school he could attend in the small farming community in which he was raised, so he left home to work his way through high school. He also worked his way through Biddle University (now Johnson C. Smith University) in Charlotte, North Carolina. Daddy used to tell us that after he had completed his first year of college, his father wrote asking if he had finished his schooling yet because he was needed on the farm. My parents were married shortly after my father graduated from college. Several years later they moved to Wilberforce, Ohio, where Daddy earned his bachelor of divinity degree at Payne Theological Seminary.

My maternal grandfather was a schoolteacher in Cokesbury, where Mamma and Daddy were raised. She was the oldest child in the family, and perhaps it followed that she was sent away to finish high school and prepare to be a schoolteacher. When they moved to Ohio, Mamma studied tailoring at Wilberforce, training that was extremely useful years later when we children had arrived. Both our parents watched over our academic pursuits, but Mamma had a special interest in our use of the English language, especially in the written form. When I went away to college, she began correcting, in red pencil, the letters I wrote in haste, sending them back to me. That process continued until my engagement to be married was announced in the newspaper. I did learn from her efforts. Once I saw the red marks on an error, I never made that mistake again.

Among my teachers in high school were a mother and daughter, both of whom influenced the direction of my academic interests. The mother taught history. She required us to memorize a chapter each night, but she also made us look for the influences and nuances of historical events. I still like to read history with an interest in cause and effect. The daughter taught some sections of junior and senior mathematics. I had discovered back in fifth grade that math was my favorite subject. Senior math was not required, so those math classes were fewer and smaller, filled only by those who liked the subject. I thus saw less of some friends because their interests were in other subjects. The teaching method used by this teacher was exactly opposite the one used by her mother. We were not required to memorize but to prove the equations, the propositions, the theorems, and thus to be able to cite them from knowledge. I was happy about not memorizing; I preferred taking the facts and arriving at the results.

After the required two years for general science and biology, I wanted no part of the other science classes. After taking four years of Latin, four of English and literature, four of math, two each of history and French, and all the other requirements, I was ready to graduate. One subject I never conquered, on any level, was spelling. My friend, Annie Mae Franklin, saw me through spelling, and I tutored her in the required math courses.

When I graduated from Booker T. Washington High School, I had not missed one single day of school. From very close competition I emerged valedictorian of my class, which permitted me first choice of the available scholarships. In the 1930s three of the most outstanding Negro colleges were Fisk University, Howard University, and Wilberforce University. There were scholarships of varying size to other schools, but my attention centered on these three schools. There were some small differences between the colleges in terms of social atmosphere and location, but I picked Wilberforce because it had the earliest opening date, a bit of information I refrained from telling my parents until years later. I have had no regrets about my choice.

As I prepared to leave home for college, Mamma made sure that I could take care of myself and my belongings, giving much advice and many warnings. Together we went over my clothes to make sure I would have what I would need, following the suggestions given by the college. I recall that we disagreed over the style of the evening dress I should have; her choice was definitely school-girlish, mine more adult. She won.

In addition to clothing, I would have to take the necessary linens needed for dormitory living, so Daddy purchased a wardrobe trunk. It was a very sturdy trunk designed for overseas travel, and he bought it with the idea that it would last the four years of college. It lasted, but we had to pay the excess baggage fee every time we shipped it because the trunk weighed 150 pounds empty, which was the total weight allowed on a ticket.

When I boarded the train for the eighteen-hour trip to Wilberforce, Ohio, my father's advice was short. "We have tried to teach you right from wrong. Just do right." What a burden that advice put on my shoulders!

I was the first child to leave home, and I was very excited. I was also scared. I did not know then how many good memories I had or how much I would miss the togetherness of our family.

College was a real culture shock. The students seemed so sophisticated I was sure anyone could tell the big-city kids from the small-town kids. Everyone was very friendly, and we arriving freshmen were a little envious as we watched the upperclass students greet each other. I was one of the taller girls among the newcomers and hoped that I looked like a junior or senior.

As an out-of-state student I was assigned to dormitory quarters in Shorter Hall, a large multipurpose building. The college administrative offices were on the first floor, with science and mathematics offices and labs on the basement floor. Floors two, three, and four were the residence areas. Besides my academic scholarship, I also had a student job, as did many other students. Seven days of the week I got up at 5:00 A.M. in order to sweep and mop (with wax or water) the steps between the basement and fourth floor on one end of Shorter Hall. To this day I consider that job to be the worst I ever had to perform. For maintaining my scholarship-level academic average for two quarters, I was assigned a less strenuous chore. I worked a student job all four years of college.

After that first year I felt more a part of the scene. There were so many PKs that we easily found common ground. I soon became involved in campus organizations and activities, among them the Women's Self-Government

Association, the NAACP, the YMCA, Delta Sigma Theta Sorority, the Literary Society. I even did some "punching," but not very seriously. The simplest definition of the word "punch" is "to walk on the campus with the boy- or girlfriend of the hour."

I had wanted to major in mathematics and history but changed to mathematics and physics on the advice of my counselor. Based on the credit hours I earned, I graduated with majors in mathematics, physics, and Latin, and a minor in history.

By my sophomore year I knew, as did everyone else on campus, that I could not carry a tune. On Founder's Day and commencement, Bishop Gregg, composer of the words to the university alma mater, usually visited the campus and enthusiastically led the singing of the school song. Several days before his arrival Mrs. Terry, director of the music department, would send for me. When I reported to her, she would say, "Now, Edna, remember. When they sing the Alma Mater, just work your mouth. Somehow, when you sing a whole section of the audience goes off key. Just remember, dear, work your lips."

During my senior year I took courses in the College of Education so that I could be certified to teach. And teach I did, in my hometown, in the same segregated system where I had been a student. Several of us who had been in high school together were back, now college graduates, teaching in a system where our white counterparts were high school graduates. Negroes had to be twice as qualified as whites for equivalent jobs. I taught junior high school mathematics and general science. I liked teaching, but my major accomplishment brought a top-level reprimand. I taught my math students the advantage of saving up in advance to make a purchase rather than buying by the "dollar down, dollar a week" (or layaway) system. One leading merchant complained. After that encounter I no longer mentioned the layaway system but continued to teach cost comparisons.

I taught mathematics and general science in Columbia for four years and, although it was pleasant, it was not challenging. I did, however, develop some traces of independence. I opened my first charge account and I bought my first car. Between school years I attended the summer quarters at Ohio State University. There was not much direction in my academic pursuits during the first two summer quarters. By the third quarter I knew what I wanted to do and I registered as a candidate for a master's degree. My major interest was vocational psychology.

As the years passed, I developed a real appreciation for certain homilies to which we had been exposed in the family circle. Their real meanings gradually became clear to me as they became applicable to events in my life:

—Don't advertise when you are down. When people believe that you are down, they press down; when they think you are up, they push up.

—Don't worry that people talk about you, just hope that the talk is good. The time to worry is when no one mentions you at all, for it means that you have made no impression.

—Don't tell a lie; you may have to tell a second, even a third, to protect the first one. Real trouble begins when you forget the order in which you told them.

—Don't look back when you have made a decision. You cannot change the past, and looking back only impedes forward movement.

I was nearing the end of my fourth year as a teacher when the invitation (it really was that) to apply for the Women's Army Auxiliary Corps arrived. The personal letter to which the application was attached stated that I had been recommended by the Dean of Women of Wilberforce University. The letter also emphasized career and leadership opportunities. I was sure that Dean Teal would not have made the recommendation unless she believed in those opportunities.

It was early in June 1942 when I mailed my application for membership in the corps. Because my hometown was in the Fourth Service Command, my application went to Atlanta, Georgia, the Fourth Service Command Headquarters.

I knew little about the military and expected the Army to be so pleased to receive my application that I would hear from some general within twenty-four hours. After a week of waiting I gave up in disgust and decided not to waste my time on an organization that was so slow in answering correspondence.

Having discarded the Army as a possibility for a job, or an adventure, I went back to graduate school at Ohio State University and forgot all about the Army. Forgetting was not to be easily done. When the Southern Railway's Carolina Special, en route to Columbus, stopped in Knoxville, Tennessee, I found my aunt waiting for me at the station with a message that I was to call home immediately. In this case "immediately" meant that I must try to call home during the fifteen-minute stopover in Knoxville. She had no trouble finding me because the "colored" coach seats were in the back half of the second baggage car. In case of an overflow, as frequently happened in September and June when college students were traveling, the "white" coach behind the baggage car was divided in half by a string, with the "white" section in back and the "colored" up front. This was at a time when long-distance communication was a high priority with the military, and I doubted my chance of getting a call through.

I did the only thing I could think of at the moment; I asked the conductor to hold the train. His answer was that he could not do that; the train would be late. It was what I had expected him to say, even though during all the years in college and graduate school traveling this same train, I had never heard of its arriving in Cincinnati on time. I asked if he would go with me to make the call. He had heard my aunt tell me to call home, so this white man had a tiny moment of compassion for a Negro woman. He followed me the few feet to the telephone booth on the wall of the depot building, where I made my call. When the time approached for the train to leave, the conductor became restless. I reached out of the booth and caught his coattail and held on until I finished talking, expecting any minute to be arrested for assault.

The message I received was that the Army had answered my application via telegram. I was to report to Atlanta, Georgia, by eight o'clock the following morning. From Knoxville, to Atlanta at that hour of the night (it was about ten o'clock in the evening) seemed a physical, if not a financial, impossibility, so I continued my trip. However, I could not forget that the Army had answered my application, and I wondered what I should do since I could not get back to Atlanta.

Upon my arrival in Columbus, I found several friends waiting for me, and I explained my dilemma. One member of the group suggested that I call Fort Hayes, headquarters of the Fifth Service Command, and ask what I should do.

In the meantime, as we ate lunch, I was told how completely out of my mind I must be to ever consider leaving the security of a teaching position to go into something as uncertain as the Women's Army Auxiliary Corps. My friends did not know that the uncertainty of the Army was far more appealing at this point than the certainty of the dullness and rigidity that the teaching profession had offered in the last few months.

Within two hours after my arrival in Columbus, I was in Fort Hayes looking for someone to listen to my problem about reporting to Atlanta. It was there I had my first real experience with passing the buck. For a while I thought the buck would never find a place to stop. I talked to lots of people, each in turn referring me to somebody else but never providing any answer as to what I should do. Finally, by some twist of luck, I was referred to a captain from Sumter, South Carolina, who had not been home for seventeen years. He was so happy to see someone from home that he forgot all about color, going to a great deal of trouble to help me. While I was in his office, he made two long-distance calls to Atlanta, with follow-up telegrams, requesting that my application and records be transferred to Fort Hayes.

The captain suggested that it might be a good idea if I took the physical examination that afternoon. At least I would know the state of my health. I joined a long line of women, Negro and white, which moved from room to room, building to building, and specialist to specialist, all of us changing to varying states of dress and/or undress as the examination required. It was really thorough. If I had had doubts about my good health before that examination began, I had none by the time it was finished. I was in good health. Completely exhausted and four pounds lighter, I was told to go home and wait until I was notified of further action.

I did not have to wait very long. Within three days I was notified to report for an interview, which I did. There were a number of women reporting about the same time. I was later to understand the look of disgusted annoyance on the faces of the officers we met. We probably engaged in the largest mass demonstration of disrespect for rank that has ever taken place. We treated all officers alike, expecting them to do gentlemanly things like opening doors and pulling out chairs. As for me, I thought that the Army was mostly made up of sergeants and second lieutenants as officers, and that personnel with higher rank stayed in Washington or on battle fronts. I did know that our country was at war.

The committee that interviewed me was composed of two distinguished-looking women of middle age and an extremely distinguished looking colonel, all white. I knew his rank because of the nameplate. They greeted me warmly and invited me to be seated in front of the desk. The colonel sat across from me, with one of the women seated on each side of him, all three smiling that sweet artificial smile that one uses when performing a boring duty. My file was open in front of the colonel. I was asked the usual "intelligence-determining" questions, some of which I thought were silly. One of the women asked me whether I did much reading, to which I replied, "I consider myself an extremely well-read person." She then asked me to tell her something I had read recently that had impressed me. I think my answer to her was my first experience at making a lengthy speech and saying absolutely nothing. If she understood what I was saying in my discourse on the psychological aspects of *The Sun Is My Undoing* (a novel about the evils of slave trading), she understood more than I did.

The colonel wanted to know whether I thought I could take a group of 10,000 women overseas and, with no other officers, feed them. My immediate thought was that it was an unrealistic situation; my second, that even with women the Army would follow the usual pattern of using Negroes for the hot and dirty work, such as cooking for and feeding thousands of persons. I found an answer: "If any other woman can, given the same training and opportunity, I can." The three interviewers smiled politely as I left the room. As I was about to close the door, one of the women leaned forward to look at the other woman and said, "Let's take her and see if she is as good as she thinks she is."

My cocky attitude and self-confidence left me as soon as I closed the door. I was appalled at my own behavior. I rushed to a chair in a nearby corner and sat down.

I had been so brave and so forward, but now I was ashamed that I had tried to show off. I need not have worried. I was only one of the many women who passed before "the committee" during the course of that day.

They had their laugh and forgot me as they must have done with hundreds of others.

I went home rather depressed, but it did not take long to convince myself that I had as much chance of being selected for the service as any other woman. Not having ever known Army wives or Army "brats," I assumed all women lived with some degree of ignorance about the military.

I began making a mental adjustment to an unknown future. When I realized that I was accepting the idea, I also realized that the only basis I had for my feeling was an optimistic hunch. I did not know how to prepare for going into the Army, but one thing I had to do was inform my family. My parents had not given much thought to the matter even when I showed them the application. I mailed the application, and there had been no further mention of the subject. Their attitude was that adults made their own decisions. At least, that is what they said, although I am sure that my mother's more immediate concern was whether I was planning to marry a man I was then seeing, of whom she disapproved.

She need not have worried. Suddenly I became aware of how much my attitude had changed. Back in Columbus in the company of my friends and associates from past summers, I had "forgotten to remember" the man I had been determined to marry. What a shock! I was going out with other people, alone and in groups, and not once had I remembered him! I knew how close to creating a personal disaster I had come when I realized that I would be annoyed if "he" appeared on the scene.

My father had occasion to be in Cincinnati on church business about this time. It seemed to be the perfect opportunity for me to break the news that I was going into the Army. I had not registered for the summer quarter since I was sure I would have to withdraw before the term was over, so I was free to take off for Cincinnati.

I found my father busy with his church meeting, and it was late afternoon before I could have a private conversation with him. By the time we were able to talk, I had been through all sorts of doubts about my assumption that the Army would accept me. I also worried about how my father would react to the news, provided it came true. I need not have worried. The conversation was short and to the point. I said that I was going into the Army.

Daddy asked, "Have you been notified that you have been accepted?"

"No," I replied, "but I have never felt so sure about anything in my life."

"How will you feel if you are not accepted?" he asked.

With great assurance I replied to his question, "I know it, I just know it."

He demonstrated the same confidence in me that he had when I left home for college, and he said, "We have tried to teach you right from wrong; just try to do right." This time he wished me well and said that he was pleased if that was what I wanted to do. Not once did my parents question my decision, not even during the period later when women in the services were branded as anything but decent.

That night I returned to Columbus rather pleased and grateful to find the same friends who a few days earlier had advised me against this unpredictable adventure now accepting my Army future with even more certainty than I. They spread the word; they discussed every detail they read or imagined; they searched newspapers and magazines for any publicity about the WAAC. They took sides in the various arguments for and against the use of women in the service, and speculated on the assignments women would be given and on their chances of promotion. They anticipated prejudice and discrimination in the Army and demeaned the type of women who would join the WAAC, at the same time praised me for my courage. A few secretly acquired application blanks but failed to file them because they feared condemnation.

I expected some attention from my friends and immediate associates, but I was amazed at the sudden interest people whom I barely knew developed in my welfare. Being human, I did develop a little ego, accepting their concern with questionable modesty, as if I had already accomplished something.

In a short time I recognized the basis for public concern. In the society of the forties, great effort was exerted to prohibit the appearance of Negroes in any activity that even smacked of the unusual, of being honorable, and especially of being first. Even in the battle areas Negroes were denied the opportunity to fight for their country and were kept in the dirty and most unmilitary positions as the unsung support personnel.

13 July–19 July 1942

One morning a letter with an unfamiliar return address arrived in the mail. I looked at it curiously, having no idea how familiar I would become with envelopes marked "Army Service Forces."

My strong faith had paid off. I had been accepted by the Women's Army Auxiliary Corps. I was to report either 13 July or 18 July to be sworn in. That was definite enough. If I reported on 13 July, I would be sworn in and put on furlough for a week. If I reported on 18 July, I should come prepared to leave immediately from Fort Hayes, Ohio, for Des Moines, Iowa. To make things easier, I had a way out. If I did not choose to go into the Army, I did not have to report.

Even with the knowledge that there were many other women receiving notices like mine, how special I felt! Not that the Army had done me any favor by accepting me, but rather that the Army had gone to the trouble to find me and to want all that I had to offer.

There were other papers attached to the letter: instructions about time and place to report, what supplies and clothing we were to have with us. I rushed out to share the news with my friends.

On Monday morning, 13 July 1942, I reported to Fort Hayes and was sworn into the WAAC. There were eight of us on that morning, and I happened to be the only Negro in the group. As our names were called out in alphabetical order, we lined up. The sergeant who read our names did not realize that the first person on the list was a Negro and, as our WAAC serial numbers were issued in that order, I was given the first number from the Fifth Service Command—A500001. That same afternoon the *Colum-*

bus Dispatch, a daily, carried individual pictures of us on the front page. And from the accompanying article we learned more about each other than we would have in conversation. The photograph of me was a real indication of how much I had yet to learn about military life.

Having been sworn in, I felt a real letdown, for my anticipation had not gone beyond that point. That is when the fear set in. What had I gotten myself into? Had it not been for my friends, I think I would have backed out. The swearing-in ceremony and the news story that followed had made each of us into minor celebrities. My friends, acquaintances, and even strangers rallied around me, gave me special attention. I, a Negro, had my picture on the front page of a white daily without having done anything criminal, a most unusual situation that added to the community's support of my actions.

I received much assistance with my purchasing and packing, and I spent money that could have been saved. The recommended list of supplies ranged from a hot water bottle and penknife to shorts and slacks, and I made a conscientious effort to secure every item on the list except the slacks and shorts. I had never owned either, feeling that I was not the type to wear them, and now was not the time to begin. My summer civilian clothes had to be shipped home; I kept for my use, while awaiting uniforms, two outfits I thought were really "sharp." Using my trunk and a series of boxes, I managed to send all my possessions back to South Carolina.

On Saturday morning, 18 July 1942, I reported to Fort Hayes ready for travel to the First WAAC Training Center. Those of us who had been sworn in on Monday just stood around while the rest of the group took the oath. With everything and everyone in readiness for the trip, we gathered for one last newspaper picture before we departed the post for our new lives.

Now, at last, we had assembled the quota from the Fifth Service Command for the first officer candidate class of the WAAC. There were twenty-five of us. Two other women were of approximately the same shade of tan, or brown, as I was, so I knew that there were at least two more Negroes. Not until we arrived at Fort Des Moines and were sent to our segregated quarters did I find out that there actually were five of us in the Ohio contingent who were Negroes. I had suspected but it had not occurred to me to inquire into the racial identity of my associates.

We left Fort Hayes in one station wagon and one truck, a type I came to know well as a 6 × 6, and were marched directly into a Pullman car. The care with which we were protected made us wonder whether it was feared we would escape, or that an unauthorized person might join us. Sleeping accommodations were strictly according to the Army system, two in a lower berth and one in an upper. The choice of berth-mate was done by friendship, and, since I was more closely associated with those women who were sworn in at the same time I was, I shared a lower berth with a young white woman who had been a member of the faculty at Ohio State University.

That was probably the last unregulated choice I would make in almost four years. One member of the group was designated as being "in charge," which meant that she carried all the records. The train then pulled out. The trip was very pleasant, and there was lots and lots of conversation. We talked about our families, our careers, and our patriotism. The only event that seemed of significance was that the air-conditioning broke down before we arrived in Toledo and, when we finally did arrive there, we were moved to another Pullman car. Our route took us through Chicago, where our coach was transferred to the Rock Island Railroad Line, a rail system I would come to know well. We were awakened the following morning, outside Des Moines, Iowa, with just enough time to perform a hasty wash-up and dress.

It was a dreary, rainy day on 19 July when we got off the train in Des Moines. Right away I learned that the weather could be predicted by whether WAAC recruits were arriving at Fort Des Moines. Later in my stay at the training center I would call headquarters to inquire about the arrival of recruits if my plans were related to weather conditions, for it seemed as if we had set the weather pattern for all recruits who were to follow us. We were told to line up by twos, and we marched into an alley near the station, where, before we boarded trucks, we were allowed to stand in the dampness until our feet were cold. The alley where we stood had been carefully picked. It was very long, and the walls on each side were very high, forbidding even a glimpse of the city. I was stationed at Fort Des Moines for nearly three years and came to know the city and its surroundings quite well, but I was never able to find that alley again, even though I made many trips from that same railroad station.

The truck ride to Fort Des Moines seemed very long as we bounced around in the back of the vehicle. Actually, it was only three miles, but with our mixed feelings of anticipation, excitement, fear, and fatigue it seemed endless. We were unaccustomed to riding in trucks, so we fell all over each other whenever the truck made a turn; we missed no experience associated with truck transport.

Fort Des Moines was a cavalry post of long standing, established before the cavalry was mechanized. It was so beautiful and well kept, one would never think of it as military. On the immediate right as one entered the main gate was part of the golf course, which ran across the post behind the homes for officers. The spacious parade ground was in front, and to the right and across this expanse was a street of barracks that would become known in WAACdom as OC Row. At the far end of the parade grounds the streets, which cut off that end of the field, circled a bandstand, and on the distant half-circle were the homes of the top-ranking

Headquarters, First WAC Training Center, Fort Des Moines, Iowa

officers. On the left as we came onto the post was the officers club and, after crossing officers row, the post chapel, post theater, post headquarters, the guard house, and the post exchange. The street behind OC Row was known as Stable Row, for here were the buildings that had been converted from stables to Training Center facilities. Behind this was another street on which could be found various warehouses, engineering offices, and general utility installations. Fort Des Moines was a small post, but in my ignorance I thought it was enormous. Later I would love the place for its security and permanence for me; but from the beginning I admired it for its serene beauty.

Our first stop on that dreary morning was at the Consolidated Mess Hall, a yellow building on Stable Row, which had been newly constructed to feed the women who were to train at the post. True to the tradition we were making, we had to step from the truck right into mud. In a line, of course, we marched into the building and right up to the steam tables, where we were served our first mess hall meal.

It was about this time that I became aware of the reporters—an awareness I have kept ever since. We had had a small experience with the press before we left Columbus, but that was nothing compared to what was in

The post guard house, Fort Des Moines

store for us. We were talked to and photographed, we held forks as directed, or continued eating as directed. We stood, sat, or saluted (which we did not know how to do). Eating does not make for glamorous pictures, so I have reserved for my private files pictures from *Liberty Magazine* that showed me with my mouth open as I shoveled in a forkful of food. All of this media pressure was to remain with us for quite a long time; every move we made was watched and recorded.

Those of us who had traveled from Fort Hayes together had some feeling of closeness because we had started out together on our adventure: race, color, age, finances, social class, all of these had been pushed aside on our trip to Fort Des Moines. The Army soon shattered whatever closeness we had felt. When we left the mess hall we were marched by twos to one of the stable buildings known as the Reception Center. We all sat down, but not for very long. Almost immediately a young, red-haired second lieutenant stood in front of us and said, "Will all the colored girls move over on this side." He pointed to an isolated group of seats.

There was a moment of stunned silence, for even in the United States of the forties it did not occur to us that this could happen. The integration

The post chapel, Fort Des Moines

of our trip did not prepare us for this. What made things worse was that after the "colored girls" had been pushed to the side, all the rest of the women were called by name to join a group to be led to their quarters. Why could not the "colored girls" be called by name to go to their quarters rather than be isolated by race?

When we did arrive at Quarters 54, our own segregated building, we found another young woman who had arrived several days earlier and had been living in the building alone because she was a Negro. A few of us may have had some idea what an Army barracks would be, but most of us were in for a surprise about how we were to live. We were introduced to some non-coms, male and white, who were to be responsible, along with the company officers, for our training. We also found out that we belonged to the First Company of the First Training Regiment and, this we should have expected, we were in the Third Platoon of three.

The day was still young when we finished settling in our barracks, having picked a living space and checked out the facilities available to us. We unpacked as much as possible and began a period of waiting that, for a while, seemed more like a wake. Once in a while one of the non-coms would pop in for a minute to ask if we needed anything, to tell us a little more about the post, and pop out again. In the meantime other groups of women were arriving. As each group arrived, we exchanged greetings and small bits of personal information. Those of us who had come early in the day began to feel like real veterans by the time the last groups arrived. We sort of took charge of the new people, helping them to settle in.

Late in the afternoon the commanding officer of the Training Center came to Barracks 54 to call on us, and, after a bit of general conversation and welcoming words, Colonel Faith apologized for the fact that we were segregated. He assured us that it was not his idea, that he had hoped that it would not be so, but that he was just following Army policy. I felt then, and a year later had an opportunity to express that feeling to the colonel, that his apology was made to ease his own feeling of guilt about not being in a position to see that the WAAC be integrated.

Even though segregated, our quarters were like the others, as we later found out. There were two floors of large rooms that accommodated about ten to eighteen women. We each had a tall locker behind the head of the bed and footlocker at the foot. We would soon learn that all of our possessions had to be stored in those two containers and had to be arranged in precise military order. The showers, toilets, basins, and laundry equipment were in the basement. These were adequate if no one lingered too long over her activities. The adjustment that was most difficult to handle was the lack of privacy. Individual shower stalls and wash basin cubicles were things of our past.

Shortly after we marched back to the barracks from supper, I was summoned to the company orderly room, which was in Building 55 across the street where the First Platoon (white) was housed. I was told that I was to be CQ in 54 for that evening. I had caught that duty because my name, Adams, was first on the alphabetical roster. My duties were to receive other personnel coming in that night, to assign them to beds, and to make sure that everything was in order during the night. Several groups did come in during the night, the last one arriving about four in the morning. When this last group arrived, I put on my bright red (and beautiful, I thought) housecoat and met them at the door. At the time I was in my early twenties, so I was rather shocked when one of the women, obviously a number of years older than I, turned to me as I was showing her to her bed and asked if I were the housemother.

After performing my duties all night and performing them well, I hope, I found out the next day that CQ was army language for "Charge of Quarters."

20 July–28 August 1942

The members of this first class continued to arrive during the next few days, and by Wednesday the Third Platoon had all reported to Fort Des Moines. We were thirty-nine strong, eagerly awaiting the arrival of number forty. She never did get there, so we were short one of the 10 percent that had been allotted for Negro women, supposedly based on the percentage of the population we represented. I have since met several women, in various cities, each of whom claimed to have been number forty and each offering an unsatisfactory excuse for not reporting. In spite of our hatred of discrimination and prejudice, we did want our quota filled because, as we understood it, other women's service organizations then under consideration did not plan to use Negro women.

The thirty-nine women in the Third Platoon, First Company, First WAAC Training Center were

Charity E. Adams	Thelma J. Cayton
Francis C. Alexander	Cleo V. Daniels
Myrtle E. Anderson	Natalie F. Donaldson
Violet W. Askins	Sarah E. Emmert
Verneal M. Austin	Geneva V. Ferguson
Mary A. Bordeaux	Ruth L. Freeman
Geraldine G. Bright	Evelyn F. Greene
Annie L. Brown	Elizabeth C. Hampton
Abbie N. Campbell	Vera A. Harrison
Vera G. Campbell	Bessie M. Jarrett
Mildred E. Carter	Dovey M. Johnson

Alice M. Jones	Sarah E. Murphy
Mary F. Kearney	Doris M. Norrel
May L. Lewis	Mildred L. Osby
Ruth A. Lucas	Gertrude J. Peebles
Veolis H. Lynch	Corrie S. Sherard
Ina M. MacFadden	Jessie L. Ward
Charline J. May	Harriet M. West
Mary L. Miller	Harriette B. White
Glendora Moore	

We were thirty-nine different personalities, from different family backgrounds and different vocational experiences. If our platoon had been referred to as thirty-nine "characters," it was meant to be complimentary. We were single women, married women, divorcees, fiancées. We were the ambitious, the patriotic, the adventurous. We were whomever our environments had made us, and that was what we had to contribute to the WAAC. The one thing we had in common, besides race, was that we had voluntarily become members of the military. As with our thirty-nine, if there were 439 members of the first officer candidate class, there were 439 unique people to start the machinery in motion.

Our reasons for joining the WAAC were varied:

"My husband is in the Army and I felt that I could help him get home sooner." This desire to hasten the end of the war applied when there were boyfriends, fathers, sons, and brothers in the service. In one case there were no young men in the family, so a daughter joined the military.

"It was time to make a change, and this seemed a good opportunity."

"I know that the draft is going to get my fiancé."

"I wanted to go back to work." And on and on.

We were all part of the same culture, we and the other Negro women who joined the corps during the war. The thirty-nine of us were more carefully sorted out and selected for the first officer candidate class, but we shared the same hopes and disappointments.

In the era leading to World War II there were no real and highly visible class distinctions among Negroes as developed during the years following the war. We were all Negroes, some with more education than others, some who had better-paying jobs than others, some who lived in less segregated environments than others, some from more structured and stable families than others. The experiences we shared were discrimination in the nation's mores and legalized segregation in many sections of the country. Following the Great Depression of the late thirties, the job picture had worsened for Negroes. "Last hired, first fired" became the pattern in industry. When economic times were severe, even domestic help was frequently sacrificed.

By 1940 the war had begun in Europe and the thunderclouds were in the air over the United States, accompanied by the economic growth of "preparedness" and a general feeling of patriotism. In the South there was a sudden demand for Negro household help because the white matrons were joining the defense effort. In other sections of the country both Negro and white matrons were joining the work force on assembly lines, side by side. When needed, mothers and grandmothers who had never worked outside the home became wage earners.

Where there was an institution, other than traditional Negro universities, whose quota was not filled, the number of Negro professionals increased. Doctors, lawyers, and teachers, were in demand in the armed forces as well as in civilian communities to care for Negroes. There were some white professionals who attended "coloreds" on special separate days with entry through special separate doors. Now, patriotism and discrimination reached an "accommodation": there were jobs for all, but some were "white" jobs and some were "colored" jobs.

There were, of course, organizations for Negroes based on common interests, in many cases, for social activities. In larger cities and among the more affluent there were more defined social groups. For the college women there were the Negro Greek letter sororities so important as networks, and there were many professional societies.

This is but a glimpse of the world we left to serve our country. I cannot pretend to recall all the women in the corps I knew, but from my review of records and memorabilia I am sure of the following list of preservice jobs we held:

beautician	insurance agent
business school operator	law student
chiropodist	musician
clerical worker	newspaper staff member
college professor	nurse
cook	office assistant
counselor	office manager
defense worker	postal worker
dietician	production inspector
domestic worker	recreation worker
factory worker	salesperson
farm worker	schoolteacher
government employee	seamstress
home economics teacher	secretary
hotel maid	social worker
housekeeper	textile worker
housewife	waitress

Of course, not everyone entering the service was employed; some of the recruits had only recently graduated from high school or college.

On the afternoon of our second day at Fort Des Moines, 20 July, the official opening day of the First WAAC Training Center and the day our training began, we were ordered to report for uniform fittings. We were asked (we still had difficulty with "ordered") to wear as little as possible to the fittings, for we were to be issued uniform items from the skin out and from the feet up. We wore as little as possible, which for most of us meant everything we usually wore. We were not ready to expose ourselves as we walked across the post, even if no one was looking.

We were fitted for every item that did not come as a "one size fits all." The only items I can recall that came in that size were the purse, the necktie, and the dress scarf. Clothing for women in the WAAC was made according to size charts drawn up by the largest mail order houses in the country, I have been informed, for these companies had the most complete range of women's sizes. Underwear, including girdles, was fitted by weight, height, and type of figure, and where alterations were needed, they were made. Bras and girdles were pink; slips and panties were khaki. After a few months we found out that dipping the khaki-colored "unmentionables" in a mild bleach solution produced a yellow-orange color. There were several different shades because the bleach solution produced a different shade for each manufacturer, depending on the dye used. Stockings were issued by foot size and height in pale brown, thick, service-weight styles. Khaki shirts, skirts, and jackets were issued, generally according to our regular size, but in most cases the waists had to be taken in and hems altered, either up or down. We quickly learned that "khaki" referred to cloth and to color. The shoe problem seemed at that time, and continued to be, the greatest one. Every conceivable size was presumed to be stocked, and yet there were some women who could not be fitted. Some of them waited many months before they received their special-order issue shoes.

The fitting problems belonged to all of us, Negro and white. An effort was made to keep the fittings segregated by sending the platoons to the clothing warehouse separately, the Third Platoon last. It had been anticipated that the women would pass before the fitters with their supplies, state the size, pick up the clothing, try it on, and move on. Things did not work that way. There were so many misfits requiring adjustments that I doubt if even 10 percent of the women were completely outfitted on the first round.

I had my problems, too, although I had never been much concerned about my size. True, in my early teens I had worn adult clothing, altered, because I was too tall for clothing for my age group. Fortunate, but absolutely unappreciated during those teen years, was my mother's ability to make most of my clothing. Now, for my fitting for an Army uniform, I discovered a number of strange things about my size. My skirts had to be taken in several inches at the waist because my waist measurement was

too small for the skirts that fitted my hips. I was too tall; skirts that were
long enough were too large, so the hems of my skirts had to be let out
the entire amount and faced. My right arm was three-fourths of an inch
longer than the left, so my shirts did not fit; the left sleeve had to be shortened. All of the slips were too short for me, and certain other items had
to be made smaller in spots. The uniform jackets fitted in the back and
shoulders, but there was not enough of me to fill out the front, and the
sleeves had to be lengthened.

Up to this point I had at least been permitted to comment on how certain items felt or looked, but at the shoe fitting I was permitted no involvement. Like the fitters for clothing, the shoe fitters were the best that money
and patriotism could hire. However, with my feet in front of them two
fitters could not agree on the size shoe I needed. One said 9 AAAA and
the other said 9½ AAAAA. It was during their debate that I learned what
the ball of the foot was and that it should be in a specific place in the
shoe and that the shoe size should be determined by having the ball of
the foot in the right place. My problem: the length of my foot called for
size 9, but with the ball of my foot in the right place the size was 9½,
although my toes were too short to fill out the end of the shoe. Since both
sizes felt all right, the gentlemen compromised and I was issued a pair of
each size. I guess they were both right, as I never had trouble with either
pair. That I was never able to wear my issue gym shoes in comfort was
my own fault because I asked for, and received, a pair in the same size
as my leather duty oxfords.

After several days most of us were at least partially outfitted; the alterations and special orders would complete the clothing allotment as soon
as they arrived. We were some sight: large dull blurs, khaki-colored from
head to ankle, with the brown shoes making us look like exclamation marks.
That was not how we pictured them, for we were proud of our uniforms,
which may have been chic for 1942 (I don't think so), but they were our
badges of service. When we had received everything, complete to brown
leather shoulder bag, gloves, handerkerchiefs, towels, combs, even tooth-
brushes, along with all the clothing we had been issued, including gym
clothes, we really had a lot of stuff.

Now we had to mark everything with our serial numbers; we were told
how and where to put these markings. I began with my cap (generally
called the Hobby Hat after Oveta Culp Hobby, the WAAC director) because, like everyone else, I had tried on about a hundred caps to find one
that fitted just right. I spent hours at the chore, marking even some of
the personal items I had brought to Fort Des Moines with me. At the same
time we were learning other things: how to make a military bed, with mi-
tered corners, so tight on the blanket fold that a quarter would bounce;
how to hang things in our wall lockers, including how to hide our civilian

Class A uniform, summer weight

clothes; how to lay out the items in the tray of the footlocker and in the bottom; how to keep our shoes shining; how to use the laundry facilities and where the dry-cleaning shop was located; and on and on and on.

We dressed up, those of us who were lucky enough to get one complete outfit, and made pictures and made pictures and made pictures. Alone and in groups. Visualize us in Uniform A: cotton jacket, skirt, shirt, and tie, with gloves tucked in the leather belt and bag hanging from the shoulder, the Hobby Hat and brown service oxfords. Now you get a picture of a very unattractive woman individually, but quite smart in a formation. Whatever of glamour that was brought by any of the women was promptly and completely eliminated with the donning of the uniform.

We were very proud of ourselves and the uniforms we had been issued. The newness of the whole thing took away the concern over lack of style. In our eagerness we thought that everything we wore was becoming, and photographers, professional and amateur, did a thriving business. We ordered great numbers of copies. When I ordered mine, I had every intention of sending all of them to family and friends, but I developed a sudden spell of modesty and kept most of them.

I did grow into my uniform. After I was commissioned a third officer, I was more concerned about the fit of my uniform. By the time the WAAC

My fatigue uniform

My officers winter dress uniform

My officers summer off-duty dress uniform

had become WAC and I had been promoted to captain, I like many other WAC officers, began to wear custom-tailored uniforms and shirts. This was expensive living, but the stores in the city of Des Moines were happy to accommodate us.

My winter outer wear

For the first OC class of the WAAC, the press personnel seemed constant companions. Patriotism competed with publicity. We had many
interviews, but pictures seemed more important. We were photographed

eating, marching, at play, at rest, in quarters, in the company area, in classrooms, at the Coke machine, in the post exchange, in the clothing warehouse, in the chapel, in the theater, while walking on the post, examining
landmarks, at drill, taking exercise, going into buildings, coming out of
buildings, greeting friends, writing letters, receiving mail, in every position
the photographers could imagine. Some of the pictures were good, some
were wonderful, some ugly, some glamorous, some bad; some of mine I
liked, some I did not, but I was flattered that there were so many. I collected copies of many of these pictures whenever possible and, of course,
clipped newspaper and magazine items about the WAAC.

At the same time we were handling the news people, acquiring our uniforms, and beginning our training, the Third Platoon was becoming as
much of a family group as thirty-nine people could. We began to be individuals who shared with each other, disagreed with each other, and supported each other as needed.

The member of the platoon who had been a practicing chiropodist lived
in the squad room where I lived, and she soon had patients from our squad.
We marched everywhere we went, and after several weeks our feet began
to protest. How much, depended on one's pre-WAAC lifestyle. We called
on squad members as if they were family members. We had joined the
Army for many different reasons, but whatever the reason, joining had
meant personal sacrifice.

Company 1, First Training Regiment, was one of the four companies
training the first officer candidate class. The company commander was Capt.
Frank E. Stillman, Jr.; the three platoons were commanded by 1st Lt. C. C.
Mabry, 2nd Lt. J. E. Glover, and 1st Lt. R. E. Barrows, the latter being
our platoon commander.

The Army had surely screened and selected well the male personnel assigned to the Training Center. Our personal concerns were about the officers assigned to the First Company and in particular the Third Platoon.
I believe that the officers and noncommissioned officers picked to work
with the Third Platoon showed the least amount of racial prejudice and,
perhaps, the most willingness to work with Negroes. We did encounter lots
of racial prejudice, but not from those assigned to work with us; their
problem was having to train women. One thing that worked in our favor
was that our trainers would themselves be rated on how well the Third Platoon performed, so it was important to them, regardless of our race or
sex, that we perform well.

On the second day of training, along with the continued press coverage,
uniform fitting, and getting acquainted, our classes began. We had pretty
much the same classroom training as male officer candidate trainees except that the tactical studies were omitted. Among the courses for this first
week were military courtesy and customs, organization of the Army, first

aid, hygiene, property accountability, and map reading. There were many other courses, but these stick out in my memory.

Property accountability, or how the Army accounts for what it has and has not, was my favorite subject. I studied the manuals with enthusiasm and availed myself of every opportunity to explain how things worked to those who had not understood as quickly as I. This stuff was so easy, I thought. That was before the instructor informed us one morning, now that we all understood, that we must forget what we had learned; circular F had just superseded circular S, which had itself been a superseder. Already I had learned that "to supersede" was one of the more important operating administrative verbs used by the Army. Later I was to learn that the most important phrase was "in extenuating circumstances, the CO may _____."

Because my college major had been mathematics, and I had taught the subject, I was sure that map reading would be a snap since it was so mathematical. What a disappointment that my worst grade came when we had our first examination in map reading. It was right up my alley, but the alley was so dark that I did not see where we were going. I passed the course with a satisfactory grade, but it was well over two years later when the Army published a simplified manual of map reading, designed, we were told, for those with less than six years' schooling, that I got the hang of it.

There were two other phases of our training that had definite effects on me. I did not like physical training because I thought there was too much of it. I had never been particularly athletic, and, suddenly, I was required to successfully execute handsprings and pushups. I managed the latter after several weeks of effort. It was a major accomplishment when I did seven pushups without falling down. I really did dislike PT, and I was very self-conscious about my long, bare legs flinging about in the air even though there were usually a few hundred other pairs of legs in the air at the same time. At that time all I thought PT was good for was to create sweat and great fatigue. Besides, it was always amazing that our schedules put PT and close order drill at times when we had to rush across the post for another class without time for a shower or even time to dry our perspiration-soaked bodies.

The other phase of our training that left an impression on me, and which became my favorite, was close order drill. I took to drill the way a duck takes to water. I read the manual and practiced. I joined any group on the practice field and quoted the manual to help others correct their movements. After several weeks of training we began to take turns giving commands to the platoon or company. I knew that I was excellent in this area, so one day I volunteered and found out that I still had quite a lot to learn. I took my place three paces to the left of the platoon, and in my loudest voice I gave a command. How bad I felt when Lieutenant Barrows called out, "Miss Adams, did I hear someone say something?" Not one syllable of my command had gone farther than six feet from me.

After supper that night five of my classmates took me out onto the parade ground, and we practiced our "command voices" until it was too dark to see each other. That's the night I learned to speak from the diaphragm, and ever since then I have been able to make myself heard.

That first week we also got shots, it seemed, for everything, though only for typhoid, smallpox, and tetanus. A few of the women were actually ill from the shots, and I think all of us had sore and stiff arms for days. Under more or less normal conditions we took the AGCT. Our arms were sore from shots, it was pouring rain, and we had to march several blocks to get to the test site. We were assured that the results of the test were unimportant. We learned later that enlisted personnel who desired OCS had to score at least 110 on the AGCT. We were already in OCS, fortunately.

After our training got up a full head of steam, I seemed to have moved into another world. It wasn't that I had forgotten my past life and goals. I wrote lots of letters to family members and to my friends, so I was maintaining strong connections with the "Before." Maybe it was that this new military life filled all my time and consumed all my energy, so much so that I had no time to miss my previous activities. By bedtime I was so tired that I was requested to finish all sentences before I started to lie down because I was always asleep by the time my head reached the pillow. During this period my only ambition was to do a good job each day and let the next day wait its turn. We were all busy, and even with the sameness of the activities of the first OC class, I was always conscious of the segregation of Negro WAACs. This put a damper on thoughts of the future. In my first classification interview, I indicated that I wanted to be a truck driver because I thought I would have a choice only between that and being an Army cook, the chores normally assigned to Negroes.

After about a week in OCS, I decided that it was about time that I really learned to make up my bed according to Army requirements. When I was assigned the bed, it was already made up in a style called "white bed," meaning the sheets and pillowcase could be seen. The fold at the top was two inches from the bottom of the pillow, and the fold itself was exactly six inches deep. The corners were properly turned, hospital style, and the two sheets and two blankets were tightly tucked under on the sides and smoothed out underneath. Up to this time, to avoid making the bed incorrectly, I had started at the top each night and squirmed down into the tightness of the bed. The mattress, just a plain quartermaster mattress, was flat and hard, so it was not too difficult to smooth the bed each morning. My first efforts at making my bed were limited to watching the squad leader, male, white, as he showed me, female, Negro, how it was done.

After two days, however, I think he became suspicious of my efforts and suggested that I try making the bed myself. It was not as difficult as it seemed, my own distaste for the job being the fact that, no matter how carefully I slept, I had to tear my bed up each morning and "start from scratch."

Once settled, the routine of our daily lives became regular, consistent. Reveille was at 6:30 A.M., most of us rising even before first call at 6:15 A.M. in order to be completely dressed by 6:30; some few were able to sleep that fifteen minutes, getting up at 6:15 and making reveille on time. When the whistle sounded, we had to race like mad from our "private" Barracks 54 over to the front of 55, where the rest of the company was housed. The breakfast schedule rotated so that no one company ate first every day. Sometimes we went to breakfast right from the reveille formation, and at other times we had a few minutes to perform barracks chores before marching to breakfast.

The first class was at 8:00 A.M., which meant that we left for class at 7:50 A.M. every morning. The classes were scheduled to be changed every week, but actually we had almost daily changes. Consequently, we might move in a different direction for a different class nearly each morning. Every place the platoon went, we marched and, when there were four or more involved, it was suggested that we march as a detail to get the practice of moving units. We were in class all day until 4:30 P.M., and it was a constant process of falling in, forward marching, falling out, and class dismissed, from morning until night.

We marched all over the post to temporary classrooms a half-mile from our barracks, to bleachers on the parade ground, to classrooms near our barracks, to classes in the theater right past our barracks, back to temporary classrooms, to the designated drill area, back to classrooms, day after day. After about the third formation of the day we would look longingly toward 54 and wish for a few minutes there. When we were fortunate enough to get a break near our barracks, it was a mad dash into the building and out again.

In the winter months Des Moines is in "Cold Country," but it was extremely hot that first summer, and the other summers I was there. When we were in OCS, half the time it was dry, dusty, and sticky, and the other half it was rainy, muddy, and sticky. I had never before been wet so often and so long. During the hot and dry weather I was wet with perspiration that dripped and rolled from under my hat and made my clothes stick to my body. During the rainy and muddy weather my clothes were wet from the rain, which leaked through all the seams of my raincoat. In a short time it became our custom to wear a large bath towel around the shoulders under the raincoat. Because of the mud we had to wear galoshes, but the problem was to keep the mud out of the barracks. This meant washing the galoshes before every entrance into the barracks. If our activities had been restricted to the permanent cavalry post, we would not have had the mud problem, but the temporary buildings were new and the ground around them was soft and porous. Perhaps Fort Des Moines had been selected for training because it afforded the extremes of weather.

Saturday morning was inspection. There was the hustle and bustle of cleaning and arranging everything in proper order; squad rooms, footlockers, wall lockers, latrines, and corridors were included. Beds were changed and made more tightly than they would be until next Saturday, and all unauthorized items were hidden with the hope that they would not be spotted. Since the person was also subjected to inspection, the person had to be made ready. The main problem was ascertaining the uniform of the day in time to be properly dressed. In anticipation of the uniform announcement the shoes were shined, clothes pressed, buttons buttoned, ties tied properly and tucked, hair combed neatly and well above the collar, nail polish and makeup applied inconspicuously.

Inspection day was a real test of whether we were tough enough to make it. As we were already keyed up for the occasion, there was no surprise if nerves gave way when the inspecting party, with white gloves, arrived. The inspectors rubbed walls, patted beds, kicked barracks bags, looked under hats, pillows, and mattresses, wiped floors, walls, and windows, measured distances. They asked questions we could not answer: we knew the answers but were unable to get the words out in order. They nearly always managed to discover one undusted spot in the squad room, one unpolished spot in the latrine, one unswept corner in the day room, one shoe out of line, one item in the wrong place in the footlocker, and one article not well hidden, especially if the article was a piece of fruit or an unauthorized object. There were also good inspections when nothing was found out of order, when platoons or companies were compared, and there was a designated winner. The opportunity to win helped us to endure inspections.

Most of the activities we engaged in had been heard about in jokes, and we knew in a superficial way what was involved. We did not know what it meant to "police an area." There was one story told about a woman who was told "to come outside and help police the area." She quickly doffed her uniform, donned a chic slacks suit brought from civilian life, and rushed out expecting to be handed a rifle to do guard duty. She learned promptly that policing meant cleaning up the area by picking up all cigarette butts and other bits of discernible trash.

There were numerous parades and reviews. There were practice parades, Saturday parades, parades for military brass and civilian dignitaries, parades to present awards, and sometimes parades for no special reason. Since there had not been women in military parades before, lots of people came to look. The first OC class was only four companies, but we frequently passed in review. After several weeks the second class began, and the parades were larger. The companies were judged on marching performance, the appearance of the company, the execution of all commands and movements, with a special lookout for such irregularities as personnel out of line, talking, or chewing gum. The company picked as having performed best was selected as the color guard company for the next parade.

One of the great problems about WAACs' marching in formation was what happened to the short people at the back of the line. In our platoon the heights of the women ranged from about five feet four inches to just a fraction under six feet, and we lined up by squad with the tallest members in front progressing to the shortest at the rear. The cadence of our marching was set by the cadence of the military band, twenty paces to the minute with thirty-inch steps. That was easy for me. I had come into the Army claiming to be five feet, eight and one-half inches tall, but by the time I had been taught how to stand correctly, my official height was five feet, eight inches. Or perhaps I was accurately measured for the first time. With the tall people in front setting the pace, the short people in the back constantly complained that they had trouble keeping up. It was comical to watch them at the rear trying to keep up and trying not to be obvious that they had to run.

As I have stated, the summer of 1942 in Fort Des Moines was either hot and dusty or hot and wet. The weather made no difference as to whether there was a parade, only as to whether we wore raincoats. During the hot and dusty days, we stood for long periods on the parade grounds, and some trainees fainted. The ambulance was driven behind the line of troops, the fainters were taken away, and never a head was turned to look. During the hot and wet days there was less fainting, but many caught fresh colds. The parades continued, and we kept trying to be the best marching unit on the field. Hordes of visitors came on the post to watch the parades, and we knew that the Third Platoon was a conspicuous curiosity as we did our thing.

The term "Third Platoon" came to be a term of endearment when we referred to our unit, even with the underlying resentment of the segregation. Everyone was so caught up in the training process that separate housing for the platoons of Company One seemed to have little effect on the coordination of company activities. Segregated housing did necessitate two duty rosters: one for the Third Platoon, one for the other two platoons. The separation did not affect friendships that developed between women living in Barracks 54 and those in Barracks 55. Those who wanted to get together for study did so. As I recall, there was only one occasion during OCS when there was a nasty expression of racial prejudice. After a gas mask drill when we were all lined up to clean our individual masks with the same chemical and the same cloth, one of the women from 55 remarked that she could not use a cloth that had been used by colored girls because she had to put that mask on her own face. There was absolute silence following that remark. Everyone turned to look, but no one stepped forward to offer another cloth. With considerable redness of face, the young woman used the designated cloth. There was no way to know what kinds of protection she put on her face for the next gas mask drill or how many kinds of disinfectants she used on her mask.

The post chapel was only about a city block from our barracks, as was the post theater, and those who cared to do so attended religious services and movies. There were many churches and theaters in the city of Des Moines, which was only a ten-cent trolley ride away. Many of our group visited Des Moines, but I did not go into the city while I was in training. All meals were compulsory except supper, which was almost compulsory as we had little time for trips off the post, except on weekends. I always seemed to have some washing and ironing and cleaning left over for the weekends, and on this day and a half off each week, after Saturday's inspections, my personal pleasure was to dress in my fatigue clothes and roam the post, country girl that I was. Lights had to be out in the sleeping rooms at 9:00 P.M. although bed check was not until 11:00 P.M. If possible, I avoided being out very long after supper because I disliked getting ready for bed in the dark even though I stayed up until bed check.

Something that was always a problem to the men who were training us was that they were never sure what was inconspicuous makeup or when a woman's hairdo was neat. While the first OC class was in training, it was never definitely decided how we should be addressed. Depending upon who was addressing us, it varied from "Miss" to "Auxiliary" to "Private" to "Officer Candidate," and in the most military circumstances it became "Soldier." We were not in the Army, just with it, in sort of a nonposition position.

In the Infantry Drill Regulations Manual, which was being used for WAAC training and from which WAAC/WAC Drill Regulations were later drafted, there was a paragraph that described the position of attention. One phrase in this paragraph read "with thumbs along the seams of the trousers." This phrase became more and more difficult for the men to use because we were wearing skirts. Without permission, they could not make the change to "along the seams of the skirt," which was the way it was written later. Dressing the line, checking to make sure a line of soldiers side by side was a straight line, required that each person look to the left to the second shirt button or the necktie of the second person down and align herself on that button or necktie. This may have worked for the men, but for the women it was hilarious. The hills and valleys varied in shape, size, and location, so we used the knot in the tie as the best choice. The men who taught us drill could never bring themselves to ask a woman what she had in her shirt pocket when there seemed to be an extra hump in view.

We were on the Army payroll, and as it turned out, the paymaster was as confused as we were. For the month of July we received U.S. Army officer candidate pay, which was $50. By the August payday our status had been clarified and we were paid as auxiliaries (privates) in the WAAC, $21. After the first pay we had anticipated the same amount, but, beginning with that August $21, the paymaster was deducting the July overpayment. What a disappointment! Fortunately, most of us still had some funds left from what we had brought with us.

The United States was at war, and there must have been many manpower experts who wondered why it took so many men to maintain WAAC training in those early days. The companies were manned with all the cadre that the Table of Organization permitted, and there were all sorts of special details assigned to the TC. For our class these special details performed the necessary chores such as cleaning and KP, chores that later fell the lot of OC classes and Basic Training Company personnel. There were lots of extra officers who were awaiting the arrival of more training units to which they would be assigned. Until then, they were attached to the first class, made up of four companies. Besides these officers were the many instructors and support personnel. Later, when I became a unit commander with only the personnel authorized by the T/O, I realized the kind of overload in personnel and cost that had been experienced at Fort Des Moines, to establish the Training Center.

Ours was not an easy life, even with lots of help and too much attention. The first officer candidate class was the guinea pig for the WAAC, and lots of adjustments had to be made on both sides, by the trainees and the trainers. We were subjected to hundreds of changes during that first six weeks. We were the people upon whom the rules and policies were tried out, changed and tried, and in many cases changed back to the first position. We were the people, as Colonel Hobby said, and said so well, beginning the tradition for women in the service. There were many unpleasant moments and disillusioning experiences, and there were the pleasant and hopeful ones.

In spite of everything, or because of it all, we were made into soldiers. Before our OC training was over, we spoke the Army alphabet language fluently. We became accustomed to the uniform, not only to the fact that women were wearing clothes exactly alike but to the fact that we were told what to put on and when. We learned to tie neckties, to shine shoes (a little Jergens lotion on the toe and a shine cloth did wonders), to make army beds, to respond almost automatically to the sounds of whistles and bugles. Most of us even recognized bugle calls and knew what they meant; I did not. My only recognition of bugle calls was according to the time of day, except "Taps." I did recognize that whenever it was played.

We adopted the courtesies and customs of the service. We opened doors for our superiors; we stood at attention in their presence unless otherwise ordered. We walked to the left of officers, and it was the far, far left in cases of two or more officers; and we learned to salute. We saluted like *mad,* indoors and outdoors, at the proper time and the improper time, the right people and the wrong people. And there were times when we had no idea what to do. Should we salute officers on horseback and in vehicles, and should we stand at attention while the horse or vehicle passed; should we salute officers when we met them in corridors; should we salute the colonel's car; should we salute naval officers; should we salute officers when we met them in the city when we were wearing civilian clothing? At times it seemed that the safest thing to do was salute uniforms: elevator operators, doormen, telegraph delivery boys, postmen, garbage collectors, truck drivers, trainmen, anyone in uniform. Somehow we restrained ourselves!

I remember one day three of us were walking toward our barracks when we spotted two men, dressed in the white uniform of Coca-Cola delivery men, sitting on the rail around our barracks porch. We saw them; we even discussed their presence there. As we came about fifteen feet from them, one of the men started to raise his right hand. Instantly the three of us came to attention and executed our smartest salutes. The man lifted his hand to his head and pushed his cap to the back of his head. The two of them had a good laugh at our expense, and we were terribly embarrassed each time we saw a Coca-Cola truck drive through our area.

From the first week there had been a great deal of discussion about whether or not we were to be commissioned when we had completed our training. At the time we entered the WAAC, the understanding was that all who successfully completed the training would receive commissions. Suddenly it seemed that there would be no need for such a large number of officers. The first rumor we heard was that 10 percent of us would make it, then 20 percent, and so on up the scale. At the 20-percent level the story was that 20 percent of the class would be commissioned and that all others who successfully completed the training would receive "Certificates of Qualifications." At such time as more officers were needed, others would be commissioned on an as-needed basis. Another story we heard was that by Army Regulations, at least 10 percent of all OC classes had to fail. These stories certainly did little for morale. Even the best students among the prospective officers became discouraged. It was difficult to keep ourselves buoyed up for the rumors continued. I managed to keep my confidence up, as did others in the class, but I did wonder at times how I could tell my family if I failed.

In the sixth and last week of our training we found out that, with the exception of a very few of the 439 members of our class, we would all be commissioned third officers. It was a jubilant day for us. There was much to be done: uniforms prepared, the ceremony rehearsed, final examinations taken, friends and family to invite to the graduation. I have never quite forgiven myself for not inviting my parents for the occasion, although I was not certain that there was money for the trip. The truth was that I did not realize that parents were invited — but it was my first graduation in the Army. How was I to know?

On 28 August 1942, in the afternoon, the four OC companies marched across the post to receive discharges from the WAAC as enlisted personnel, for the convenience of the government, to accept appointments as third officers in the Women's Army Auxiliary Corps on the following day. On that particular day I was acting company commander and in charge of the march across the post, and I kept thinking of the one other time I had been assigned to move the entire company. I was to move the company from one of the classroom buildings to the front of Barracks 54 so that Captain Stillman could talk to the group. I followed my instructions to the letter, but when I turned and saluted the captain, he returned my salute as he said, "Adams, your troops are standing in the sun, facing the sun and you are in the shade."

Many lessons from OCS have stayed with me over the years, but none more than the one that afternoon. With great embarrassment, and a passing dislike for Captain Stillman, I found the required commands to move the company so that I was facing the sun and Company 1 was in proper formation in the shade.

I was proud of my ability to move a unit around, and things were going quite well the afternoon before graduation until we approached a circle around which our unit had to march. Mentally I was going through the whole drill process trying to think of the right command to get the company around that circle. I could not think of any such command. I looked at the guide officer, Lieutenant Mabry, whose purpose was to help us out in such spots, and he said not a word. He was probably thinking that since I was to become a commissioned officer the next morning, I should be able to get myself out of this spot. The moment arrived when I had to say something or, I thought, the unit would march right across the untouchable post lawn. In my loudest and most precise command voice I sounded off, "Swing on around the circle, march!" How was I to know that the unit would follow the street?

Lieutenant Mabry spoke then, and his sarcasm was appreciated by all. "All right, Major Adams, are you writing your own drill regulations now?" It was quite a while before I recovered from a new embarrassment, but I did, and I hope that Lieutenant Mabry did find out that two years later I *was* a major and one of the people responsible for drafting the first WAC drill regulations.

29 August–31 December 1942

Graduation day, 29 August 1942, arrived beautiful and hot. The heat was felt early that day, and it dulled our spirits, for we knew how we would look, soggy and damp from perspiration, in our cotton khaki uniforms. However, since we would have open ranks inspection before the ceremony, we did our best to look like the well-groomed soldiers we thought we were. There was excitement and anticipation in the air.

After a review we marched to our seats at the bandstand. All around us were the bleachers upon which the visitors sat. The great and near great of the Army (at least that is what we thought) sat on the bandstand. The post band, which had seen us through many formations, from reveille to marching to tunes like "Jingle Bells" and "Dark Town Strutters Ball," was in place on the left side of the bandstand. Cars were parked all over the post, and the number of people attending our graduation indicated the public's interest in our activities. Reporters and photographers were very busy with the participants in this history-making event.

Army ceremonies and services are short and to the point. Our graduation exercises followed this pattern: there was a prayer, followed by greetings, the introduction of the speaker, the address, the oath of office, the awarding of diplomas, the National Anthem, and the benediction. It was over quickly, and we were deeply impressed with the purposes that had motivated our organization. Among the VIPs visiting for the occasion were Maj. Gen. F. E. Uhl, commander of the Seventh Service Command; Col. Oveta Culp Hobby, director of the WAAC; and Representative Edith Nourse Rogers, sponsor of the bill that created the Women's Army Auxiliary Corps.

Graduation day, 29 August 1942: (*left to right*) Congresswoman Edith Nourse Rogers, WAAC director Oveta Culp Hobby, Maj. Gen. Frederick E. Uhl, Third Officer Charity E. Adams, Capt. Frank E. Stillman

I was very happy on that day. The fact that I had been the first Negro woman to receive a commission in the WAAC was nearly as impressive as the fact that we had "arrived." Whatever doubts we might have later, that day we knew ourselves as members of the great fraternity of officers. The only authorized insignia available for us was the gold bars of the second lieutenant, so with obvious disregard for the prescribed manner of wearing insignia, we put on our gold bars and were third officers of the WAAC, comparable to second lieutenants in the U.S. Army.

There was one historic change that took place at our graduation. Traditionally, at Army graduation exercises the candidates are presented according to the company roster, which is the way we were listed in the program.

For our graduation the class was presented by platoon, which meant that the Third Platoon, the "colored girls," came last in the First Company. My name was Adams and, alphabetically, I would have been the first WAAC officer to be commissioned. There were four other Negro graduates whose names began with the letter A.

When it was all over and we were free to pursue our own interests for the rest of the day, we realized that now we were in position to have the courtesy of the salute extended to us first. Because we were self-conscious and insecure, three of us, new legal third officers, returned to Barracks 54 right down the middle of the parade ground. We were not sure how we would handle being saluted first — we had not been on that end of a salute before.

One other thing happened to us when we received our commissions. We received new serial numbers; we dropped the A and picked up the L. Mine went from A-500001 to L-500001.

Classification, or "job assignment" came next. Most of us had heard some strange stories about Army classification; a civilian butcher assigned as a surgeon's assistant, an auto mechanic assigned as a pastry cook, a telephone operator assigned as a typist. These examples were usually offered in jest, but there were a few authentic cases. When I had successfully completed OCS, I believed that I must have learned something that could be used in the service of my country. With that bit of self-confidence I went for my first classification interview on the afternoon following graduation.

I remember that interview quite well, although the only thing I recall about the captain who conducted the interview was that he had beautiful white hair. He hardly looked up from the card on the desk in front of him. When I reported, he said, "You are Charity Adams?"

"Yes, Sir."

"You taught school?"

"Yes, Sir."

"Do you know anything about public relations?"

"No, Sir."

"Are you interested in recruiting?"

"I don't know, Sir."

"Well," the captain said, "we'll see what we can find for you to do. You are too young to be put in charge of people and I don't have any idea what we're going to do with you young women."

"Yes, Sir."

"That's all, Miss."

I was not encouraged by that interview. After the hectic six weeks of OCS, I did not feel so young, although I was among the youngest members of our class. I later found out that all the younger women had been told the same thing, so we rather felt that we would not have a chance to do anything worthwhile, that we might be the people stuck with all the assignments no one else wanted.

In the meantime, after graduation we had moved from our training barracks, 54, into various officers quarters. Some of us moved into houses on Officers Row, and others into more temporary quarters while awaiting assignments. Eleven of us from the Third Platoon moved into Quarters 1, a large double house on the circle around the bandstand. In the other side of the house, Quarters 2, were eleven white third officers who had graduated with us that morning. We had some trouble understanding why we were assigned to Quarters 1, but we finally realized that we were on the end of Officers Row. To put us in any other house on the circle would have mixed us in, and that would have been integration.

Little did I realize when I moved into that house that it would be my home for nearly two and one-half years. That first day I unpacked my footlocker and arranged the room to be as homelike as I could. This activity did not take long and, after the interview I have already described, I suddenly felt very lonesome and homesick. To alleviate this feeling, I put on a civilian outfit for the first time since I had been in the service and made my first trip into the city of Des Moines, where I wandered around for about an hour before returning to the post.

Our graduation had taken place on a Saturday morning, and it was on the following Monday morning that we received our first assignments. During our last weeks in OCS several hundred women had reported to Fort Des Moines for training as auxiliaries, and several basic training companies had been formed. One member of the Third Platoon was assigned to WAAC Headquarters in the Pentagon because she had worked for a Negro adviser to the president of the United States and had been promised this assignment. Some members of our class were assigned to various administrative offices for training, but most of us were assigned to the new basic training companies for training as company officers.

Those of us in training to be company officers were assigned to the Third Company, Third Training Regiment. This company was similar to our OC company in that there were two platoons of white women and one of Negro women. The only Negro auxiliaries then at the Training Center were in this company. At the time that we began our assignment with Company 3, there were fewer than forty Negro women at the TC. As a result there were almost as many officers as there were enlisted women. We, the new officers, had to be divided into groups to work with the Negro platoon, some accompanying the platoon to classes while the rest of us remained in the company to learn all the duties connected with running the company. At any time when it was necessary for all personnel of the company, new officers included, to be in formation together, there was a complete platoon of officers. Even for parades we had this strange forma-

Company 1, First Training Regiment, company officers (the four men in the center of the front row): (*left to right*) Lt. J. J. Glover; Lt. R. C. Barrows; Capt. Frank E. Stillman, CO; Lt. C. C. Mabry

tion of three platoons of enlisted women followed by a platoon of third officers.

Here began the confusion as to what third officers would be called. It was agreed that we could no longer use civilian terms of address because we were now definitely part of the military. "Third officer" was certainly a cumbersome title to use, as would be "second officer" and "first officer" at such time as some of us would be promoted to those ranks. For non-commissioned officers the titles were even worse: "auxiliary," "leader," "junior leader," "staff leader," "first leader." It was finally agreed, since we had grades equivalent to Army grades, that we would use the Army titles when addressing each other but that we would sign our names with official

WAAC titles. I rather liked being addressed as "Lieutenant Adams" and, except for my signature, I referred to myself that way.

We were learning something about company administration while we were detailed to the Third Company, although I was feeling some impatience with what appeared to be a waste of time before getting on with whatever we could contribute to the war effort. In the meantime we began to respond to the small health problems that we had ignored during OCS. For several weeks I had been conscious of some numbness in my left index finger, so I made my first sick call to the infirmary. There was absolutely no doubt that instructions had come from high places that nothing bad was to happen to women in the WAAC. I never did know what was wrong with my finger, but the prescription was that I report to the hospital every morning for a week, where my hand was submerged in a tub of whirling hot water. It must have worked because I have had no further trouble with that finger.

There were only a small number of Negro auxiliaries reporting for training, and we wondered whether there would ever be a sufficient number so that we would get assignments. We did not know whether the Army was discouraging Negroes or whether there was just slow response.

Our concern was not to last very long. Two weeks after we were commissioned, we received the assignments we had wanted. Two Negro companies were formed—a Basic Training Company and a Specialist Training Company. This latter company was in the Second Training Regiment and would be housed in hotels in downtown Des Moines. The Basic Training Company was part of the Third Training Regiment and was located in Boomtown, the new part of the post. My assignment was as company commander of the Basic Training Company, and, since the specialist group would not be operative for a while, the commander of the unit and the other officers were detailed to work with those of us assigned to the first all-Negro company.

Capt. Jack Wagner, CO of the Third Company to which we had been attached, sent for me and the other officers assigned to our new unit. When we reported to him, he told us to go out to Boomtown and activate Company 12, Third Regiment. I asked him what we were to do in order to follow his orders. His reply was brief and to the point, "Go activate the company."

We saluted the captain and left the office. As company commander I assumed that I should come up with some suggestions as to how we would get started on our job, but I was as confused as the others. After a bit of discussion we decided that the best thing to do at that moment was to go to the company area. So, each of us armed with a copy of "The Officer's Guide" and a copy of "Company Administration," we left OC Row

Practicing my official stance

Maj. Joseph Fowler, regimental commander

Capt. Jack Wagner, my first company adviser

to locate Company 12 out in Boomtown, officially listed as the Winn Area, after Gen. John S. Winn, but never called that in my time.

If a place could be called "completely unfinished," Boomtown would have fit the description. This area was filled with new temporary buildings

First Lieutenant Young, my second company adviser

that, by comparison with many other temporary buildings, could be called permanent. The company areas were composed of three barracks buildings and a company headquarters building, which also housed the supply room and the day room. Between each two companies was a mess hall. Four companies were located so that they formed a square, with the company

Captain Crowley, my third company adviser, and I, with the mud of Boomtown in the background

buildings facing four different streets. Behind the buildings within the square were the company areas. There were not yet any sidewalks in Boomtown, and because of the constant rain, the area was extremely muddy. In some spots the mud was so gummy that it would pull a shoe right off the foot. From the outside the buildings appeared complete, but they were definitely not. The walls, the floors, the ceilings, and the roofs were completed, but the doors and windows were missing from many of the buildings.

When the officers assigned to Company 12 arrived at Boomtown and located the buildings assigned to that company, they were faced with the problem of what to do with the unfinished buildings. We were rather quiet as we looked through our three barracks and the company headquarters building. The windows were installed in the barracks, but they were grimy with construction dirt. There were no doors. There were neither doors nor windows in the orderly room.

We held a "pow-wow" and decided that the first thing to do was to clean up the place. That decision raised the problem of cleaning supplies. Since Army supplies were issued on the basis of troop strength, we could not

Lieutenant Wright, my fourth company adviser

draw supplies from the quartermaster. We suddenly remembered that we had learned something about company funds, and, assuming that we would surely have such a fund and with no knowledge of where such funds originated, I went to the post commissary and bought cleaning supplies on a "ghost company fund." Incidentally, before we ever did establish a real company fund, I had paid that bill and thanked my lucky stars that I had gotten away with it. Having secured the necessary cleaning supplies and a few old razor blades, we set about cleaning the buildings. We put on our oldest and most appropriate clothing and looked as little like WAAC officers as was possible. Cleaning involved scraping manufacturers' stickers from every windowpane and other parts of the structures. While we were working away at the windows and floors, Colonel Morgan, assistant commandant of the Training Center, came through the area. When he saw what we were doing, he informed us in no uncertain terms that, as officers, we were not to perform such chores and assured us that he would see that we had a detail of enlisted men to clean up the place. We got the detail, but that work had been easier than some of the other tasks we performed setting up the company.

The first Negro company made history, even if only in terms of what happened at the First WAAC Training Center. This history began with the announcement that we were in the wrong building. Company 12 was scheduled to be in the buildings across the street. When Maj. Joseph Fowler, our regimental commander, made this announcement, I almost cried. I was very discouraged, especially after all the cleaning we had done. I did not have long to nurse my disappointment because in less than thirty-six hours the TC Headquarters changed company designations; Company 12 became Company 14. (Several months later there was another number change, and Company 14 became Company 8. At this point the number designations did not really matter to me, since my attachment to the company was based on the people and the activities.)

As could be expected, new WAAC officers knew very little about what their duties were when they received their assignments. Actually, they knew only those things that they had observed in the OC companies and what classroom knowledge that might apply. For this reason a male officer was assigned to each company to show us how to succeed. Our company had for its tactical adviser the same officer with whom we had been associated when we were assigned to Company 3. I am indebted to Captain Wagner for all the help he gave me as I learned to be a company commander, although a great part of his help was in letting me do the job as I wanted. He believed in learning by doing.

For several months we had a full cadre of male officers assigned to each company. As the months passed, these officers were gradually reassigned away from the Training Center until there were no male officers left except the battalion commander. During this period we had four different tactical officers assigned as advisers, and each had characteristics we remembered long after they were gone. Captain Wagner, our first adviser, liked to talk and to have drill classes. An immaculate Cavalry officer, he had many Army stories to tell, and between stories he supervised our company drill sessions or taught us officers more about close order drill. Our second adviser was a First Lieutenant Young. He was a southerner, and because he was so uncommunicative, I thought he was unhappy about being assigned to a Negro company. As I got to know him better, I realized that he was just shy and retiring and really did not like to talk. He would sit in the office for hours at a time and never say a word unless he was addressed. The only time I ever heard him speak up in a vigorous manner was when one of my officers griped so much about the denial of a special request that she irritated the regimental commander, the battalion commander, and me, the company commander. Everyone understood how he felt.

Lieutenant Crowley was our third tactical officer, and he was assigned to Company 14 and Company 16. He would appear in the office at exactly 8:00 A.M., sit down in a chair near the potbellied stove, and start talking. He collected guns and told many tall tales about his guns and how he collected them. Although Lieutenant Crowley talked all day, he did not interfere with my work. When something required my attention, he would stop talking until I finished and would take up again at exactly the point where he had stopped. He would be interrupted many times during the day, sometimes for hours when I had to leave the office, but he would take up his story just where he left off before the interruption. He rode a motorcycle to the company area every morning, and the most strenuous labor I ever saw him perform was pushing the motorcycle when it sometimes refused to start. Our last tactical officer was Lieutenant Wright, who was outstanding because he seemed to do everything in exactly the right proportion. He spent several hours in the company area but not all day, he talked only when he had something to say that had a lesson in it, and he dressed as we expected an Army officer to dress, without too much flair. Maybe more than anything I learned from each of these officers before I was left on my own to run a company, that efficiency and knowledge comes in all shapes, sizes, personalities, and vocalization.

When all the male officers had been removed from the company level, we still had a male battalion commander — my immediate superior and a real character. A very small man, about five feet, five inches and 140 pounds, he dressed with extreme care and emulated, to the best of his ability, the over six-foot-tall regimental commander. Because he always fell short in this, he developed a personal idiosyncrasy. We called him "Gestapo" because when everything was in perfect order by everyone else's standards, he could find something wrong. Many times I had to listen to him berate me, the officers, and the company about something he disapproved of when the Training Center commandant or the regimental commander would come in, while he was talking, and tell us that the same thing was superior. Because he wanted to feel important, he would stand around in places where people were certain to pass so he could be saluted. We would watch him from the window as he drew himself up to his full height and waited for a salute, even when the approaching party was a block away. He, too, served his purpose, for we learned to appreciate the consideration we received from other officers.

I was very fortunate to have gotten along with all the officers with whom I worked, and I actually became friends with some of them. Besides Captain Stillman, CO of our OCS company, I think our regimental commander, Maj. Joseph Fowler, most influenced my success as an Army officer. He was military to the letter of the regulations, tolerated no foolishness, and gave none. He demanded the best of every member of his command and as a result kept all of us in a state of fear. "The Major," as we usually referred to him, was about six feet, three inches tall, slender, blond, extremely well groomed, and he was a striking figure in his Cavalry uniform. We never saw him without his riding crop, and I always wished that I could have carried one.

After what was to us a terrible struggle getting supplies, beds, sheets, pillowcases, pillows, blankets, office supplies, and the like, we were ready to receive our first basic training group. In those early days the training schedule was issued from the Headquarters Training Section, so we did not have to worry about what to teach, who would teach it, or where it would be taught. The instructors and classrooms were assigned. Our job was the administration of the company, the housing and feeding, and getting the troops to the right place at the right time.

The day came when we received our first auxiliaries for training. There were twenty-two of them for the twenty-seven officers in the company. The women had already had some training because they had been members of Company 3, where we had been assigned as trainees. In spite of their previous training, we went at our jobs with determination and set out to make real soldiers of them.

There were no WAAC noncommissioned officers when we started, so we used commissioned officers in those spots. All the jobs from first sergeant to squad leader were filled by third officers. In our case there were so many officers and so few troops that we had to change the duties frequently so that everyone had a chance to perform. There were so few Negro women coming in for training that we were rather depressed about being in excess so early in the service of our country. Along with this was the ever-present concern for our chances for success. We did not know whether our progress was to be in an all-Negro world or in the all-WAAC world.

There was no reception center for recruits coming into the Training Center, so this job was performed by the basic company to which the troops were assigned. The company supply officer was responsible for getting clothing from the warehouse for the recruits reporting. At times it seemed that the warehouse had sufficient supplies of everything in every size except those we needed. Our troops were coming in individually or in small groups of two or three, which meant that every day we had to requisition clothing. Almost every day we tried to begin a new training group with the latest bunch of arrivals. After several weeks of this, it was decided that instead of starting so many new groups, we would hold the new recruits until we had a group of reasonable size.

Because we had some difficulty getting uniforms in the correct sizes for our troops, sometimes the company made a strange appearance when in formation. It was required that any part of the uniform that fitted would be worn so it was not unusual to see a woman in a WAAC hat, khaki shirt, and plaid skirt. Many of the officers had not received their complete uniforms, and we were still without insignia. On 25 September 1942 there was a sudden snowstorm, and we were wearing summer uniforms. There were no winter uniforms available; snow had not been expected so early in the season. We put on our civilian clothing along with the uniform, anything to keep warm. By this time there were several thousand women at the TC and, with all the bright civilian clothing being worn, we were a strange army, which precipitated prompt action "at the highest level." Every woman in the service was issued an enlisted man's overcoat. We soon found out what was meant by the saying that GI clothing came in two sizes—too large and too small. I was five feet, eight inches, and although my coat reached my knees, the sleeves struggled to approach my wrists. The small people were completely lost in their coats, which reached the ankles and covered the hands.

In a short time these overcoats became standard issue for new recruits, along with knitted wool caps, brown leather gloves, and arctics. With these, any woman could lose her identity. Of course, the women were also issued the standard WAAC items and equipment, but none of that was visible under the coat. We third officers wore those coats for a long time and proudly pinned our shiny gold bars on the shoulders. We complained about the coats, but we made many jokes about them and made pictures of ourselves in them. Second to the enlisted man's overcoat was the enlisted man's raincoat, which was also issued. The raincoat came in the same two sizes as the overcoat but was lighter weight and easier to carry when walking. The raincoats were uglier because they were constantly wrinkled and creased from the custom of rolling them in the hood for carrying.

After several weeks running the company, we began to feel rather secure in our jobs. The second OC class graduated two weeks after we had, and by the time they were assigned to Boomtown we felt that we were in a position to teach them a great deal. Though all our neighbors were white, we had established excellent rapport, for we were all learning our way at the same time. We had little equipment to use in our activities, so we shared and borrowed from each other without hesitation. We created a friendly rivalry that spurred enthusiasm and work, and when our company was on the drill field along with other companies, each company tried to outdo the others.

Part of learning more about what was expected of us led to the mastery of the morning report, a daily log of unit strength, status of personnel, record of events, and changes of location when applicable. About this time the Negro company in the Second Training Regiment was activated, and the officers assigned to that company, who had been temporarily working with us, left for the hotels downtown. This meant another shift in the assignments of the officers holding noncommissioned officers' jobs. Follow-

On the parade grounds at Fort Des Moines. *Women's Army Corps photograph*

ing this, a decision was made to send some Negro officers on recruiting duty. We were pleased with this move, for surely it would mean more recruits for the Negro companies. The problem we had with these new assignments was that as soon as we had a person completely trained for a job, that person would be transferred to another unit.

Soon there were two Negro companies in the Second Regiment, one for training motor transport personnel and the other for clerical personnel. We sent our first groups from basic training to bakers and cooks training, not to motor or clerical training. These women were not housed with the bakers and cooks company because that company was primarily white. They were housed with our basic training company, which meant that their schedules and equipment gave us more headaches.

Finally, there were enough jobs for us so that all Negro officers had real assignments. The time had come when we had to have real noncommissioned officers to handle the duties that third officers had taken on. A few of the women who had completed their training in the clerks company were sent back to Company 8 for housing and administration until they were given assignments in the field.

When we received the orders sending the clerical school graduates back to us, my officers and I looked over the list and, without knowing the women, picked a group to serve as noncommissioned officers. When they arrived, we put them right to work. Most of those we chose that day remained with us for many months and became the first group of Negro WAACs to become noncommissioned officers and wear stripes. They gradually worked up the ranks until they had the appropriate stripes for the jobs we gave them. We selected as company first sergeant Margaret Charity, who

Bicycle drill on the parade grounds at Fort Des Moines. *Women's Army Corps photograph*

became the best there was. First sergeants from other companies would call her for information and advice. Adding to the general confusion was the fact that my first name was the same as her last name. There were times when callers were unsure to whom they should ask to speak.

Early in December of 1942 the first group of WAACs was assigned to various Army posts where the post commanders had been convinced that the women could be effective by relieving the men from certain duties so that they could take on the more rigorous ones. Among this first group to leave was a detachment of Negro WAACs assigned to Fort Huachuca, Arizona. The women of this group had been trained as drivers, cooks, bakers, clerks, and basics. This last group had no special training.

As the Negro women graduated from the specialist companies, most of them returned to our company to await assignment, while a few were waiting in the downtown hotel quarters. We had looked forward to the day when we would finally see the trained personnel leave for duty, so the day that the group left for Fort Huachuca was busy and exciting. I was choked with pride as I watched the women leave. Some of them had received all of their basic training under my command in Company 8, and all of them had received a few days' training with me.

Even if the America of 1942 had not embraced formal segregation, it probably would have been practiced at the First WAAC Training Center to accommodate the color prejudice. We were different in color and therefore hated or feared because of this difference. The routine schedule for WAAC recruits was one week in the reception center to receive equipment and orientation, followed by basic training, from which trainees were sent to the specialist companies to develop skills, followed by assignment to a staging company to await assignment in the field. Because there were not many Negro WAACs, all of their routine schedules were done in Company 8 except for the specialist training. The result was that I commanded a receiving company, a basic training company, and a staging company. My officers and I learned in one company, in a short time, what other officers learned over long periods of time.

I did not let these adverse circumstances affect my desire to be a good officer. I was hardly aware of how much I was learning. My satisfaction came from watching a group of civilian women arrive in my company and seeing them leave six weeks later as well-trained soldiers. I knew there were no better trained troops at the Training Center than those who left Company 8.

It was probably during my tour of duty as a company commander that I developed what I later came to call my "lightly attached shoulder chip." I had been raised in the South, and I knew that there was no such thing as separate but equal, but I had become determined to see that any troops I commanded would have every opportunity that was afforded others. I knew that there was no such thing as personal success, that success came only if we all succeeded together.

We began to feel at home on the job, and the activities of the Women's Army Auxiliary Corps were better organized and moving forward. We lost the feeling of hopelessness and insecurity about the service and recognized that there was real purpose to the corps. Company 12 had become Company 14 then Company 8 but because we were the same personnel, certain unit traditions were established. The officers and noncommissioned personnel were more or less permanent, as such things go in the Army, and we had our goals set. The male officers, with the exception of the regimental and battalion commanders, had been released from their duties with the companies, and women officers were performing those jobs. Several more officer candidate classes had graduated, and there were quite a number of Negro officers in addition to those of us who had been in the first OC class.

There had also been promotions for members of the first class. I was really surprised when on 23 December 1942, all members of that class were promoted to second officer except twenty-four of us who were promoted to first officer, over four hundred promotions. At the time there must have been at least a thousand third officers in the corps, and it was necessary to make promotions for the purposes of organization, discipline, and command structure. There were four Negro officers among those promoted to first officer: Alexander, Donaldson, West, and Adams. We would call ourselves captain, although we would sign our names with the official title of first officer. In anticipation of promotions at some point, some of my

Soprano Marian Anderson, with accompanist Franz Rupp, visiting Company 8 officers ([*left to right*] myself, Jessie Ward, and Ruth Freeman), 3 December 1942. *Women's Army Corps photograph*

officers and civilian friends had supplied me with silver bars, the insignia for second officer or first lieutenant. I even had a pair given to me by Captain Wagner, our company adviser, when he had been promoted to captain from first lieutenant. With all my collection of "promotion gear" I was unable to find any captain's bars. There were so many new promotions that the post exchange had exhausted its supply. One of my company officers had to go into the city to secure my first captain's bars.

After graduation I had looked forward to going home for a visit, but my assignment had kept me so busy that I had not had a chance. When, on 10 December 1942 I did get a leave, I was still a relatively new "spit and polish" second lieutenant, and I wanted my family to be proud of me. The visit was very pleasant, and it eliminated any fears my parents may have had about my venture into the unknown. I was feted as the "home-town girl who had made good."

There were, however, several unpleasant events associated with my first visit back to my hometown. The Carolina Special, of the Southern Railway system, was segregated, as were all trains and other accommodations in the South. There were sometimes provisions made, such as they were, for Negro passengers to eat in the dining car in a small curtained-off section. I had boarded the train at night in Cincinnati, and the following morning I went to the dining car and joined the line of people waiting for a seat. When the line moved, I moved, and I finally made it to the door of the dining car when the steward put his arm across the door and announced that the car was full. I stood there in front of the line and waited. After a rather long time the steward called, "All persons in uniform first." I stepped forward. He thrust his arm across the door again and said, angrily, "I said all persons in uniform first." Before I could answer, I heard a voice behind me.

"Well, what in the hell do you think that is that she has on? Get your _____ _____ arm down before I break it off for you."

The voice was so obviously southern that I turned around in surprise. That voice belonged to a very tall, very blond second lieutenant, and he was so angry that his face was quite red. He continued to talk, and loudly. "What in the world are we fighting this damned war for? She's giving her service, too, and can eat anywhere I can. And, by Jesus, I am going to eat with her in this diner."

By this time I was rather alarmed and wondered what would happen next. When I looked at the steward, he had stepped aside and was waiting to show me to my seat. I followed him to the middle of the diner where he seated me at a table for four. The lieutenant came right behind and sat down opposite me. The dining room was absolutely quiet until we were seated, and when people resumed eating there was only the sound of flatware being used. We did have breakfast together, and as we ate, the officer kept up his tirade against "crackers" and "cheap whites" and "what this war is all about." He did all the talking, and when the meal was over, he escorted me back to my seat, bowed, and left. I never saw him again, but I still think of him as a southern gentleman.

The Negro Ministerial Alliance and the NAACP (National Association for the Advancement of Colored People) had been very active in Columbia, especially about the mistreatment of Negro soldiers by white military police stationed at Fort Jackson. The pressure forced authorities to put Negro MPs on the streets, but they were unarmed and subject to the same mistreatment that other enlisted personnel received. To even things up, the Negro ministers armed themselves and patrolled the streets, one minister for each Negro MP. There were never any incidents with this system, and finally the military armed the Negro MPs, which, of course, did not go over very well with many of the more bigoted citizens.

As it happened, my first visit home was in December 1942, and while I was there the NAACP chapter had its annual meeting. My father was president of the branch and was presiding at the meeting, which was also attended by the state president of the NAACP. As I sat listening to the proceedings in a church auditorium, I heard someone whisper my name. I looked toward the side door, where a man whom I had known all my life beckoned me to come to him, which I did. He wanted to make sure that my father knew before we left the meeting to go home that the Ku Klux Klan had surrounded our house, as well as that of the Reverend Hinton, the state president. With great difficulty I refrained from rushing up to deliver the message. As soon as the meeting was over, I told my father and asked what we were going to do. We went home, to find a line of cars parked in the street in front of the house. It was not possible to surround the house without entering private property, but the Klan was lined up, in hoods, in considerable strength along the street. Daddy got out his double-barreled shotgun and shells, gave instructions to Mamma, my sister who was home from college for the weekend, my younger brother, and me, and then he left to join Mr. Hinton because his family was out of the city and he was alone. We sat in darkness following our instructions, which were to make sure that we did nothing that could be considered provocation. It had been just dusk when we came home, and we could see the men clearly. They had made no move when we came in and none when Daddy left, but they continued to sit in front of the house as the night passed. We could peep through the slats of the venetian blinds and would occasionally see one of the men light a cigarette. About dawn the cars left. It must have been a prearranged time, for they left Mr. Hinton's house about the same time. The whole thing had been reported to the police, but they "couldn't do anything about men parked on the street."

1 January–21 May 1943 . . .

☆　☆　☆　☆　☆　☆　☆　☆　☆　☆　☆　☆

I was to make many trips away from Fort Des Moines while I was stationed there, most of them on official business, but I also used some leave time. On orders issued 10 February 1943 I took my second trip, an official one, for I was the convoy officer for the second group of women assigned to Fort Huachuca, Arizona. That was my only visit to that post, and more than anything else I enjoyed the reunion with the officers who had been my classmates and with the women whom I had helped train. My friends took me on a trip to Mexico, my first away from the United States, and I purchased souvenirs. In my few days at Fort Huachuca I experienced strange weather for February. In the morning we put on full winter uniform with overcoat; by eleven the overcoat was off; and by two in the afternoon we shed the uniform jackets. Then the process was reversed, so that by ten in the evening, if one happened to be out of doors, the overcoat was needed. My lasting impression of the post was that it was large and desolate, so completely surrounded by mountains that I was puzzled as to how we got into that valley. My train ride back to Des Moines was long and lonely, especially after the excitement of the trip to Fort Huachuca.

On the way to Arizona we had traveled on a troop train. Since our group was small, we were all in one sleeping car, but there were about fifteen hundred other military personnel aboard that train: soldiers, sailors, and new recruits, all male. To prevent any difficulty we locked our doors securely at night. As we expected, on the first night some men, apparently intoxicated, attempted to break into our compartments. They tried to force each door, found each one locked, and departed. On the second day of the trip as I sat in my compartment getting dressed, there was a very precise knock on the door. One of the women who shared the compartment with me answered the door. I heard a man's voice.

"I beg your pardon, but may I speak to your officer?"

She looked at me, and I nodded my head. A well-dressed first sergeant stepped into the room and saluted.

He said, "The captain in charge of our groups would like permission to come back and speak with you."

"Of course, Sergeant. Tell him to come back, by all means."

The sergeant saluted and departed. I knew that all the personnel on the train except for my group were white, but I had seen no officer among any of the groups, so I was intensely curious. I put on my complete uniform and waited. In about fifteen minutes there was another knock at the door, and this time I answered. At the door stood a very handsome young captain.

He spoke very pleasantly and said, "Good morning, Captain, I hope you will pardon this intrusion, but since I have never met a WAAC officer, I was anxious to meet you when I heard you were on the train."

I invited him in, and we talked for about half an hour. During the course of the conversation I told him a bit about the WAAC, of which he was quite supportive, and found out that we were both southern raised. He asked if I would be kind enough to have dinner with him that evening at eight. I accepted. That evening after I had seen to the feeding of my troops, I dressed in my "pinks" and tried to look my very best.

Promptly at ten minutes to eight the captain came to take me to dinner. I had not paid very much attention to the number of cars making up the train, but it seemed that we walked through at least twelve cars and, as we walked through each one, the men stood at attention. The captain led the way to the second dining car, and there in the middle of the car stood a table covered with a flowing white cloth and a vase of roses in the middle of the table. I do not know what happened to the other tables, for there was only this one. We were seated, and the steward himself served the meal. It was a wonderful turkey dinner complete to the last detail; at that time turkey was still special. I sat facing the door, and several times during the meal when I happened to glance in the direction of the door, I could see uniformed men looking in at us in utter shock. When the meal was over, the captain escorted me back to our car, bid me good-bye, and left. The cars on which he and his men were traveling were switched from the train during the night, so I did not see the captain again. He certainly had a unique way of satisfying his curiosity about the Women's Army Auxiliary Corps.

As spring approached, Boomtown began to look like a different place. The mud was not as thick as it had been because concrete sidewalks had

As convoy officer, I visit Fort Huachuca, Arizona, in February 1943.

been laid all through the area. On the drill area the grass had come up with the warm weather. The members of Company 8 had pitched in to make our area the most beautiful in Boomtown. We drew sufficient garden tools from the quartermaster to do a real landscaping job. We raked our area over and over to keep the ground smooth and clean. Headquarters had promised that all of Boomtown would be sodded, but we were impatient; we wanted grass right then and there. We bought and planted grass seed all over the place and guarded the area carefully, practically threatening anyone who dared walk on our grass. Not content with just having grass, we had a fence built, eighteen inches high, and put it around the orderly room and planted flowers next to the building. The fence had been painted white, and it was kept white at all times.

The post commander had conducted a program of shrub planting, and there were small trees growing in the area. Beside our orderly room were cedar trees, much improving the appearance of the area. There was one chore connected with the small trees that was disliked by all. Every day before sundown one bucket of water had to be poured around the roots of each tree, which necessitated a tree-watering detail.

One set of Company 8 officers: (*left to right, standing*) Lieutenants Jones, Bright, Berry, Murphy, Clark, and Campbell, and (*seated*) myself.

We extended our beautification program so far that we were eventually asked to slow down because Company 8 was beginning to look more civilian than military. What really brought this request on was the rose arbor. Having learned the ropes about how to legally acquire almost anything available, we secured the lumber and employed the boiler room fireman to build it. He had assured us of his carpentry skills, but the item he made was an absolute monstrosity. It was extremely large, too large for a one-story building, and it looked topheavy. We set this thing outside the rear orderly room door and looked at it in despair. To avoid offending the creator, we left it there for several days before we told him that the major had ordered us to remove it. In the meantime we had planted morning glories under the pretty little white fences around the company, and they were growing wildly, as morning glories will. They were beautiful, but they required trimming to keep them off the sidewalks.

The military insists on cleanliness and order for health and appearance and, it seems most important to me, discipline. The rule at the Training Center was that all boiler rooms be kept clean and neat. I had trouble in our area because our fireman had no concept of military order, and he did not care to learn. One wall of the boiler room where he spent his time was lined with bottles and boxes and other odds and ends. In one corner was a homemade table with a lawn chair beside it, both in desperate need of repair, and he insisted on keeping them there. Every morning after his inspection, the major would remind me of the condition of the boiler room. The truth was that I was afraid of the fireman, and reminding him was as much as I was willing to do. The major was more emphatic each morning, and in turn I would try to be more emphatic when I spoke to the fireman.

Then came the Saturday when the major did not remind me about the boiler room. He sent for me to report to him at regimental headquarters. He was most emphatic that time and, instead of reminding me about the boiler room, he ordered me to see that the job was done, and he seemed to suggest something about efficiency reports. I had never really been on the carpet before, and I hesitated no longer. I went straight to the troublesome area where the fireman was relaxed and comfortable in his chair. He expressed surprise at seeing me, since inspection had been over for quite a while. I told him that he would keep this boiler room, as well as the ones in the barracks, neat and clean, and that his junk would have to go. I have always talked loudly, so I had seldom had the need to raise my voice. This time I did, and the man stood up. To emphasize how serious I was, I suddenly threw the table and the chair out of the door and into the street. I surprised myself with this act. I stomped out of the place and returned to my office to wait for him to come and knock my head off. To my surprise, I had no more trouble from the fireman, and I think that he was actually afraid of me after my outburst.

Company 8 was the showplace of the First WAAC Training Center. We had the most beautiful and best maintained area, we won many inspections, and we won first place in many parades. When the TC was at full strength, there were many companies, among them several Negro companies, some with white officers. We did have some advantage; our officers and noncommissioned officers stayed with us longer because there were fewer assignments for Negroes. Whenever there were distinguished visitors on the post, they were brought to Company 8 to see how things were done. We were very proud of our company and adopted a policy of "standing ready for inspection" every weekday between the hours of 8:00 A.M. and 4:30 P.M. This was not nearly as hard on the troops as it sounds because they were in one or another form of training during those hours. The only times we were hesitant about having visitors look us over was during the first two weeks of training of a new company of recruits.

One set of Company 8 Cadre: (*left to right*) Corporal Jones, Private Gravely, Master Sergeant Charity, Sergeant Carter, and Corporal Dunlap.

The number of trainees and officers had greatly increased and parade formations were larger, although we still had parades at every opportunity. Being selected as the best performing company in a parade still meant serving as the color guard for the next parade. Company 8 was the color guard so often we wondered whether we were as good as it seemed or other units were just not good. Unintentionally we built a grand reputation for the company, and we worked hard to live up to it. Whenever there was available time, the company would be formed and we would practice close order drill movements and march in review all around the company area.

We were very proud when we received the colors on the parade grounds, but our proudest moments were when we escorted the colors back to post headquarters and executed the required ceremony. These were moments when we felt how strong our patriotism really was. The patriotism was always there, but we were usually too busy with routine activities to let it come to surface. When I stood at "present arms" and watched the flag go down with "The Star-Spangled Banner" sounding in the air, I was always filled with a deep and rich feeling.

While things were going smoothly and pleasantly at the Training Center, the American public had lost part of its love for the women in the service or their love for the idea. It had heard nothing but glowing reports during the first six months; now, new stories began to hint of less savory things, that women in the service were strange and frustrated, looking for men or women associates. Many had forgotten that the military had not promised to change the character of any adult but only to train her for service so that she could replace a man for duty closer to the war. There were those who were thoroughly convinced that the WAAC was a system of organized prostitution for the Army. We lived through that period, too, with its cartoons and dirty jokes and vile insinuations.

One of the things I enjoyed most during my days as Basic Company CO was watching new recruits as they reported to the area, especially since my company was a reception center for Negro WAACs for many months. (Later when the number of women reporting increased, a Negro reception company was activated.) The women would be driven to the area in the large Army trucks and invited to jump to the ground. They ranged in age from twenty-one to fifty, and it was fun to note the amount of vigor in each one's jump from the truck. When they were all out of the trucks, they were marched into the supply room through the side door.

I usually sat in the corner behind the heater and looked the newcomers over as they came through that side door. This afforded an excellent opportunity to spot troublemakers by their attitudes as they received and signed for supplies and equipment. As I look back, I have wondered if we were completely fair with the newcomers. We had forgotten how frightened we were when we first arrived. Even though the women had their luggage with them, the supply sergeant promptly gave them two sheets, a pillowcase, and two blankets. When they were so loaded that it was hardly possible to walk, the platoon sergeants marched the new recruits to the barracks and assigned beds. They were immediately marched back to the supply room where they were issued an overcoat, a pair of arctics, a pair of heavy leather gloves, and a knitted cap. The non-coms would have them try all of these items on right in the supply room, so we could observe their dismay over their new attire as compared with the chic outfits they had worn to Des Moines.

The supply room was always crowded on the days when new basic training groups arrived because all the permanent members of the company wanted to hear the comments made by people who were as ignorant of the military as we had been when we arrived. Some said that they had come

Company 8 in formation at Fort Des Moines

into the Army to be officers because they were sure that the present officers did not know what they were doing. Others said that they were not going to have anyone telling them what to do because, after all, they were grown. Very few of them could tell officers from enlisted personnel, and the eager beavers saluted privates as well as officers. The younger women treated us like schoolteachers and the older women treated us like schoolchildren. It was cruel fun, for we knew that in twenty-four hours they would have learned about officers and non-coms and authority and would be overcome with humility, fear, and anger.

In one group of recruits there arrived one day a very lively woman, whom I later learned was forty-four years of age. The day was quite cold, and I had my corner chair close to the heater because the supply room door was open. This woman came in, broke out of the line, and came over to the heater, where she dropped her bag and starting rubbing her hands. When the supply officer told her to get back in the line, she replied that she was cold and was going to get warm before she moved. When she raised her head, she saw me sitting in my warm corner and reached over and pulled my shoulder as she said to me, with my captain's bars and all, "Get up, Missie, and give me that chair. You are younger than I am and I want to warm my knees."

The mess hall between our company and the next one, Company 7, pro-

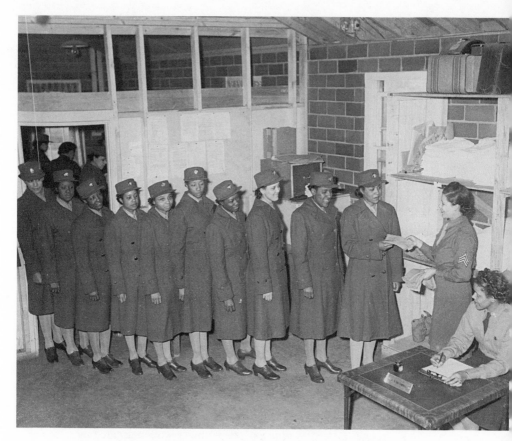

Lieutenant Campbell (*seated*) and Sergeant Carter issuing supplies to Company 8

vided us with three meals each day, as well as with a thorough understanding of the term "mess hall." Along with Company 7 we carried our beautification program to the interior and exterior of that building. We shared all its activities with our neighbors, who happened to be white. Both companies provided people for KP duty, and there was a pleasant association among the women, depending on whether the current mess officer could control her racial bias.

The Training Center was exactly what its name implied. As personnel were trained, it was assumed that they would be sent to an assignment in the field. Officers and enlisted personnel changed rapidly all over the post as more and more openings were created for WAAC personnel. This was true for all units except Company 8. Somehow, we managed to keep our personnel fairly permanent, although there were occasional changes in the officer roster. Even with the few changes in the company, we had to work extremely hard. Some months the instructors were assigned from head-quarters and at other times company officers had to do the teaching. How-ever, all classroom instruction was supervised by headquarters personnel.

Among the people on the supervising staff was a WAAC captain who, in a few months, had grown notorious for her skill at bullying junior offi-cers and enlisted personnel. I had never met the captain and knew her only by reputation until one rainy day she felt the time had come to bully the members of my company. During her visit to one of the classrooms of Company 8 she spotted one woman asleep in the classroom. When the class was over, she had the guide officer take the troops out into the rain in company formation, where she kept them standing in pouring rain for ten minutes while she told the officer how terrible she was, what poorly trained personnel the company had, and everything else she could think of that was unkind and uncomplimentary. I could make no excuse for the woman sleeping in the class, but I surely could not find any excuse, or even tolerate, any supervisor's trying to embarrass personnel in my company. With a bit of official nudging after considerable prodding from me, less than twelve hours had passed before we received a "voluntary apology" from the captain.

In the spring of 1943 a large number of women, both white and Negro, came to the Training Center from two southern states. There were greater numbers in these groups than had been received from any state at any one time. Although some of the most qualified women we were to train were members of these groups, it was evident that the recruiters had dropped all standards. Nearly every member of the corps had been homesick at some time, but these women were the worst that I had seen, and they were unhappy about being in the service at all. Our standard line about how you volunteered for this organization and would have to take what it dealt out had no effect. Seeking the cause of their extreme unhappiness, I asked the officers and non-coms in the company to talk to members of the com-pany. There had been a great deal of talk about drafting women into the WAAC, but to the best of my knowledge it never happened; however, many of this group claimed to have been drafted. This is the story we finally got from the women: in these communities when a male member of a woman's family was leaving for training camp after having been called up by Selective Service and the woman would go to the railway or bus station to tell the man good-bye, an Army officer would rush up after the draftee had departed and ask if she wanted to do something to bring her man back home sooner. When she answered "Yes," she was asked to sign a paper the officer had. Many of them had thought they were merely signing a peti-tion, but several days later they would receive notices to report for induc-tion into the WAAC. Both white and Negro women told this same story, and the various COs reported it to headquarters. We only had the word of the women, but we did notice that, after that, a bit more care was taken in the selection process.

In spite of the recruiting methods used, there were some outstanding WAAC soldiers among these recruits. And there were some bona fide characters. One woman was a bully. On Friday evenings when cleaning for the Saturday morning inspections was at fever pitch, she became a real slave driver. She introduced liquid bleach to the floor cleaning process, where a strong soap and stiff brush had been used to do the job before. Our barracks floors were the cleanest on the post. She would sit on the edge of her bunk and yell instructions and exhortations: "Scrub that floor! Make it white! The Cap'n wants us to win this inspection." She had a few personal techniques for special cleaning jobs, but I was never privy to these because she felt that I would not approve.

Then there was the woman who, after two weeks in training, decided that she was too tired to get up and go through "all that stuff," so she planned to remain in bed all day to rest. By the time the matter was brought to my attention, the squad leader, the platoon leader, and the platoon commander had all ordered the woman to get out of bed, but she had refused. The matter now rested in my hands. After conferring a bit, we decided that the company executive officer would go to the barracks and order the woman to get up, put on her uniform, and report to the company officer. After Lieutenant Campbell left the office to go to the barracks, my thoughts stayed on the situation. If the woman defied Lieutenant Campbell, my turn was next, and if she refused to get up for me, the commanding officer, where did I turn? I simply could not let this reach the point of calling the military police. By the time Lieutenant Campbell returned and informed me that Private _____ refused to budge, I had made up my mind.

Wearing my best "I am in command" attitude, followed by an entourage of the platoon commander, the platoon sergeant, and the squad leader, I marched over to the barracks and up the stairs right to the woman's bed. Her back was to me as I approached, and she made no move to turn in my direction. The squad leader stepped forward and addressed the woman by name, requesting that she turn over. She turned. I had to be careful that I said nothing to which she could give a negative answer, so I said, "I understand that you want to stay in bed and rest, Private. I am going to oblige you. You are hereby confined to bed for the next three days, with guard. You may get out of bed only to go to the latrine, and you will be accompanied on that trip. Your meals will be brought to you. Have a good rest." It worked. After twenty-four hours I began to get messages containing the request to lift the punishment. I did not, and I am sure that my refusal prevented some other problems that might have come up later.

With all my concern for having the perfect basic training company, I developed some rather rigid inspection methods. When the troops marched away each morning to the various classes, I expected *everything* to be in order, and, generally, all was in order. However, with one group of trainees there was found to be a strange problem that actually required about a week of investigation to solve. Each morning after inspecting the troops and seeing them march off to class, I would go through the barracks to check personally. One morning as I walked through the second barracks building, I glanced up at the third window on my left and saw a brown spot. I was annoyed. After all, this was the company that was prepared for visitors at all times. I turned the matter over to the squad leader. The brown spot was there the next morning, and this time I had the two women, between whose beds this window was located, report to me for a reprimand. The third morning I saw the brown spot I was somewhat more than annoyed, and this time I gave company punishment. All the time the two women were insisting that they washed that window each morning before they came out for the company formation. I had to believe them, because no one would keep repeating a punishable offense. I sent the non-coms to look outside the building for birds' nests. Of course there were none. On the fourth morning we went outside to examine the brown spot and discovered that it seemed soft and slightly runny. Unknowingly we came one step closer to the answer when we decided that the spot was wind blown, possibly bird droppings. But whoever heard of a bird that kept such exact time? On the fifth day, Friday, the appearance of that spot did not help my disposition, but it led me to the action that solved the problem. For the Saturday morning inspection I stationed a non-com in the building just before the whistle sounded for the company to fall in for inspection. Her report: "Right after the whistle blew I could hear all the girls upstairs running to fall in. I was watching the window and suddenly that brown stuff hit the window with a 'plop.' It had to come from upstairs."

I asked the squad leader to do a little investigating and report to me. She found that, regardless of the weather, there was one young woman who opened the window for thirty seconds every morning to spit after the whistle sounded. I was indignant that such a nasty habit had caused so much trouble and, on Monday morning, had that private report to me. I am afraid I was carried away with my ideas of what was ladylike, feminine, cultured, and refined and did not hesitate to point this out. The only thing nice I did in that conference was ask her to sit rather than stand at attention as I had to do when I was called on the carpet. After I had carried on for a while making sure that I had made my point, I asked the woman if she had anything to say.

"Captain Adams, don't the officers in this company smoke?"

"Why, of course," I answered, surprised at her question.

"Well, Ma'am, that's tobacco, and so is snuff. You all takes your tobacco your way and I takes tobacco my way."

I felt about two inches tall, but she was right. To save face, I asked if
she had known how much trouble she had caused the women who lived
below her.

"No, Ma'am, I didn't know, but I knew I would not be allowed to keep
any kind of container in the barracks so I just spit it out the window."

From then on she was allowed a small can, provided it was neither visible or otherwise offensive, and I had learned a new tolerance.

In the 1940s much of the country had laws and customs of segregation
that supported the general practice of prejudice and discrimination. It was,
therefore, very difficult to understand how anyone who was Negro might
not know all this, but it happened. A group of young ladies from a small
town in the northernmost section of the United States, all classmates and
good friends, decided to make a patriotic move for their country and sign
up for the WAAC. The town celebrated and sent them off to Des Moines
with love and support. The group traveled together and looked forward
to sharing their experiences in the Army. When they arrived at the TC,
the dreams of one of the young ladies was shattered. From the reception
center all the women were sent to the same company of white women — all
except one. She was sent to Company 8 because her birth certificate had
a "C" in the box showing race.

The woman was not prepared for segregation from her friends, and she
had never seen Negroes before she left her hometown on the way to Fort
Des Moines and had never been close to a Negro until she reported to our
company, in tears. She tried very hard to adjust to us, but after three days
she was still crying. Since the platoon sergeant and platoon commander
were unable to find out the reason for this great unhappiness, I felt that
the time had come for me to get into the matter. My first move was to
talk to the CO of the friends of my company member. She had learned
a little from them because they, too, had been surprised by the separation
and asked questions about it. With great effort and many conversations,
I learned the story. This woman had been the only Negro in their town.
Years before, a young Negro man became snowbound while passing through
the town, remained to work, and married her mother; she was born, and
then her father died. Since she looked white and everyone else was white,
the matter of race never came up. As a matter of fact, the issue had not
come up since the time her birth certificate had been recorded.

This young woman suffered the most extreme case of cultural shock that
I have ever known. Her discovery of her racial identity had filled her with
hatred of her mother and grandparents back home and filled her with fear
of these strange people among whom she was living. We provided her with
lots of counseling as well as acts of reassurance, and in time she made

a reasonable adjustment. Among other things, we were prepared to grant a discharge "for the good of the service" so that she could go home and not face her new world. She found that unacceptable; she did not even want a furlough to visit. More than anything she wanted to complete her training and receive an assignment away from her former friends, and that is what happened.

... 1 January–21 May 1943 (continued)

In time the training programs were quite well organized, based on the kinds of assignments available to women. Most of the male personnel who had originally handled the training had departed, and women were in charge of most activities.

Col. Don Faith, the first commandant, had moved on and had been followed by Colonel Hoag, who did not stay very long. The commandant whom I knew best and who remained at the TC longest was Col. Frank U. McCoskrie, affectionately referred to as "Colonel Mac." He was a large, well-groomed man and was never seen outdoors without his swagger stick. Colonel Mac was genuinely interested in all phases of our training and was fair and compassionate. One of the most valuable members of his staff was Mrs. Ella M. Putnam, resident counselor. She was there for all, officers and enlisted women, when anyone needed to talk to someone outside the military. She helped thousands of women with their problems, sometimes just by letting them blow off steam. I felt free to go into her office and talk to her, and when I felt down, I could always get an encouraging word.

As the organization grew, the processing system was perfected, or at least scheduled routinely. Recruits would come to the TC and spend the first week in a reception company. From there, in groups of approximately two hundred, they would move to a basic training company for six weeks (at first, basic training had been eight weeks). After basic, the group would be assigned to various specialist schools, with some members of a class being sent into the field as generalists to be trained at the new station.

As for Negro personnel, there were still some problems in the receiving battalion and worse ones in the staging area. When the Negro recruits were too few to form a whole separate company, those who had arrived were kept waiting until the needed number accumulated. By the time this happened, much of the recruits' enthusiasm had cooled. There was a serious problem in the staging area because there were few Army bases willing to accept Negro women even when they were well trained. When assignment requests did come, they were for jobs where segregation could be maintained and for which basics with no special training were used.

In the spring of 1943 there were so many Negro women awaiting assignment that it became necessary to house them in company day rooms, which meant the company recreational space was sacrificed. The furniture from seven day rooms was stored in supply rooms, and twenty-five double-decked Army beds were placed in each day room, fifty people in each room. My company had 208 trainees as it was, and when I received an additional 200 from those housed in day rooms, we had absolutely all that we could handle. The one other Negro basic company at that time was Company 20, commanded by 1st Lt. Geneva Ferguson, and that company received 150 additional people. The crowded living conditions, the scheduling of meals, and maintaining our high standards for Company 8, plus the fact that these conditions existed because post commanders did not want Negro personnel, created a morale problem. It was difficult to understand the logic that refused the use of trained personnel whose services could help end hostilities.

It did not take very long to learn that military rumors are like kudzu, the most prolific plant I have ever heard of. It was even said that when the top-level brass was unable to make a decision, it resorted to doing things according to the latrine rumor. Before my service was completed, I had begun to believe that because there always seemed to be some truth in the rumors. I found out that a rumor could begin with a few phrases, as in the case of two rather aggressive young women who overheard my end of a telephone conversation. Within half an hour they had most of the troops practically packed and ready to move. Actually, the conversation dealt with the problem of meeting and housing a group of women arriving from California during the night. My end of the conversation upon which the rumor started sounded something like this:

"Captain Adams speaking. A lieutenant who from Transportation? Oh! What? When did you get the orders? How many? Is it San Francisco or Los Angeles? Four days? What a trip. How can they stand it? How many officers do you want? This is awful short notice but will do the best I can. What time will the trucks be ready? This is going to rush me but we'll be ready. The old Army spirit, you know. Thanks, Lieutenant, and I'll see you when you pick me up."

Sometimes rumors are started by the very people one must depend on to stop them. Normally, when a company commander received a report of the AGCT scores, she looked them over with the platoon commander, and the report was returned to the Classification Office. One day when I returned to my office, I found the whole company in an uproar. The first sergeant was angry, as were the other non-coms, and some of the trainees were in tears. After a time I was able to piece together what great disaster had befallen the company during my absence. The AGCT scores had come in, and the only officer present saw the report. She decided that this was her chance to exert authority by taking action. She called the troops together and announced that all the people who had received a score of 110 or better would go to OCS and that all the others would automatically go to bakers and cooks school. No wonder the troops were alarmed. Very few wanted to go to either school, and as for going to OCS, they were entitled to the right to make up their own minds.

Bulletin boards were the primary source of information for members of a unit: duty rosters and post, regimental, battalion, and company regulations and assignments are posted there, KP duty and inspection gigs being the most unpleasant. Individuals were required to initial their names when they read their assignments. The difficult part was posting notices as required by some higher headquarters; even mops and brooms were to be placed as the major wanted them. Once, when all the officers agreed that the present arrangement of cleaning equipment was not practical, we had a meeting of company commanders in our area to decide on a recommendation for hanging the mops and brooms. The meeting lasted for two hours, and as I recall, we were unable to reach a decision on this weighty matter.

One problem I faced all the time I was in the service was keeping up with all the items for which I signed on memorandum receipts, or M/Rs. The signature on the M/R made one responsible — we were told that the post quartermaster was accountable. That was not the way it worked; WAAC officers were also accountable. The most mobile items seemed to be the folding chairs, folding tables, shovels, coal buckets, brooms, and GI cans. Arctics especially had a strange way of disappearing. One week a company might have twenty pairs in excess and the next week be short ten pairs. The fact that all items were carefully marked meant absolutely nothing because sometimes they would show up a half mile away. It was more important to keep up with sheets, pillowcases, blankets, and comforters, always checking against a laundry short count. We counted the items as the laundry went out and when it returned and seldom came out even. We wondered if the quartermaster used different mathematics than other people did. It seemed impossible to beat the system as far as blankets and comforters were concerned, but there were ways to take care of the number of sheets and pillowcases. I approved a policy initiated by the supply officer and supply sergeant: we always keep a little excess until that excess turned into eighty pillowcases and two hundred sheets. We called every company on the post and, to our amazement, every one had an accurate M/R count. That was the day I learned that it was better to be short than long. The linen was finally given to the laundryman to find out where the items belonged, along with a strong suggestion that he had left us the excess.

A properly fitting uniform was vital equipment for appearance, morale, and performance, because looking good enhanced self-confidence, and thus performance. Which reminds me of Supply Sgt. Vera Carter, probably the most efficient at the Training Center. In addition to her successes with keeping the women well dressed, she developed skills and contacts that kept the company supplied with whatever we needed or wanted. The man at the quartermaster warehouse who was responsible for issuing WAAC clothing was known on the post for his unpleasant disposition and was the despair of any conscientious supply sergeant. Although she never told us how she knew, Sergeant Carter knew that Tuesday was the only day in the week when this man was reasonably pleasant, and she was able to keep us well supplied by holding her requisitions until Tuesday whenever possible. She was pleasant to have around because she was always cheerful, even though she had the impossible task of impressing recruits with their responsibility for issue items. She even smiled when she was reprimanded, which occurred often since she insisted on wearing her Hobby Hat pushed back and tilted over her right ear. Even when she had every member of the company perfectly uniformed, she wore a sweater.

One of our major supply problems was the WAAC shoulder bag. The original bag, such as I was issued, had been a large synthetic leather bag with a shoulder strap. Inside was a smaller bag that could be kept inside the large bag or worn on the belt. The next bag issue was of rough real leather and shaped like a half-circle, but the old bags were still used until the manufacturer's contract was completed. As the old bags wore out, we had to collect them to exchange for new ones. Sometimes the "new" bags were from the original design and sometimes from the new design, which meant that the troops were unhappy because one group thought the other had better bags, and vice versa, and I was unhappy because I was unable to have my company all dressed alike. Eventually the supply of originals was used up and we accomplished the sameness we desired.

Only someone who has sold women's shoes can appreciate what enormous difficulties were encountered in issuing shoes to the new recruits. To begin with, the shoes were made by several different manufacturers, and consequently the sizes varied slightly. Second, more women than I would have believed were accustomed to buying their shoes by size rather than by fit, which made for lots of uncomfortable feet. The quartermaster general had obviously secured some real shoe-fitting specialists, and they were the butt of the complaints that some women were being forced to wear shoes larger than their size and that they were not accustomed to wearing shoes as large as were issued to them. These complaints became so numerous that it was decided that, as nearly as possible, the women would be given the size that they wanted. This created another problem. After a week of wearing the shoes that they wanted, some of the women complained that their feet were giving them trouble. Some of them really were having trouble, for their shoes were too small. This meant that the shoes had to be turned in for new ones, and in some cases, with all the required walking and marching, the feet had been damaged for life. This system soon became too expensive, and the decision was made to issue shoes by fit rather than by size.

It was amazing the number of women who had never had shoes properly fitted until they joined the service. However, shoes were just a part of the problem. Many had their own ideas about how they wanted their clothes to fit and applied these ideas to the uniform. They were constantly altering and realtering garments that had been correctly fitted at the clothing warehouse. The company officers and non-coms were always reminding the offenders that the uniform was designed to have a specific cut and fit for comfort and performance. There were some cases that demanded an official refitting according to military needs. Then there was the girdle. This was the item of issue that was not required to be worn unless needed, but often those who needed it most would not wear it, and some who did not need the girdle would wear it. It was really getting rather personal when one had to call someone in for a conference to suggest that wearing a girdle might make for a more attractive appearance. That was just one of the less pleasant chores.

There were, of course, those women who felt that wearing a uniform meant looking as masculine as possible, although I had never heard even a hint of such an idea from the authorities. During the first year of the corps's existence there was a small amount of this thinking, but as the organization grew, those of us responsible for the training used all the skill and ingenuity we could muster to discourage it. Occasionally we recommended makeup to women who had never even worn lipstick before. The regulation requiring that the hair be worn "neat and well above the collar" was not intended to suggest that the hair had to be cut short, as many believed. We became a divided camp: those who cut the hair short, those who managed to pin, curl, or roll the hair so that it was as desired, and those who were forever on the carpet because their hair was "down." One morning when I completed the inspection of my company and before they moved out to class, I said to the group, "Two of you have forgotten this morning. Your hair is down and I want you to fall out and do something about it before we move."

Two women, not the two about whom I was speaking, ran out of the formation into the barracks at top speed. The platoon sergeant then spoke to the real offenders. Later in the day, Sergeant Carter said to me, "Captain Adams, you really embarrassed those two women this morning."

"What are you talking about, Carter?"

"Those two women who flew into the barracks this morning both wear wigs, and they hang them on the corner of their bunks at night. When you said 'hair down,' they thought they had left their wigs hanging on the bed."

By the time the TC was at full strength, we had among the trainees women from all levels of the economic scale. For many, military life offered a real improvement in the standard of living. Some of us were surprised to learn that the everyday amenities we took for granted were unknown to scores of fellow WAACs, Negro and white. It was difficult to believe that there were women who had never been to a medical doctor until they reported for the physical examination required to join the corps or who had never seen a dentist at all. There was such fear of a dentist that some refused to report for appointments; they threatened to go AWOL and lived in anguish for days. There were a few women whom I had to personally take to the dentist and stand beside the doctor while he did his work, after having promised them that I would not let anyone hurt them. I was especially concerned about the large number of Negro women who came from poor rural areas. I tried diligently to see that they had full benefit of the services available. It was not easy, because changing habits is a slow process, the unknown being the source of much fear.

We worked hard at making soldiers out of civilians. All classes were being taught by company officers by this time, following the outline provided by the Training Office. It was assumed, I suppose, that because we had been exposed to concentrated training in OCS that we were well versed in all the subject matter. This was not absolutely true, and the officers spent a great deal of time preparing for their classes. Periodically there were refresher courses to keep company officers up to date. As a company commander, with many extra duties, I had not assigned myself to any major or long courses, but I was willing to serve as a substitute when an officer needed to be away from a class. With officers going out in the field so rapidly, I was constantly reassigning the personnel left, until there were just enough officers remaining to get the job done.

One day, about fifteen minutes before a class was to meet, I received word from headquarters that the officer who taught the class had received orders for a transfer and would be leaving immediately. With no one left to whom I could assign that particular class, I had no choice but to pick up the course outline and prepare to give the class a lecture. I realized that I knew very little about the subject matter, but not how very little that little amount was. After twenty minutes of the fifty-minute class period, I had covered all that I could remember about hygiene and was fishing for some interesting subject to discuss for the rest of the period. At that point one of the few male supervising officers left at the TC walked in the door, planning to supervise the content and method of instruction. I was desperate, searching for a way out of the dilemma, when I had a brilliant idea. I cleared my throat, paused dramatically, and announced to the class, "We will now discuss the subject of female hygiene. Feel free to ask any questions you might have." The visiting officer blushed and hurriedly left the classroom. To my surprise there were a great many questions, and somehow I managed to bluff my way through the remaining half hour. I never again tried to teach unless I knew the material.

In just a few months a great deal had been accomplished, and Company 8 was at its peak. There were even requests to be transferred to the company, and some jealousies were expressed about us. Our members were very proud and boasted about how great we were, even after the short training period. I kept my personal pride tightly under control when I found out that the word from members of other companies to members of my company was "Your company commander can't be as good as some of you say, even if she is a captain."

Company 8 continued to be the show company of the post, and I credited this to the fact that my officers and I had been assigned to one spot longer than had the officers in other companies. We learned all the tricks for getting things done. My personal pride came from the sheer beauty of my company's execution of close order drill and their near-perfect marching in the many parades and reviews. Because I was not an athletic person, I was amazed at how much I liked this part of the military. Perhaps it was the discipline that appealed to me. One day when the company had performed especially well, even receiving a round of applause as it passed the reviewing stand, I was so proud of the group that I marched backward just to look at them as we marched back to the company area. At one point I forgot to look around for the six-inch stakes on the parade ground that we used to guide our lines. Suddenly I fell flat on my back, but I kept on counting the cadence as I got to my feet, still marching and brushing the dried grass from my uniform. Pride made me continue to march backward for about fifty feet, and I noted the great effort required by the women to keep from laughing at their company commander who had just fallen flat. We kept going until we were well off the parade grounds and out of the view of the reviewing stand. I brought the company to a halt and said, "Now, go ahead and laugh. I remember thinking it was funny when I saw an officer fall down."

We finally had a cadre of noncommissioned officers with the proper stripes for their grade. They were 1st Sgt. Margaret Charity, Sgts. Evelyn Cunningham, Vera Carter, and Oleta Crain, and Cpls. Virginia Dunley and Vera Jones.

Despite all the general concern for intensive training and my personal concern about having the show company of the TC, we did not ignore the social side of life. In civilian life there had been a saying that the only qualification for call-up by the draft was "breath and britches." When the TC opened, it seemed to us that the only qualification was "britches." The draft boards seemed to have had some strictly private instruction to clear out as many men as possible from the Des Moines area. So there were very few available and unattached men left in the city. However, the Army and the Navy had stationed great numbers of men in several cities not too far away. And there were weekend passes. There were the post service clubs, including a separate one for Negroes, of course, where troops received their guests. Other activities on the post were movies, visiting shows, company shows, and company parties. The city of Des Moines had many eating places, movies, and a good theater season.

Company 8 had its fair share of company and platoon social events, generally in the company day room. The only outside guests were regimental and battalion staff members and officers from neighboring companies. The games and refreshments were simple, and everyone was reminded that good companions made for great fun, even with the childish activities.

Sometimes we had elaborate company affairs complete with costumes, scenery, and live music, which could be accommodated only in the service club. Usually each platoon would be responsible for a part of the show, and it was amazing the amount of talent and skill that was discovered among the women. Two of the most delightful concert voices I had heard belonged to two members of Company 8, and we were proud to show them off to others. Among other talents were a concert violinist, several excellent pianists, dramatic artists, comedians, and a seasoned mistress of ceremonies. Our shows included musical selections, patriotic scenes, dramatic skits, comedy acts, and whatever else the members thought of, including some real surprises.

On the occasion of one of our shows for which I declared there would be no censorship, the TC "big brass" had been invited. I was proud as I sat on the front row between the regimental commander and the Training Center commandant watching the performance. It was magnificent, as amateur shows go. The costumes were complete, the music was excellent, and the mistress of ceremonies was really doing a great job when she announced an act for which I was not prepared. A young WAAC came on stage to do a comic monologue, followed by a short poem about the clothing she was issued and about orders telling her when to wear them. Suddenly, she began to take her clothes off, reciting a funny line with each item. She removed a pair of arctics, a pair of service oxfords, a pair of socks, and two pairs of service stockings. Then off came an enlisted man's overcoat, a utility coat, a WAAC overcoat, a suit jacket, a suit skirt, a shirt, a fatigue dress, a pair of fatigue pants, a WAAC slip and a WAAC bra, leaving her, back to the audience, in only an issue girdle, so far as I could see. She paused to look over her shoulder at the field grade officers who were watching, and as she reached to pull off the girdle, I closed my eyes. When I heard the applause, I opened my eyes, and there she stood looking very good in a nearly nothing white bathing suit. She asked me later if I had not trusted her not to let me down. I told her that sometimes I would rather be let down than be frightened to death.

The mistress of ceremonies for that show was in basic training at the time. This woman was a livewire, but she remained clear of the orderly room. Her first trip there had been to complain to the first sergeant that everyone else in the company had been on the KP duty roster except her, and she wanted to know why she was being ignored. We needed a mail orderly at that time, and we gave her the job. We had not noticed her particularly before this time, but from the moment she became mail orderly she became one of the most valuable members of the cadre. She later became a platoon sergeant and was one of the first women to get sergeant's stripes.

As we grew more certain about what we were supposed to do and more confident about our skills to do it, those of us who had been at Fort Des Moines since the TC opened began to get acquainted with the city. Most of us had found reasons to shop in the city, but now we began to know the people, dine in the better eating places, and to attend the theaters. One member of the Third Platoon who was more sophisticated than most of us had very friendly relations with many of the big-name entertainers who appeared on the stages of Des Moines. I was pleased that she asked me to accompany her several times. We always had the best seats in the house and visited backstage after the performances. I am very proud of my collection of personally autographed pictures of Cab Calloway, Katherine Dunham, and Lionel Hampton when they were at their peaks — even though the collection is relatively small.

Des Moines is the capital of Iowa, and, compared with my hometown, it was a very large city in the forties. When we inquired of new acquaintances about the size of the city, the answer was always the same, over 100,000 with about 5,000 Negroes. The official 1940 census reports the count as 153,426 whites and 6,360 Negroes, so the amateur guesses were not far from the truth. The city was easy to get around in because of the way the streets were planned, and its most striking feature seemed to be the state capitol building with its golden central dome. I always wanted to visit the building, but twenty-five years passed before I had the chance to do so, when I attended a national convention in the city.

My impression was that the citizens of Des Moines were tolerant, at best, of the members of the WAAC, but more understanding about the benefits of the Training Center presence. There was no apparent segregation, although there were separate "everythings," except perhaps schools. However, discrimination was present even though frequently underground. It seemed to me that before the WAAC TC was established, there had not been enough Negroes to cause concern. They were not just a minority, but a less-than-1-percent minority. The city public schools were reputed to have one Negro teacher.

I gradually became aware of latent discrimination. Many of us were from the South, and we were always careful not to set ourselves up for overt rejection and embarrassment. The stores in Des Moines were quite willing to receive us as customers. The tailors offered custom-made uniforms, and I must admit that I was one of the officers who took advantage of the opportunity. As a matter of fact, it was here that I had my very first charge account that was truly mine (my father had always signed for me when I lived at home).

More than anything we looked forward to having a meal away from the mess hall and the military atmosphere. Several of us frequently dined in the city at the nicer restaurants and always felt that we were welcome. However, when we reported to fellow officers that we had eaten at a particular place and suggested that they would find it very pleasant, there were some who expected the worst. They would enter the restaurant and ask if they served Negroes. The same place others of us had eaten the day before would now have a hostess or cashier who would reply, "No, we do not." The very next day the original group would go to that restaurant and have no problem. Eventually the practice of asking about service stopped.

While I was stationed at Fort Des Moines I met several people with whom I had pleasant associations. I met the Reverend William F. Ogleton, pastor of the A.M.E. church in the city, and his family. Twenty years later, Mr. Ogleton was transferred to the same position at another A.M.E. church where I was a member.

The one person I met for whom I felt great closeness and upon whom I depended at times was Charlie Howard. He was a lawyer, a photographer, a newspaper correspondent, and the editor and publisher of the local Negro newspaper. Charlie was a real character, and, once we set the ground rules of our relationship, we grew to be great friends. Charlie needed a contact on the post, and I needed a "kitchen cabinet" for advice on area civilian matters. I never needed a lawyer, but Charlie was nice to refer to when it seemed that I might. Charlie was an activist when I knew him and later achieved some national publicity in the 1947 presidential campaign of Henry A. Wallace.

We were sure that the Selective Service had been ordered to clean out the Des Moines area, but they missed a few men, and occasionally one or two would return home for a while. My friend Capt. Sarah Murphy and I found a couple of escorts among the few. Sarah's friend was an instructor at one of the southern Negro state colleges who was home recuperating from major surgery. My friend was a very handsome young man (he looked like Alan Ladd) whose job was classified "necessary for the war effort" and so was exempt from the draft. We always double dated because Sarah and I were careful to set good examples for the troops and, of course, we had to avoid compromising situations. My friend was as quiet as he was good looking, which meant that he seldom said anything. We were allowed to wear civilian clothes when off duty, and although we had sent most of our clothes home when we arrived, by borrowing and sharing Sarah and I would manage attractive outfits. The four of us would go into the city for dinner or a show or a nightclub and "H" would be silent most of the time. When he did speak, his ideas were usually well thought out and, for those who saw little of him, his words were profound. It was really quite nice to be seen with him since he was so good looking, but, to give an example of his profundity, when I asked him why he wore a watch on each wrist, he replied, "I like to have time on both hands."

Play Day, as we called it, was celebrated in May; it was actually the anniversary of the passing of the bill creating the WAAC. All training was suspended and all personnel participated in the activities. In the morning there was a big parade for all the important visitors who came for the occasion. In the afternoon there were competitive games with representatives from every company taking part. The parade ground was marked off in squares, and troops were assigned to the squares for certain games. After a specified time all the troops rotated to another square. This was a festive occasion with thousands of women playing on the grounds in exercise suits. Play Days were truly democratic, with the troops playing together in complete accord without regard for color or race or religion or rank. When the day was over, the post was one giant sleep-in from utter fatigue.

A few days after one of these play days I turned Company 8 over to the new CO, 1st Lt. Alma Berry.

22 May–31 December 1943

Before I turned the company over to Lieutenant Berry, we had the routine going excellently, and most of the time all that I had to do was be present and sometimes make a suggestion or two. The company executive officer delighted in relieving me of all my duties that she was able to handle, and even the matter of correspondence required little of me. Because everyone was "on the ball," I had the easiest job on the post. But, alas, such a state of near perfection could not last long. We had already learned that the only thing permanent in the Army was change.

One morning I received a telephone message to report to headquarters immediately. I was not exactly alarmed, but ordinarily I had so little business there that the message did create some concern. When I stopped at the adjutant's office, I was told that the commandant was waiting for me and that I should go right into Colonel Mac's office. At this point I did worry a bit because there was none of the lighthearted banter with Captain Crumm and Warrant Officer Machuta to which I had become accustomed. I was not prepared for what the colonel wanted of me.

"Adams, how long would it take you to turn over your company property and be prepared to leave?"

"Why, Colonel, I could do that within a few hours for we have tried to keep everything in order should I have to be away for an extended time. Sir, I am not leaving the company, am I?"

The colonel answered my question with, "Yes, you are leaving Company 8. I have decided that we will bring you up here in headquarters."

"I don't want to leave my company, sir. I am enjoying my work, and

I am not qualified to do anything else. Really, Colonel Mac, I can do more good where I am."

I realized as I spoke that I was going beyond the limits, especially when my opinion had not been invited, but I dreaded the thought of leaving Boomtown, where I felt at home and, because of my seniority, I was sort of a local authority. And the truth was that I could think of absolutely nothing else that I could do and could see no logic in leaving a job that I did well for something about which I knew nothing.

"Captain, I have decided that you must move," the colonel continued. "We are very pleased with the job you are doing. In fact, the reason that we are moving you is that you are doing your job almost too well. It simply adds up to the fact that you have learned how to be a good company commander and should you remain on that job you would become stagnant. We don't want that to happen. You have done so well that you have qualified yourself to move."

I was almost in tears. I had organized Company 8 and had been its only CO, and I felt that I should spend the rest of my Army service right in that spot. But when I realized that those good days were over, I adopted an attitude of resignation and asked, "When do I have to move, Colonel?"

"We will give you two days to turn over your company and give any instructions that you think should be given to the new CO. I am sure that you will enjoy being with us here, and I know that you will do just as good a job in the Training Section as you have done with your company."

The conference was over, and I left the building. Slowly, I started back toward Boomtown and Company 8, but I kept feeling more and more depressed. I should have realized that eventually I would have to leave the unit, but I had assumed that I would receive some special training for my next assignment. It was ironic that I was going to the Training Section. That was the one section for which I had the greatest dislike, feeling that it was unnecessary and designed just to get in one's hair. I did not look forward to going back to the company area and breaking the news to the staff. I was not concerned about what they thought of me as CO, for we had all been together so long that there was genuine affection for each other. I hated the thought of working with strangers.

I decided to stop by Major Fowler's office and ask him why he had permitted me to be moved. I learned that he did not even know that I was to be moved. Since the major was most noncommital about things in general, except following regulations, the news of my assignment served some purpose, for it was then that I found out that he thought I was a good officer and that he felt that I would be missed by the entire regiment. The compliments did help me to prepare myself to go back to the company.

In utmost confidence I told my officers and NCOs about the move — and I should have known better. No one betrayed my confidence, I am sure, but within a few hours every member of the company knew I was leaving. I hoped that some of the sadness expressed about my departure was sincere. There were a great many expressions of regret made, including get-togethers in my honor; the more kindnesses that were heaped upon me, the sadder I felt. During the two days I had been allotted to rid myself of the company property as well as my sentiment about the company, I worked hard at both tasks. The property matter was easy, but a great part of the buildings in the company had been completed under my supervision, in some cases by my own physical labor. I had helped paint, hang screens, police and clean the areas, and decorate the interior and exterior of Company 8, and I knew that I would be leaving a part of me there when I left. Most people complained about being stuck in one place, and I was complaining about leaving.

Within two days I had moved out of the company completely and reported to TC headquarters. I was to be a training supervisor, but I did not find out what that meant until I had been in the section for some time. The day I went to work at headquarters, I reported to Major Mumm, who was then in charge. He invited me to sit down, told me he was happy to have me join the staff, and said he hoped I would like my new assignment. He then asked me to follow him across the hall to the office of the supervisors. The room was filled with desks and people sitting at them. When we walked into the room, Major Mumm turned to me and said, "These are supervisors here. There are now ten of you and nine chairs. The first ones to arrive in the morning get to sit down."

He left the room, and even now I do not know whether that introduction to my new job was made in jest or not. I stood there inside the door for several moments before one of the officers decided to say something. I was invited to have a seat, and several of them attempted to explain to me what we would be doing. The job was to supervise the training of the auxiliaries, to participate in organizing new phases of training that might be introduced from time to time, and to see that materials were provided where needed.

It did not take me long to get acquainted with the people in the Plans and Training Office, the section's official title. I had known some of the officers before, and I wasted no time getting to know the others. I spent my work days observing the classes of the trainees. At no time did anyone suggest that I devote my supervision to classes for Negro troops, so I often was in classes for whites too. As happens when a large group of people work closely together, several grew very friendly. At first there were four of us who spent much of our spare time together. I was the only Negro in the office, or at headquarters for that matter, but that presented no problem.

Capt. Eleanor Sullivan, who was from Boston, mentioned how she missed home and seafood, especially lobster. The other three of us expressed no enthusiasm because none of us had ever eaten lobster. Captain Sullivan took it on herself to remedy that situation. Because she felt that it was part of one's education to know how to handle various foods, she took us into the city of Des Moines, on one of those "special fresh seafood flown in" days, and taught us how to eat lobster. It was our first experience wearing the bib, cracking the shells, dipping in hot butter, and so forth. A lesson in living.

During my stay in the Plans and Training Section, one of the jobs we undertook was writing courses for the training of WAAC officer candidates in overseas theaters of operation. This required a great deal of time and energy. Some of our staff spent long hours at night working on these courses. After everything was finished and we had individually and collectively approved the courses, it was decided that no officers would be trained in any theater of operations. We were overcome with a feeling of futility: all that work for nothing. But the experience taught us to put unused projects aside and move on to other duties.

So long as one was at the Training Center, one was presumed to be in training. As a result there were always classes for officers as well as for enlisted personnel. Besides the regular refresher classroom courses, which never seemed to end and which made company officers very unhappy, there were perpetual drill classes. One night each week all officers were required to attend a drill class held in the riding hall. These classes were under the supervision of the few male officers still connected with the TC, but quite often the instruction and supervision was delegated to some of the WAAC officers. I was one of the few who liked the drill classes. Having been assigned to a basic training company for such a long time, I had developed considerable skill and enjoyed sharing my knowledge. The truth was that what I missed most about being at Company 8, besides the people, was being in command of the expert marching unit.

There had been a time at the TC when we had a surplus of fresh basic training graduates with no duty assignments. There was suddenly a surplus of officers. Recruiting had not reached its anticipated peak, but OC training had been only minimally curtailed. Consequently, with officers still being commissioned, there were scores of them without assignments. Installation commanders over the country were now beginning to accept WAACs and the officers who commanded their units, but they were still reluctant to accept officers for noncommand operational jobs. There were now three training centers turning out trained enlisted personnel, but these centers did not use all the officers being commissioned. In an effort to keep the officers occupied, the Army brought them to Fort Des Moines and put them into what was called Intermediate Officers School. Later, as the number of surplus officers grew, there was a second session of this school called

Advanced Officers School. For most of the officers, going the IOS and AOS did nothing for morale, but, as in any large group, there were those who really needed the additional training. The proportion of Negro officers who returned to Des Moines to wait assignment and attend these special schools was no higher than those from the white officers' groups.

In addition to my duty as a training supervisor, I assumed some other chores, such as trying to improve the morale of the disappointed privates awaiting assignment. I later included the waiting officers in my group discussions, and that is exactly what the sessions were. They were completely unstructured: no theme, no minimum or maximum attendance, in fact, no particular persons, just whoever wanted to sit around and talk. I am reasonably certain that I helped some people quite a bit and some others not at all. The real lessons learned during this period were for me. I realized that I was fortunate to have a very satisfying job, so I gave up looking back and developed a technique for group handling without having the power of command.

One of my favorite spots for supervision was motor transport school, where I actually learned a great deal from observation. Suddenly, one day, I became conscious of how few Negro women were being trained in this area. It seemed strange because this was one area in which Negroes were used extensively, since it was classified as semiskilled. Investigation revealed that this was one of the few areas in which field commanders had agreed to accept Negro WAACs. I tried very hard to get more of the women assigned to motor transport school, pointing out how useless the women felt just waiting when they could be on the job. It was finally revealed that the quota had been set at WAAC Headquarters in Washington, and this precipitated my first visit to the Pentagon.

On June 29 I received orders to go to Washington on temporary duty, and one of my missions was to convince the powers that be to increase the quota of Negro women for motor transport training. I was the house guest of fellow officer Capt. Harriet West, who was assigned to WAAC Headquarters. Without her assistance I would never have found my way to and about the Pentagon. One had to see this building, inside and out, to believe it. A story going around at the time was that a woman had gone into the building carrying her baby son in her arms, and by the time she found the office for which she was looking, the son had been commissioned a second lieutenant in the Army.

After my mission was accomplished, I received another assignment while in Washington. Captain West and I were sent on what amounted to an inspection trip to see what was happening to Negro WAACs in the field. The tour included visits to the Second WAAC Training Center at Fort Devens, Massachusetts; Fort Dix, New Jersey; and Fort Bragg, North Carolina. When we arrived at Fort Bragg, I called my family in Columbia, South

Carolina. My parents, sister, and brother drove up to see me. The last time we had visited together, I had been a second lieutenant (third officer). On this occasion I was a captain (first officer).

During my second TD assignment to the Pentagon, Captain West was away on TD and I had no one to lead me around by the hand, so I had a problem when I tried to enter the building. When I showed my AGD identification card, the guard would not permit me to pass. He had two concerns. One was that rank among WAACs was rare so he doubted mine. The other was that my resemblance to my ID picture seemed questionable to him. After he looked at my orders, I was permitted to enter, only to become lost immediately. I had arrived about nine o'clock in the morning, after most people had reported for work, so there was little traffic in the corridors and on the ramps. After I had wandered around for about ten minutes, I took out a five dollar bill and held it in my hand, planning to offer it to anyone who would lead me to the WAAC Headquarters. Fortunately, I did not have to use that system; a kind young civilian woman came by and asked if she could help me. She could and she did, and I did not tell her why I had the money in my hand.

The other women's service organizations were already going strong by the summer of 1943, and we in the WAAC felt very bitter because those groups had begun as members of the various services while we were just an organization of women who worked with the Army. Finally, Congress did get around to making us a part of the Army, and we were given the opportunity to withdraw from the service or become members of the new organization, which would be the Women's Army Corps, removed from its auxiliary status. A number of women took advantage of the opportunity, but I did not feel that in losing them we suffered any great loss, since they were unhappy in the service.

At Fort Des Moines we had two great ceremonies for the "swearing in," as we called it. The enlisted women were sworn into the Army en masse several days before the officers were. For both occasions we had large formations on the parade grounds, and there was great seriousness about taking the oath that made us a part of the United States Army. We felt that now we had some status that counted. On 1 September 1943 the WAAC became the WAC, an official branch of the Army. On 1 November we became eligible for GI insurance.

In August, just before we were sworn into the WAC, there had been some additional promotions to higher ranks than had previously existed in the corps. A number of officers had been promoted to staff director, the WAAC equivalent to major, among them Harriet West, a Negro officer to whom I have referred already. Even though she was stationed in Washington, we were very proud to have one of us promoted. In September, Major West visited Fort Des Moines, and we were especially pleased to

Turning my command of Company 8 over to Lt. Alma Berry (*left*). *Women's Army Corps photograph*

have her because there was one WAC major on the post, Maj. Mary Lou Milligan, who was white. Major Milligan and I were among the last of the first officer class to still be stationed at the TC, and we were good friends. However, the presence of Major West gave hope to all Negro officers that promotions could lie in our own futures.

It was during Harriet's visit that I received one of the few real surprises in the Army. September 20 had been unusually hot, and for the first time since I had been at Fort Des Moines I left my office early and went home. It was about 3:30 when I left the office, and the half-mile walk to my quarters did nothing to improve my disposition. As soon as I walked into the house, the telephone rang and Captain Crumm, the TC adjutant, told me that Colonel Mac wanted to see me right away. I knew that a large group

My promotion to major, 20 September 1943. *Women's Army Corps photograph*

of school principals was visiting the post and that the colonel had been with them all day. I assumed that he wanted me to dig up some information for the visitors. That did not make me feel better, but I trudged back across the post to headquarters. When I arrived, Captain Crumm told me that the colonel wanted me to meet him at the reviewing stand on the parade grounds at 4:45 P.M. I loved Colonel Mac, but by this time I was truly being tested. I cooled off a bit as I waited in my office.

When I reported to the colonel, I noticed that his visitors had departed. He asked me to join him and Major West in reviewing the parade. There was nothing special about his request; it had happened before. Suddenly, both he and Major West reached up and pinned a gold leaf on each of my shoulders. It was then that I realized that all the running around I had been subjected to was because my promotion to major had come through. It had not occurred to me that I had been recommended for the promotion, so I was genuinely surprised. I laughed with pleasure as tears rolled down my cheeks. The public relations office had a photographer on hand, and one of the pictures she made was the ugliest ever made of me while I was in the service.

Later that year I was sent to Staten Island as convoy officer for a group of WACs who were being assigned there. That afforded me another opportunity to see a WAC unit in the field. Before my departure from Des Moines, I had requested and received leave time, so when I had delivered the troops to Lieutenant Barnes at Staten Island, I returned to Washington, where my leave was to begin. When I was ready to depart for Columbia, I decided that I wanted sleeping accommodations for the trip in spite of the wartime load and in spite of the fact that I was not on official business. I walked up to the ticket window in the D.C. train station and asked the agent if she had a reservation for a Major Adams.

"No, I haven't," she replied. She had not even raised her eyes.

"Will you look and be sure?" I asked. She looked at me then and looked through some papers.

"I am sorry, but I do not have a reservation for you."

I had my briefcase with me, and I pulled it up on the window ledge as if to look through it. Then I said, "But you should have one. Are you sure there is not a telegram requesting that you hold a reservation for a Major C. Adams? I have to get to Columbia, South Carolina, right away. That's where Fort Jackson is, you know."

Even before she looked again I knew the answer, for no telegram had been sent, but so far I had not told a lie. I had just asked a few questions.

"I am sorry, Major, but your wire is not here. Just a minute, I'll see what I can do." She picked up a telephone and told someone about an insistent WAC whose reservation had not been held.

In about three minutes more I walked away from the window with my reservation for Columbia that same night.

Not long after I was assigned to the Plans and Training Section, we lost most of the men who had been detailed for duty with the staff. Major Mumm, who had been in charge of Plans and Training, departed and was replaced by a WAC officer, Maj. Frances Clements. WAC officers were replacing the men in most Training Center activities. By the time I received an assignment away from the training section, the only male officers were the commandant of the Training Center and two or three men on his staff, although the Fort Des Moines personnel were all male.

Early in 1944 I was assigned to be Training Center control officer. Even before the position had been created, I had been performing some of the duties required in this job. The easiest way to describe my new job is to say that it was comparable to a civilian efficiency expert who moved around a business and "improved" things. Actually, I looked at and discussed operation procedures and organizations, and made recommendations designed to increase efficiency and save time. The greatest problem I found was duplication of work. As I learned more about the job and as instructions were received from the Service Command Headquarters, I found there was more to my position than it had seemed at first. Soon the days were too short, and I needed additional help in my office.

My assistant was Lt. Aubrey Stokes, a very conscientious person with considerable civilian stenographic experience. Her skills were invaluable, considering all the paperwork involved, and I did not have to worry about the confidential nature of much of the work we handled. Lieutenant Stokes had one very annoying habit. She insisted on writing with a straight pen, which meant that there was always a bottle of ink on her desk. At least twice each week she would leave the office on some errand without first capping her bottle of ink. Just as often she would return to the office having forgotten the bottle was open and would turn it over. Our greatest office expense was the number of desk blotters used by Lieutenant Stokes.

I kept up a continual effort to make an organization chart for the Training Center. The Army Services Forces, of which the WAC was a part, had prescribed just how each unit would be organized, and I worked hard to see that we followed directions. Each day I would draw a chart of the TC organization, with all the boxes and reporting lines, according to the plans of the War Department, and carry the chart in to the colonel for approval. He would approve it and tell me to go ahead with plans to have it printed and distributed. Usually it would be decided immediately after the printing that some change had to be made. Sometimes I even got as far as distributing the copies to all the various units and sections before Colonel Mac, or the War Department, decided to make a change. The most recent copies would then be collected, and new ones printed and distributed. In one two-week period I drew up eleven charts, all of which were changed.

In spite of this, I found the work interesting and learned more about the Army every time I had to do my work over. One part of the job of control officer was that of being officer in charge of work simplification and job methods training. Fortunately, most of the job methods training applied to civilian employees, and I did not have to handle that. However,

I did have to concern myself with work simplification. This is the process of making work easier that people are already doing by making the work twice as difficult trying to find out how to make it easier. For example, I would go into some section and sit around by the hour watching people work, counting the movements required to perform specific activities, looking for methods to make the job simpler. There were times when I would ask a section chief to have her personnel keep a log of how many steps they took with a procedure and, when we had recommended a new procedure, have a log for comparison to determine if we could save time and energy and thus reduce the number of people used to perform certain jobs.

I read all the manuals carefully to find out how to apply certain steps in the work simplification program. One illustration had to do with the eye movements of a shirt inspector. The inspector stood with the shirt flat on the table, front side up, checking for missing buttons by beginning at the collar button looking down the front, then to the right cuff and finally to the left cuff. After a great deal of study it was determined that the more efficient method to inspect for missing buttons was to begin by looking at the right cuff, then up to the collar button and down the front, then to the left cuff. That seemed all right, but with all the things I had to do I knew I would never make work *that* simplified.

Forms control was another phase of my job. The Training Center was a large organization, and every company, department, section, and unit of any sort had created its own forms, in addition to regulation forms, many of them duplicating the same material and information. There were forms of biographical sketches, for surveys, for questionnaires, and for reports. The same information was collected on many different forms. My job was to consolidate, eliminate, revise, prioritize, and assign an appropriate control number for all forms used by the TC. Since this job was directed by the Seventh Service Command, I had to report to that headquarters and sometimes to the War Department. All of these reports had either Service Command or War Department control numbers, and had regularly scheduled submission dates. More than one night I worked very late preparing reports to forward to the next highest headquarters. I became so involved in forms control that I was able to recommend several changes to higher headquarters and had the satisfaction of seeing changes made that concurred with my recommendations.

After my promotion, Major Milligan and I were the only two field grade WAC officers at the First WAC Training Center for some months. Major Milligan was assistant to Colonel Mac and was beginning to assume some of his duties. There was no problem deciding who would take on the assignments that the male officers were leaving, so I was not surprised when nearly every morning Captain Crumm would say to me that Colonel Mac thought I should be assigned to a new detail because someone had to do the job. At one time, when my main duty was control officer, I had nine additional assignments, and I managed, somehow, to keep up with all of them.

I was aware at this time that none of my work had racial implications. Every one of the previously mentioned assignments concerned all units of the TC, one as much as another. I had felt for some time that had the mores of the times been different, the Women's Army Corps would have been desegregated, if not fully integrated, even during the early days of World War II. There had been so many "working together in racial harmony" situations which were forbidden and eradicated when confronted with the Army reality of both segregation and discrimination.

Perhaps this harmony was in part responsible for the "separate but equal" plan proposed by WAC Headquarters and sponsored by the White House. The plan was also attributable in part to the recommendation made to the president by his Negro adviser. The plan was to create a Negro training regiment, parallel to the regular training regiment, in order to provide promotional opportunities for Negro officers.

A meeting of all Negro officers stationed at the TC was called, and the plan was explained. The whole thing sounded very good—at least to the most junior officers. Lots of questions were asked, but the answers were not very satisfactory to a few of us. I remember that meeting very well for a number of reasons. I had been raised in the southern United States, and I knew that there was no such thing as separate but equal, so I objected to such an organization, pointing out that although it appeared to afford opportunity, there was an extremely low ceiling on where we could go. The top would be reserved for whites; I had seen it happen too many times. When I asked who the commanding officer of this regiment would be, I was informed that as ranking Negro officer I would have that assignment. My response was that I wanted no part of it and was informed that I had no choice.

"I will not command such an outfit."

"Would you disobey a direct order?" I was asked.

"I want to make it as a WAC officer and not as a Negro WAC officer. I guess this is the end because I will not be the regimental commander."

The meeting was over. Each and every officer, including the ones who had been closest to me and those for whom I had done the most, walked out of that assembly without a word to me. I was hurt that none understood that I was thinking of all our futures and that my position had not deprived them of any chances. I finally walked across the post to my office all alone—and I had learned one of life's greatest and hardest lessons: do not depend on the support of others for causes. Later my friends did express some agreement for my stand, explaining that the plan had seemed such a marvelous chance at the time. I have never forgotten.

In the meantime, a temporary draft of the new regiment was drawn but never published. I have never known by whose authority or influence the plans for the Negro regiment were dropped, but I have always considered it a very wise move.

One of my many duties was that of summary court officer, which included the trial, and I use the term advisedly, of personnel charged with minor offenses. This was not a pleasant task, as none of the court-martial duties were pleasant. I did learn about many of the problems of many women and the causes for some of the misdemeanors. I tried earnestly to do justice in every case and hoped that the talks I had with them contributed to their adjustment after the summary court was finished.

Ordinarily, these trials were held in the company area to which the accused person belonged, and on one occasion as I was going to one of the companies, I met an enlisted woman who spoke very politely to me but did not salute. I stopped her and asked, "How long have you been here at the Training Center?"

"About three weeks."

"Haven't you been taught that you are supposed to salute officers when you meet them outside of a building?"

"I do salute officers when I see them," the young woman answered.

"Well, why did you not salute me when I spoke?"

"I didn't salute you because you are not an officer."

I was startled by this answer, to say the least, and I am afraid that I became offensive. I said in very firm tones, "Don't you see these leaves on my shoulders? That means that I am an officer and that my rank is major. I do not see how you could have missed my insignia."

"Oh!" the woman answered, smiling at me, "I saw nothing but captains and lieutenants out in Boomtown. I am sorry, Ma'am."

At that point I suspect that I gave her the longest lecture on military courtesy that she would ever hear. When I dismissed her, she executed a smart salute and went into a nearby building. The incident stuck with me, for it made me realize that whenever we get to feeling rather too well satisfied with ourselves, there is always something to bring us back to earth.

The time I spent working as surveying officer, one of my added duties, was devoted to chasing down lost property. This job seemed limited to keeping officers from paying for lost property and, whenever possible, to clear them of any liability associated with the loss of the property. These cases dealt mostly with company property, and since I had been a company officer for a long time and remembered the difficulty I had keeping up with certain items of equipment, I made every possible effort to see that no one had to pay. I would go into a company, ask questions about the circumstances leading to the discovery of the loss, and help the officer count the property on hand to determine whether the items were actually missing.

It was rare that anyone had to pay, for the property was certainly not the kind that would be stolen for personal use or for sale to others.

I had a most interesting life as control officer and did many interesting things. More important, I learned to do many things I had never heard of before but that would serve me well in later assignments. I was a member of the Special Court Martial Board and the Officer Candidate Selection Board. I did routine reports and special reports when required. And I continued to try to simplify work and to control forms. I went on recruiting trips of short duration, and I went out to speak for bond drives.

For a long time I was the only Negro officer with the TC Headquarters, which put me in line to take on many odd assignments that were not in the scope of any other job. I was called upon to help with the morale problem of women who were long overdue for field assignments. One of my strangest assignments was that of getting pregnant women to sign their discharge papers. It was expected that these women would sign, but some had problems believing that their condition was real. The most difficult I had in this area required four sessions. The young lady said, "All those cowboys on my father's ranch never knocked me up and I can't believe one little old private in the Army did this to me." In a few weeks it was obvious to her that she was pregnant. She was finally convinced that a soldier had done what a cowboy had not.

1 January–15 December 1944

From TC Headquarters I traveled frequently on short periods of TD. I was frequently sent out as convoy officer when troops were moved to other posts. Since my college days at Wilberforce University, I had wanted to attend one of the Negro football classics: Wilberforce versus Tuskegee, played at Soldier Field in Chicago. I was finally able to be at one of the games when I was sent as convoy officer for one of the Training Center bands when the band marched in a parade for the event.

At the request of the convention committee of my sorority, I was sent to the national convention of Delta Sigma Theta, which met on the campus of Wilberforce University in August of 1944. I could not have planned things better. My sister, a member of the same sorority, attended that convention; my younger brother had just completed his freshman year at Wilberforce and was working on campus during the summer. I performed my recruiting and public relation duties while on the trip, and I also had a great visit with family and friends.

Some of my travels provided interesting, and sometimes scary, experiences. One Negro WAC officer had been beaten while waiting for a train in a segregated waiting room in the railroad station in a small town. The reason for the beating was anger that a "nigger" could be a captain and expect white people to salute her. I was fortunate never to be touched, but I did encounter much resentment and bias. On one long train trip when I had sleeping accommodations, there was one incident related to me in which I was not actually involved. During the afternoon ride while the berths were in the seat mode, a well-dressed white woman across the aisle just sat and stared at me. Even when I turned toward her, she never stopped staring. As on all trains in those days, military police patrolled the cars of the train because of the number of military personnel who were traveling. They had come through our car several times, in pairs or singly, but there had been no reason for them even to pause. Finally, when one of the MPs came through the car just before dusk, the woman stopped him and said, "Check on that 'negra' woman sitting over there."

"What do you mean by 'check on her,' Ma'am?"

"That woman over there is wearing an officer's uniform," she replied, "and I am sure she is an imposter. Why, she's a 'negra.'"

The MP sergeant turned to look at me as I sat looking at the page of a book, but listening. The MP turned back to the angry woman and said, "I am sorry, Ma'am, but I have no reason to bother that officer."

"Aren't you going to ask for her identification and then you will see that I am right," she insisted.

"Ma'am, I am here in case of trouble, or a problem of some kind. There is no problem here. If I check, to use your word, that officer and she is not an imposter, I might not be a sergeant tomorrow. Besides an imposter would not pick a rank that high; there are too few WAC majors in the Army."

He saluted smartly and departed. When the porter came around to make up the berths, the woman inquired about the availability of another berth. There was none, and we both had to sleep in the same sleeping car that night.

Traveling by train seemed to create "situations" for me. Once when I was meeting some family members in Atlanta, I had a small encounter with the military police. I was waiting with my parents in the small, dirty, and crowded "colored" waiting room in the Atlanta railroad station. There were very many military personnel roaming around the station waiting for people or for transportation, so the MPs were constantly moving through the crowd. After walking past our waiting party about ten times, two white MPs stopped in front of us and addressed me.

"Excuse us, Ma'am. May we speak to you for a minute? Privately."

Thinking that perhaps someone of the many women from the various services, also waiting there, might need help, I replied, "Of course." I followed them into a corridor where they stopped.

"May we see your identification and orders, Major?"

"Why?" A long pause and no answer. I said, "What have I done to warrant you to even approach me? I know what your orders are, so what do you want with me?"

"Well, Ma'am, er, er, some people have—there was a question—I mean —well, you see—"

"Yes, I see. You want to know if I really am a major in the U.S. Army."

"Some one asked—."

I opened my purse, took out a notebook and pen, and said, "Now, I have some questions to ask. Names? I can see your rank. Your serial numbers? Your unit? Location? The name of your commanding officer?" I was writing all the information down in my notebook. "I suggest that it will be easier on you if you report this incident to your CO before I get my report to him. You are dismissed." They saluted, held the door for me, and disappeared in the opposite direction. I did not have to report the incident because when I called, I learned that the two MPs had indeed reported themselves. I do not know whether they received any punishment (I doubt it), but I know that two MPs learned a lesson.

There was the time I was returning to Des Moines from a southern city when I went to the dining car for dinner, and the steward met me at the door only to inform me that the places were all taken and that I could not be served. Looking over his shoulder, I could see that there were several empty tables in the car. The steward turned back toward the dining car and discovered that all the waiters (all Negroes, of course) had put down their trays and had started moving toward the pantry area of the car. He got the point, for he turned back to me and said, "I see I have one space left." The waiters all picked up their trays to continue service as I was seated at one of the empty tables.

At the Training Center we operated with as positive an adjustment to multiracial living as there was anywhere in the United States. However, we were not without problems. After all, the women brought with them their own attitudes about people who were "different," so occasionally I was called upon to mediate disagreements, both verbal and physical. Once there was an altercation between one of the Negro cooks and a white KP who was unhappy about having to work with Negroes. The KP expressed herself rather too freely about what they did to "niggers" in Texas. The cook responded with what she wanted to do with "crackers," punctuating the remarks with a slap to the face of the KP. The mess officer and other personnel prevented any further exchange of words or blows. When asked how this case should be handled, I recommended that both women be punished. Although it had racial overtones, this was called a clash of personalities as other personnel present had not chosen to be involved. Sometimes lots of effort was required to keep the lid on threatening situations, and we did not always succeed.

Late in the summer of 1944, my brother, who had been stationed in the China-Burma-India Theater of Operations for over two years, returned to the States. In November he came out to Fort Des Moines to visit me. We had never seen each other in uniform, and we enjoyed getting accustomed to our changed appearances and our personal adoption of military behavior. I was able to get my third leave home, and we went to Columbia together where we had a real family reunion.

My brother, Staff Sgt. E. A. Adams, Jr., visiting me at Company 8 after his return from the China-Burma-India Theater of Operations. *Women's Army Corps photograph*

It is difficult now to recall all the unpleasantness and bitterness I felt at times during my time in service. The pleasant things keep coming back. Those things that seemed so terrible when they happened look very different now. At times I have made my life sound like one big happy adventure, but of course it was not. I was as upset about things when they had happened, as afraid about what could happen, as complaining about events, as critical about conditions as everyone else; and I received my fair share of reprimands, just and unjust. I hurt with the same hurt that others felt.

Late one afternoon near the end of the work day, as I was walking from Boomtown back to the TC Headquarters, I met Major Fowler, who invited me to join him for a drink at the officers club. This was the closest to a social encounter I had had with the officers assigned to get us started. I accepted the invitation even though it seemed so out of character for the major. I finally decided that the gesture was his way of saying that he accepted me as a fellow officer in the U.S. military. Anyway, that trip to the officers club created some strong ripples.

By the time Major Fowler and I walked to the officers club, it was well after five o'clock and other officers, all male and part of the post contingent, were arriving at the club. We greeted the people who were close to us and took a seat at a small table. The atmosphere seemed rather subdued, but I credited that to the early hour. When the major asked what I wanted to drink, I searched my memory for something appropriate since I was a nondrinker, rather than a teetotaler. I answered, "Scotch," and as an afterthought added, "with Coke."

He turned to me and said, "Adams, don't ever let anyone else hear you say Scotch and Coke. It's club soda or water."

I had no idea how Scotch tasted, but I managed to get that one drink down. It was what happened the next morning that made that visit to the officers club memorable.

Early the following morning I received a message to report to a colonel whose office was also in the headquarters building. Using my best military manners, I reported to the office.

The colonel was seated at his desk. I walked up to three paces in front of the desk, came to full attention, and saluted as I said, "Major Adams reporting as directed, Sir."

He recognized my presence with the most casual salute I had ever seen. I expected him to put me at ease, but he did not. Instead, he got up from his desk and walked to the window, while I remained standing at attention, which is how he let me stand for the next forty-five minutes while he repeatedly berated me.

"So you are the Major Adams, the 'negra' officer who went into the officers club last night. I don't think any colored person has ever been a guest there before. What were you doing there? Who had the nerve to invite you there? I don't believe in race mixing, and I don't intend to be a party to it. I understand you are from South Carolina. Well, I am too, and that makes it worse. I'll never accept whites and coloreds mixing socially, but I think that I might be able to ignore it if you came from any other state. I can't stand having a negra from the same state that I came from socializing with the same people I do. Don't let being an officer go to your head; you are still colored and I want you to remember that. You people have to stay in your place. Why, your folks might have been slaves to my people right in South Carolina, and here you are acting like you are the same as white folks. I don't care if you are a part of the Training Center; the officers club belongs to the post, and you can't be a member, etc., etc., etc."

That was the gist of what he had to say for three-quarters of an hour. I was proud of the fact that I maintained the position of attention for the whole time. The tirade was interspersed with rhetorical questions, but the theme never changed. He finally worked his way back to his seat behind the desk. When he finished talking, he just looked at me for a moment, then said, "You may go now," to which I answered, "Yes, Sir," saluted, and received his reluctant salute and departed.

Since my message to report to Colonel X had come through Colonel Mac's office, the commandant wanted to know what was going on. Of course, I told him. I was happy to talk to someone about that interview, for I was still in a state of shock. As I stood listening to Colonel X, I learned a lot about the feeling of superiority that whites felt in relationship to other races. More than anything, I realized that racial prejudices existed over the entire United States, no matter what declarations were made. I suspect that I knew it all before, but having lived under circumstances in which I had learned how to avoid confrontation and humiliation, I had not fully recognized what obstacles we had to overcome.

I did not go the the officers club again, although I knew that there was a rather strong confrontation between Colonel X and Colonel McCoskrie, followed by assurances that the club was open to all WAC officers, and although I received several invitations to join small groups there. I told a very few people about what had happened, as well as about some of the pain and humiliation, and I told most of them only after more than a year had passed. I did have one more encounter with Colonel X, but with less trauma for me.

A short time after the unpleasantness with Colonel X came the time when the wives of the most senior officers entertained, opening their homes to wives of junior officers stationed at Fort Des Moines. Although it had not happened the year before, some WAC officers were also invited to attend that summer of 1944. I certainly did not want to go, but Colonel Mac insisted since only the officers at the TC Headquarters were invited.

I went along with several others who were friends of mine, but I was the only nonwhite face there. I was treated coolly but politely, which was exactly the way the wives treated the white officers. Colonel X was almost polite, but he did not say "Welcome."

All things considered, I had become well adjusted to my life on an Army post and began to feel at home. I sometimes complained that others were constantly being sent to new stations while I remained a permanent fixture, but I did not think that I actually wanted a field assignment. I had a good job and pleasant quarters. I had decorated my room and, along with the various officers who lived in Quarters 1, I had shared in decorating the house. It was well furnished and well equipped and had a homelike atmosphere. I was as content living there as I would have been any place except my real home.

Earlier, I had gotten ambitious enough to follow the post commander's suggestion and planted a victory garden behind the house. It had started out as a cooperative affair with all the officers in the quarters agreeing to take part. The afternoon that we planted our plot there were three of us working, and we measured and planted until we had all the plants we had purchased in the ground. When we stopped, we saw that not one row of plants was straight, but we refused to be discouraged by the appearance of our garden. It would just have to grow in crooked rows, and that is how we left it.

The others did help for a while, but I was the one who got stuck with that garden. After a full day at the office with my many duties, I would rush home, put on a pair of slacks, and get out in the garden. The afternoon sun was very hot, and I would be wet and worn from my yard work. The worst part about keeping that little piece of land cultivated was keeping the weeds out. My father had had a small garden in our backyard as far back as I could remember, and, recalling his efforts and my own experience, I have recanted anything I may have said about the necessary amount of time spent among garden plants. But the garden was a success, even if we did not eat very much of the produce. Frankly, after working so hard, I was not interested in how the vegetables tasted. Lt. Mary Lewis, who also lived in Quarters 1, was one of the TC mess officers, and she would sometimes prepare us a meal using some of our produce, but most of it we gave to the officers mess, for there was far more than we would ever use.

I did use the flowers we grew. I took special pride in cutting them and putting them in my room and around the house, pleased that I had had something to do with their growth. However, I suspect that Mother Nature is due most of the credit for the success of our victory garden, and I do not look forward to undertaking such a project again.

Our house was quite well furnished, considering that most of the equipment had been issued by the quartermaster and was very antiquated. If the stuff had belonged to me, I am sure that I would have handed it over to the first taker. We did have one piece of furniture that was not antique and that we liked very much in spite of its limited use. It was a baby grand piano that had been given to the Negro officers by a very kind lady in Des Moines. Although we had had considerable success in breaking down racial segregation, we had no luck whatever with officers clubs and service clubs, so this piano had been used in Service Club 2 for quite a while. (Segregated facilities for Negroes were always number 2, even when there was no facility for whites. Number 1 was reserved for them.) With great effort we secured a decent piano for that service club so that we could feel all right about moving our piano into our own quarters. Some of the officers were very capable musicians, but I was one of those piano players who would wait until everyone left the house before sitting down at the keyboard. Even when my housemates were in their most tolerant moods, I hesitated to annoy them with my lack of talent.

The officers mess at the TC was in one of the new temporary brick buildings situated behind and off to the side of headquarters. I would guess that it accommodated approximately two hundred people per sitting. It was well equipped, and the chinaware bore the WAC emblem, Pallas Athene. The cost of the food was, of course, more than the subsistence allowance that we received. All of us complained about having to pay but agreed that it was worth it. We knew that we could not feed ourselves or eat in a restaurant for even as little as twice the cost. On holidays we had very fine meals with all the trimmings. My favorite meals were those we had on Thursday and Sunday evenings when all the leftovers were served in individual servings and I could pick my favorites from the buffet. I was always early for those meals.

That year I became a faithful patron at the post theater. I had tried going to my quarters after the evening meal and doing my chores, but that meant my having too much time on my hands, especially when darkness came early and I could not be in the garden or busy at other outdoor activities. The post theater had first-run movies, all of which I managed to see. Besides these, there were the USO shows I have already mentioned, class X "shoot 'em ups," class Z horror movies, and love stories that were so corny I would never sit through the whole thing. For a long time I went alone, but when Capt. Mildred E. Carter returned to the post for duty, I had company for my regular moviegoing. Our friends would look at us at the end of the day and say, "I know you two are going to the movies."

There were also the WAC Shows, which were actually revues with numbers representing all units on the post. These shows were completely written and produced by WAC personnel, assisted by enlisted men stationed at Fort Des Moines. The revues assembled a surprising amount of perform-

Victory garden at Fort Des Moines, 1943

ing talent, and the professionalism was created with a minimum of cost, the scenery being made by the women. Negro personnel were included in these shows, usually in all-Negro acts, some of them controversial in their content. I recall particularly the second show, in which the Negro women did a dance number using their fatigue dresses, hems shortened, for costumes. There was concern in advance of the performance that the costumes indicated that the women were all on KP, but the actual performance of the dance number soon dispelled that feeling.

The post chapel was typical of the Army, but beautiful. Its simplicity made it easy to feel a sense of peace and serenity, and it was used by all faiths. I was among those who attended the Protestant services regularly, and when I needed a few moments of quiet meditation, I would go in the chapel and sit alone. Sometimes I felt the urge to attend a service of my own denomination, and I would go into the city and visit the A.M.E. church. After I became a major, I received invitations to attend various churches and organizational meetings. I came to know some of the local leadership and made some friends.

One Sunday morning, on the invitation of the pastor, I attended service at a large Negro Baptist church in the city. I had met the minister and his family. There was one son, in his late twenties or early thirties, whom we in Quarters 1 thought of as shiftless, with no redeeming qualities. To our

Attorney Charlie Howard and myself

surprise he had managed to date several enlisted women. Once, when the time in the church service came to introduce visitors on this particular Sunday, the reverend stated that he wanted especially to introduce the fine service women. Then he looked at me as I sat in the pew and said, "Major, just keep your seat. I want to introduce you last."

I remained seated as all the other WAC personnel were presented and stood to be recognized. Then it was my turn.

"We have with us this morning a young woman of whom we are all very proud because of her accomplishments and because she is such a fine representative of the race, and we want to welcome you. Will you stand, Major Adams? Ladies and gentlemen, this is Maj. Charity Adams." There was polite applause and I sat down.

The minister continued, "I am especially proud to have the major here this morning because my son, _____, tells me that he and the major will announce their plans to be married very soon."

I was stunned! I was outraged! I recovered my composure and stood again. The congregation had started to applaud again, but when I stood, my face betrayed my anger and the applause stopped. Addressing the minister, I said, "Sir, I have never even spent fifteen minutes with your son and certainly not had a date. For this embarrassing announcement you have made, my lawyer will wait on you tomorrow morning." I sat down.

There was a long silence. Then the minister apologized for embarrassing me. I did contact a lawyer, my friend Charlie Howard. I had no idea what purpose a lawyer could serve in this situation, but it was the strongest response I could think of at the moment. Charlie Howard did find out what had brought on that surprising announcement. The reverend had reprimanded his son about the amount of time he spent at Fort Des Moines instead of looking for a job. The son had then told him "not to worry" because he was getting married soon, and his new wife was in a position to help him get a "position." When asked whom he was going to marry, the son had, with hesitation, told him he was engaged to a WAC major; I was the only Negro WAC major at the TC. I did not attend that church again. Besides, I was quite busy and had accepted the additional duty of traveling with a WAC band.

There were two WAC bands at the First WAC Training Center, although there had been considerable difficulty getting the second one authorized by the Army Service Forces Headquarters. The first band, the 400th ASF Band, was all white and determined to remain all white. The second band was composed of Negro women who had been brought together and thoroughly trained. Since there was no authorization for this second band, its members were carried as permanent training personnel on the various reports. Then came the day when it was necessary to cut the number of assigned personnel to the absolute minimum, and the struggle to get authority to retain the second band began in earnest. Bands were assigned to Army posts on a proportional basis, as was everything else, and there were not enough personnel at the TC for two bands. For a time the unit was disbanded. Finally, after much persistence by those of us who were responsible for organizing and training the band, and the continued refusal to

The 400th ASF Band. *Women's Army Corps photograph*

accept any Negro musicians in the 400th ASF Band, the second band was authorized and brought together as an official unit.

The 404th ASF Band, as the unit was designated when its existence became official, was very important to me. Even when I was a company commander, I kept sending, as did other COs, qualified women to try out for the WAC band. Regardless of their experience, whether they were private and public school music teachers, teaching and performing majors in college and graduate school, amateur and professional performers, no Negroes who auditioned were found to be qualified to play with the white band. For a race that was reputed to have the best sense of rhythm in the world, with exceptional dancing and singing skills, this constant failure seemed odd. We were slow to "catch on," but we eventually did. A few of us decided to organize our own Negro WAC band.

By the time authorization of the band became a reality many of the women who were qualified musicians had been trained at the TC and had been sent out on other assignments. Thus, relatively few of the women in the group, either from the beginning or some of those who joined later, could have been classified as accomplished musicians. Most were familiar with some instrument. They had much to learn, and with perseverance they did become highly qualified musicians. The first few months were filled with hard work and discouragement. Watching the 400th ASF Band per-

The 404th ASF Band. *Women's Army Corps photograph*

form made the women realize how far they had to go. Lt. Thelma Brown, the band officer and instructor, was patient with the group, and many people worked with her to keep their spirits up. The success of that band was very important to Negro morale, and I tried to squeeze in a little time to visit the practice sessions every day and to express my confidence in the band. I was elated the first time I saw the group march outside. The lines were crooked and some of the women had trouble marching and playing at the same time, but they were on their way. Another moment of elation was the first time that Band 2 played for troops to march.

There were many requests for a WAC band to participate in bond drives and other patriotic activities and, as their confidence grew, Band 2 was called upon to share these activities. I was detailed to accompany the band on many trips since bond drives required a speaker to make the appeal for bond sales. I was the escort officer and Lieutenant Brown was the band director as we made the rounds of the state of Iowa, going to such places as Altoona, Grimes, Greenfield, Burlington, and Davenport. We traveled by government vehicle, which meant an Army bus; approximately thirty of us sat on uncomfortable seats with all our equipment piled in the rear of the bus. Most of the places were towns with a bandstand in the town square in the center of the commercial area. When we arrived in the town, we were usually met at the square by the bond drive committee and such town officials as the mayor. The band would set up in the bandstand, and as the sound of their tune-up began, the citizens would emerge from the buildings around the square or drive up and park for the concert. We were always provided with a meal, which would be served picnic style and shared by the citizens. Sometimes we hit two or three towns in one day, playing at one just before noon and two in the afternoon.

I liked the towns that had the bandstands in the town square. There seemed to be a kind of cohesiveness about those communities. Where I grew up, the town had a commercial town square but not a bandstand. Maybe the difference was that in Iowa there was no urge to keep people separated.

Many of the bond drive trips that took me all over the state with WAC Band Number 2 were in communities where no Negroes lived, and I do not recall any expressions of resentment or racial bias. On these trips I was the main speaker, and my audience could not have given me more attention, and for what message I gave I am sure another speaker of any other race would not have received more applause. At least in Iowa, citizens were living in a high state of patriotism that overrode active racial prejudice. It must be added that we sold lots of war bonds on these trips.

The WAC TC remained a source of curiosity for Army brass and civilian VIPs of every type. They continued to visit and receive recognition. Even high-level churchmen from all faiths came, I suppose to check on their own. I was visited by a bishop from my church and a national officer of my sorority. Maj. Mary Milligan and I spent a great deal of time being hosts to all the visitors. We also accompanied Colonel Mac to many different official affairs.

Fort Des Moines was a Cavalry post, and many of the officers carried riding crops as part of their uniforms. Colonel Mac was an Artillery officer and carried a field baton. (He gave Major Milligan and me each a baton of teakwood with silver tips on each end, which we carried very rarely, only when in official situations with the colonel.) During 1944 I developed my own personal idiosyncrasy derived directly from an authorized clothing item. Yellow cotton gloves were authorized wear for dress; dark brown gloves were worn every day. I bought a supply of bright yellow pigskin gloves, which I wore at all times. I kept waiting to be told to stop wearing them, but all that happened was that I could be spotted from quite a distance because my gloves were distinctly visible.

Some of us were convinced that our contribution to the war would be to fight the "Battle of Fort Des Moines," as we became more and more settled. We kept telling ourselves that the day had to come when we would

Staff, First WAC Training Center, 19 September 1944: *Front row (left to right):*
Capt. Albert Preston, Jr., Capt. Katherine Stull, Maj. Mary Louise Milligan, Col.
Frank W. McCoskrie, Maj. Charity E. Adams, Capt. Eleanor Sullivan, Capt. Clifton J. Crumm. *Second row:* Capt. Margaret E. Onion, Capt. Frances K. Marquis,
Maj. Joseph Fowler, Maj. DeVere H. Woodruff, Capt. Mena R. Orr, Capt. Charlene E. Hawes. *Third row:* Capt. Dorothy Ruth Feiser, Capt. Lorene S. Horton,
Capt. Elna Anne Lombard, Capt. Mary Will Wakeford, Capt. Maryline Barnard,
Capt. Cecelia Marie Berry, Capt. Ruth Ihle. *Top row:* Lt. Eleanor Louise Marion,
Lt. Reida Longanecker, Lt. Dorothy Y. Groff.

leave, but we kept on accumulating "stuff": books, odd pieces of furniture, dishes, cleaning material, curtains, bed linens, and other items of household equipment, a collection that was frequently increased by what was left behind by transferred personnel.

Every few months some of us would decide to brighten the place up, and off we would go buying more stuff: draperies, curtains, bedspreads,

A.M.E. church officials visiting the First WAC Training Center. *Women's Army Corps photograph*

dresser scarves, and the like. In most cases making such expenditures meant almost immediate transfer, but for some of us the more we spent on quarters, the more permanent our assignments seemed to become. All this buying necessitated frequent trips into the city. Unless one had an automobile or a friend with an automobile, the two modes of transportation available were taxicab and the "Toonerville Trolley." The latter was the more commonly used mode of travel, for it was part of the Des Moines public transit system and was much cheaper. The cars were just like thousands of others in other cities, just as old and dilapidated and with questionable speed ranges. The name "Toonerville Trolley" was taken from a popular cartoon of the time because we thought the rock and roll of the streetcar and the uphill and downhill route seemed to be lifted from the cartoon. I was a faithful user of the trolley, at ten cents a ride, except during the really cold weather when the few hundred yards' walk to Quarters 1 would mean frozen appendages.

Social life did not improve with time. There were thousands of women at the TC, and the proportion to the men left in the area grew to be out-

My father, Rev. E. A. Adams, Sr., visiting me at Company 8. *Women's Army Corps photograph*

rageous. Under normal circumstances there were not many Negroes in that part of the United States, and the only increases seemed to be female. As officers we must have been the original social "sad sacks," for the enlisted women had better social lives than we did. Des Moines did not seem to be en route to many other places, but one could come through on the way to Omaha and Denver, so there were a few people passing through. One break in our lives would be the arrival of Negro pilots training with the 99th Pursuit Squadron, stationed at Tuskegee Institute, Alabama, on their cross-country flight training. During the winter months these flights always seemed to be followed by severe winter storms and blizzards, so that frequently they would be grounded in Des Moines. One of those pilots even found his future wife on one such trip. There were some Navy trainees not far away in Ames, Iowa, but the enlisted women found them first. A few officers and civilian men did find their way to Des Moines, but their attitudes toward WAC officers seemed to say, "you have your rank for company."

My father came to visit me twice while I was stationed at Fort Des Moines. I was a company commander when he came on his first visit, which was a genuine surprise for me. I was at service club 2 attending a company party when I just happened to look toward the back of the club and see him sitting there. He assured me that he had sent a telegram from Chicago that morning, Saturday. Several hours after he left Des Moines the following Tuesday, I finally received the telegram. On his second visit I met him at the train station, but I had difficulty sharing a few private minutes with him because my friends were so busy entertaining him while I worked that they forgot to include me in the activities.

I was so settled in at the TC that I began to feel like a "mother" figure, having been at this station longer than any other Negro officer. I kept going on war bond drives in the state of Iowa and on temporary duty trips to such cities as St. Paul, Minnesota, twice, and Omaha, Nebraska. I was so settled that I took steps to improve myself. At my request Lieutenant Brown agreed to take me on as a piano student, in addition to her band duties. I had studied piano for a number of years, but I never told her how many years, since my skill was not what it should have been after those years. The most that my teachers ever said was that I could read the music faster than most of their other students but that what I played on the instrument was not to be believed. Since I had the time, I wanted to get the reading and the playing of the music at least related to each other.

In November 1944 a small group of us were informed that the U.S. Army Command and General Staff School at Fort Leavenworth, Kansas, would accept its first group of WAC officers early in 1945 and that we were the people who would be members of that group. We were 100 percent excited and twice as scared. This was the Army's highest level of school, and its students were generals and field officers, most of them with combat experience, and many, many more years of service than we had. To compensate for the advantage that the male officers would have, Colonel Mac set up a series of "blitz" courses for us, covering the areas in which we had the greatest deficiencies.

Map reading was the first of our blitz courses, beginning the first week in December, and it was the one in which I expected to do best. We had three sessions before I had to withdraw because I received transfer orders. I think that the only regret I have had about my years in the service was that I never got to attend Command and General Staff School.

15 December 1944–28 January 1945

About mid-December Colonel Mac called me into his office and asked, "How would you like to go overseas?"

I smiled, assuming that the question was rhetorical. I knew that the Negro press had a campaign in progress to see that Negro WACs were assigned overseas, as white WACs had been. To date that campaign had elicited the response that Negro WACs would create great problems in the overseas arena.

"I haven't given the matter any thought, Sir. When I first entered the service I wanted to go, but since none of us are being sent overseas, I have not permitted myself to think about it."

"But do you want to go?"

"It makes no difference to me, Colonel Mac. If I get orders to go, I'll go, so what can I say?"

He picked up a letter on the desk in front of him and continued, "I have a letter here which states that it is anticipated that a group of Negro WACs will be sent overseas, and you are to go with them if I am willing to release you."

"Is this another rumor?" I asked.

"No, this is really the move, the real thing. You know, Adams, I have always refused to release you from the Training Center because I could see no advantage for you in letting you go unless you have an opportunity for a promotion. Here you have received as much as we can give, but there was no more opportunity in other assignments until this came along. I wanted you to know. How do you feel about it?"

I answered truthfully when I said, "I don't know how I feel, Colonel Mac. This comes as a surprise, and I have to think about it. I think I am excited. Yes, I guess I am excited, but, gee, I hate to think about leaving Fort Des Moines after all these years."

After that interview I did not give the matter much thought. My only military experience had been at the TC, and I could not imagine what was needed overseas, or even whether I was qualified for such service. However, there was not much time for thinking about it, for almost immediately the TC began to receive requests for enlisted personnel for overseas duty. As I helped with screening the women for the shipment, I did begin to feel a bit of excitement. The truth was that I had been involved in so many firsts that I did not want to be left out of any new venture. At the same time I felt bound to the TC by a strong feeling of security and comfort.

The first groups of WACs sent overseas had not only been carefully screened as to their physical and psychological fitness for such duty but they had been permitted to decide whether they wanted to leave the country. By the time Negro WACs were being selected, the women were still being carefully screened but the choice as to leaving U.S. soil was no longer personal, except when the fear was so strong that it would impair efficiency. There were some women who could not make up their minds about what they wanted to do, frequently waiting for family reaction, who found themselves stationed in Europe before they decided.

With the request for officers for this assignment there was the usual hustle and bustle, physical and psychiatric examinations, as well as the indecision about the assignment. When I found out that I was included in the shipment overseas, I took advantage of an opportunity to check on what kind of clothing was authorized. It was winter clothing. I wrote my friend Capt. Abbie Noel Campbell, who was stationed at Fort Oglethorpe, which was the overseas training center, and asked her to buy me an overcoat in preparation for Europe. To accommodate all the heavy winter uniforms I anticipated wearing, I asked Noel to get me a size 18 overcoat and to have the sleeves lengthened. Buying that coat was a real adventure for her. The quartermaster sergeant did not want to sell her the coat because it was too large for her, and the tailor did not want to let the sleeves out because he could not understand why she wanted to cover her hands with the sleeves. She succeeded in getting the coat but vowed never to buy for me again. Other equipment I secured for myself.

The day finally came when we knew just what personnel, officer and enlisted, would be going to the overseas training center. With boundless energy we packed and shipped home all the excess property we owned and wanted kept for future use. When we were informed as to what supplies to purchase, and how much, we bought twice as much because we thought the war might go on for years and we felt that we could not live without

Reviewing an honor parade before leaving Fort Des Moines for overseas duty, 9 January 1945: (*left to right*) Maj. Charity E. Adams, Capt. Mildred E. Carter, 1st Lt. Mary E. Lewis, 1st Lt. Mildred V. Dupee, 2nd Lt. Gussye D. Stewart, Capt. Ruth Ihle, commander of troops. *U.S. Army photograph*

all the personal items to which we were accustomed. We arrived for EFS, extended field service, loaded.

We all left Fort Des Moines together and proceeded to Fort Oglethorpe. We had a rather long layover in St. Louis, and the officers in the group went with me to visit some friends there. As we moved around St. Louis, visiting my friends and being mysterious about our troop movement, we realized that we were quite excited about going overseas. I recall that the trip to Chattanooga, Tennessee, the railroad stop for Fort Oglethorpe, was long and uncomfortable in a dirty Pullman car. We arrived early in the morning, when we boarded motor vehicles for the trip to the post. We were greeted with a series of questions and the usual questionnaires, which we had come to expect in the service, and then were directed to our quarters. The enlisted women were led away in one direction and the officers in another. The quarters to which we were assigned was a temporary building of weather boarding, and that was about all, since it was unfinished inside, with the building framework completely exposed. It was a typical barracks with the large open sleeping room and several small rooms at one end. As we entered, there was a quiet and subtle suggestion that I might, because of my rank, want to take one of the small rooms for myself. I ignored the suggestion because, in addition to being lonesome in the small room, I would miss some of the fun in the big room.

A few officers were already in the barracks when the Fort Des Moines group arrived. They gave us the "lowdown" on the setup as they had learned it, and showed us the facilities. Right away I could see that I was now in the Army with all the comforts of Fort Des Moines behind me. I had never been a user of showers when bathtubs were available, even though it meant living with cleansers ever at hand. The barracks had six showers all in a row without curtains or partitions. I had never before had to sleep in a double-decked Army bed, but that was what we had, although there were enough beds for each officer to sleep in a lower bunk, using the top one to hold supplies.

That day, and the following one, other officers and enlisted women who were to belong to our outfit arrived and, with the arrival of each group, we had another reunion. We told stories about what had happened to us during the time we had been away from each other on our various field assignments. We were all in a state of high excitement and found humor in all kinds of situations. We all remembered the second lieutenant who could never remember to respect rank, forcing me to remind her quite often. This officer, now a new first lieutenant, arrived late one night and, entering the barracks, paused right inside the door and waited as if expecting something to happen. The silence was "loud," as she continued to wait. I had already gotten in bed, so I watched along with the others. Finally someone called out, "Major Adams, you had better get up and come to attention because THE first lieutenant just came in the door."

There was much laughter, but now, having been duly recognized, she came on into the room.

Just as the officers were having their reunions, so were the troops. At the same time, we were finding out about our schedule of activities and training. We would have classes of many types, outdoor and indoor, climbing and marching, and we would receive many types of equipment. Our special equipment included helmets and helmet liners, wool trousers with outer covers, khaki-colored wool undergarments, field jackets and wool liners, wool gloves, and field equipment such as musette bags with shoulder suspender, duffel bags, and many other items we were sure we would never use. It was also strongly recommended that we discard much of the extra supplies we had purchased.

The troops were divided into four companies for training purposes, and the officers were temporarily assigned to the various companies. This way the troops and officers began to know each other. I had been responsible for the basic training of many of the enlisted women, and I was pleased to see so many whom I had known arrive for our outfit, although there were a few I wished had not arrived.

Our preparation was intense: gas mask drills, obstacle course drills, classroom training, clothes packing exercises, physical examination, and close order drill. The officers and I were busy with equipment requisitions even though we knew neither where we were going nor what we were going to do when we got there.

One of our jobs was to reduce the number of personnel to fit the T/O prescribed for our unit. Some people were physically disqualified, some were unsuccessful in various training activities, some were afraid, some just did not want to leave the country, and there were a few troublemakers who had to be scratched.

I had always enjoyed commanding my company when we marched in parades, and there at Fort Oglethorpe I was in command of four companies as we marched along the streets of the post. I had been the company commander for many of the women when they were in basic training, and they knew that precision marching was what I expected and what we had had. In a very short time we had a superior marching group.

Except for one woman. Imagine how pleasant it sounds to a drill master to hear seven hundred left feet touching down as one on the appropriate count, followed by seven hundred right feet touching down as one on the next count. The turns were perfect, the "to the rear, marches" were precise, "mark time," "double time," and so forth all in order.

Except for one woman. We knew she was there because we heard her. She turned our beautiful precision marching into 699 feet touching down as one followed by one foot touching down one-half beat later.

After a few rounds of conversation and inquiry we knew who the woman was, but we had to catch her deliberately marching out of step. I had encountered this young woman before, and she had been considered a troublemaker. When some of us questioned how she could possibly have been considered for an overseas assignment, the answer came quickly; this had been the first chance her CO had had to get rid of her. Two days after her arrival at Fort Oglethorpe, Private X had tried to organize the troops against all the officers who were part of our training group. She could be very persuasive, especially among people with insecurities. We certainly did not want to begin a new job in a new command knowing that we were taking trouble with us. The officers and non-coms became a vigilant group, and with success. Fortunately, we still had too many people and had to reduce the size of the unit.

The hustle and bustle of our training continued with classes, drills, demonstrations, examinations, conferences, training films, and lectures. I had opportunities to speak to each of the training companies and devoted the time to pointing out the necessity for our unit to be the best WAC unit ever sent into a foreign theater, making sure that each person remembered that the eyes of the public would be upon us, waiting for one slip in our conduct or performance. I talked about the necessity for cooperation and goodwill and, above all, the elimination of prejudice and pettiness toward each other.

I felt that there was no better time than this to remind the troops of the stigmas which some segments of the public had attempted to place on the corps as a whole and pointed out that these stigmas would be re-emphasized in reference to a Negro unit since there had been such strong opposition not only to such units going overseas but even to their membership in the corps. The degree of cooperative response was remarkable and certainly indicative of the overwhelming success which the unit enjoyed during its existence.

I had been warned that I might be called to Washington in connection with the duties and organization of our unit, so while waiting for whatever was to happen, several of us decided to take advantage of the facilities available at Fort Oglethorpe. We made reservations for dinner at the officers club on a Sunday. As it happened, it was the Sunday before I left the post. I learned that on the telephone racial identification is not readily made.

The arrival of a group of Negro male officers would have surprised the management, but Negro WAC officers created a state of shock. We were kept waiting a long time before the steward got around to recognizing our presence, whereupon we were told that there were no available spaces for us, that the club had overbooked that day. He was assured that we were perfectly willing to wait for an empty table. And wait we did for quite a long while. When it was obvious that we planned to wait it out, we were ushered into the dining room. Two unfamiliar sounds occurred simultaneously: the gasps of indrawn breaths and the clatter of silverware falling on china. Even the waiters (German POWs) stopped to watch the drama.

There were several loud remarks. "What the hell are those niggers doing in here?" "Get them out of here." "They have some nerve." When it was apparent that we planned to remain for a meal, most of the diners left without eating their meals. It seemed that the only way to get rid of the intruders was to feed them. We had a very nice meal, and the POWs provided more than usual service.

The following Wednesday, Capt. Abbie Noel Campbell and I did receive orders to proceed to Washington and were granted two hours to pack everything we had and be ready to take off for parts unknown. Our instructions were to pack everything but to pack in one bag sufficient equipment and supplies to live at least three months just in case our other baggage should be delayed in arriving. We would never have been able to follow our orders had not all the other officers in the barracks chipped in to see that our stuff was packed and ready for shipment with the unit. The one regret we had about all the help we had was that we did not learn how to pack the bedroll, a most important item of equipment, and on later moves we had to solicit help. Being commanding officer and executive officer of the outfit did give us some advantage when we needed help in packing. In addition to packing, getting clearance papers, and copies of orders, we squeezed a noon meal into the two hours. It was a memorable meal because I was to see it again.

Within two hours we really were on our way to the Chattanooga airport to board a plane to Washington. It was our first plane ride, and I quickly became acquainted with motion sickness. For years I blamed the sickness on the thick pork chops we had eaten for lunch before departure. In our hasty departure I had been the only one who found time to cash a check, and that for only $50. When we arrived at the airport and learned that we would have to pay our own plane fares to Washington, we suffered a moment of alarm, but by pooling our resources, we found the necessary funds. We left Chattanooga for Europe with approximately $11 between us, but we knew that eventually we would be reimbursed for the cost of the trip.

We had to change planes in Nashville, Tennessee, and during the layover there it occurred to us that since we would be arriving in Washington at about 10:00 P.M., we would need a place to spend the night. As men have always been accused of doing, we pulled out address books and began looking for people we knew in the city. Our "little black books" revealed only the names and addresses of unattached men, with whom we certainly could not invite ourselves to spend the night. When we were on the plane and almost at our destination, I remembered that I did have friends in Washington but did not have the address in my little book. Our only choice was to call them when we landed, provided we could get the number from the telephone directory. We were successful, for Mrs. Simons and her daughter, Josephine, my friends, told me that they would be happy to take us in for the night. We took a taxi to the Simons home and, as Mrs. Simons served us a late supper, we talked a great deal but could not tell very much because we did not know much.

Our orders had read "Report to Room _____, Munitions Building." Early the following morning Captain Campbell and I were up and ready to report. Mrs. Simons fed us again and wished us well. I am sure she did not know how much we appreciated her good wishes, for never have two dumber people set out for world travel. We managed to catch the right streetcar, and, though we walked in the wrong direction for several blocks, we got to the Munitions Building. When we found the Room _____, we learned to our dismay that we were reporting to a civilian, who instructed us to catch a shuttle bus that would carry us to some other building that was actually in Virginia. We caught the shuttle bus, transferred to another bus at the Pentagon building, and proceeded to our destination. Our concern about getting lost must have been stamped on our faces, for as we approached the building an Army major asked if he could help. We told him our problem, and he gave us directions that were easy to follow.

Things moved rapidly from that point. A very kind WAC sergeant took us in hand and directed our processing. We learned with certainty that we were going overseas somewhere. We made out vouchers for the money we spent on plane fare to Washington and, to our surprise, received the money in a very short time. When we went in for one more medical checkup, I discovered that I did not have my immunization record with me. The regulation, I was told, was that I should have all the shots again, and a new record would be made out for me. I already had a three-year collection of shots, plus two I had received during my short stay at Fort Oglethorpe, so I was permitted to take an oath that I had had all of the required shots. Finally, we received orders, all sealed up in envelopes, and were told not to open the envelopes until after we had been in flight for at least an hour. The sealed envelope made me more curious about the orders than I would have been normally. The sergeant then asked for our address while we were in Washington so that we could be reached with information about our departure. We explained about moving in on my friends and how we planned to find someplace else that day. We were told that we *would* remain where we were and that we would ask that the telephone be kept as free as possible so that we could be reached. We returned to the Simons home feeling that we were the Army's representatives taking over a civilian home, as we heard that the Army did in wartime.

We explained to Mrs. Simons why we would have to spend one more night in her home. That evening, Josephine took us to dinner, and even while we were having a great time, Noel and I remained apprehensive every moment, thinking about what was happening to us. We began to get caught up in the excitement of the whole process. The following morning, after carefully reviewing all we knew and generally assumed, we convinced ourselves that we were part of the military "hurry up and wait" process, that we would probably be in Washington several weeks, considering all the more essential personnel who would have higher travel priorities than we had. When Mrs. Simons started out of the house to go to a store, we decided to accompany her, but as we reached the front door the telephone rang. It was the message we had been waiting for all night. We were directed to report to the air depot at 2:30 P.M. Our limited flying experience had taught us that one should arrive at the airport at least one hour before departure time. It did not occur to us that this extra hour was included in the reporting time given us, so that when we did get to the airport, we were two hours ahead of flight time.

To our surprise we were traveling on a Priority II clearance (Priority I was reserved for the president and his top commanders), which meant that we had dumped some congressmen. It was the first time I had heard of a "junket." Although I was not exactly sure what it was called, I do remember what it was.

The ATC Terminal was a large, beautiful building, quite modern. We sat in the huge lobby and after a few minutes ran out of conversation. We were very aware of the stares directed at us and recognized the reason for them: two Negro WAC officers with rank, a captain and a major. The curious never seemed to be satisfied. Some continued to walk around us, looking, and a few said "Hello." They called their friends to take a look at us, and when the friends had looked, they called anyone who happened to pass, just in case they missed seeing us. We just sat there with nothing to do. Once we walked to the concessions stand and bought one package of chewing gum and returned to our seats to wait. Every few minutes one of us would reach in a pocket and carefully finger the motion-sickness medicine we had received at the first processing station; because I had been so ill on the flight to Washington, we wanted to be sure we had the medicine for the long flight.

Finally, at about 2:45 P.M., a voice blared over the speaker spelling out instructions for passengers of our flight. Slowly, Noel and I joined the line of passengers. We were neither eager nor frightened but tried to learn as much as possible without asking questions and exposing our ignorance. One of the first steps in the processing was to be weighed with all apparel and equipment. I was surprised to discover that with full winter uniform, winter overcoat with woolen gloves, loaded musette bag, and full WAC utility bag hanging over my shoulder, my weight had increased to 171 pounds. For the rest of the "briefing" we were herded into a small room with all sorts of equipment on display. An officer came into the room and began the session. He explained that it was not anticipated that anything would happen to us or the plane in flight, but just in case there were certain things we should know about the equipment and what our specific assignments would be in case we had to ditch. When he got to the part about being able to live for thirty days on the supplies in the rubber boats and the fact that there was fishing equipment in the boats, I began to think that I should make one effort to convince the Army that I was not needed in Europe.

After the briefing, we went directly to the plane, a C-54 cargo plane with bucket seats. What a disappointment! My visions of resting on plush reclining seats faded as we took seats on the long metal benches that ran along each side of the plane. As passengers we sat in two long rows facing each other. Later we learned that on its return flight the plane was a hospital plane, returning wounded military personnel to the States. The flight clerk, a corporal, appeared from the crew's compartment and made his speech. It was obvious that he had made the same speech many times, for his manner proclaimed his boredom with making this speech again to a new bunch of dumb ones.

"Fasten the seat belts on all take-offs and landings. No smoking back here. Passengers may go up two at a time and smoke in the crew's compartment. Men will use the facilities back here, women will be using the crew's up front. Just call me if you need me. I'll be back here most of the time."

We heard the motors start, one at a time, and watched the propellers get up to full speed so that they became invisible. The engines roared, warming up. No one spoke; all of us just sat. No one looked at anyone else. Then we were moving to the runway. Then the take-off. We felt ourselves leave the ground, and I thought, "These people are probably used to this. I have got to act like a real flyer, too. Look how cool they are. Gee, I hope I will not be sick." In silence we flew over Washington, out over the bay, and then over the Atlantic Ocean.

The passengers began to study each other. There were nineteen of us: three women, Campbell and I and one civilian woman whose entrance at ATC Terminal had annoyed us. We were lugging flight bags, field bags, pistol belts, canteens, and gas masks all by ourselves. *She* arrived with a strange assortment of boxes, hat boxes, suitcases, cosmetic kit, and the like, with almost an entire squad of enlisted men bringing these packages into the building for her. "Poor helpless creature," I thought, "she should have joined the WACs." During the entire trip over the ocean she did not speak to Noel or me but devoted her attention to one man. I suppose she knew what she was doing, for we learned very soon that he was a real VIP, and whenever we stopped, he received much special attention, and so did she. Near the end of the trip, in Scotland, we three women were assigned overnight quarters together. Suddenly, our helpless civilian fellow passenger was afraid, and we enjoyed it.

The other passengers included one major, several captains, first and second lieutenants, mostly with thick southern accents, and three civilian men in Army uniforms without insignia. Two of the civilians were experts (I believe they were called technicians), and the third was a war correspondent. The correspondent began writing as soon as we were aboard the plane and continued to write during the entire trip, stopping only to take care of whatever bodily needs he had. As could be expected, certain people gravitated toward each other and formed small support cliques for traveling. A very young captain, blond and blue-eyed, decided that he preferred our company, probably because he thought that the three of us were the most lost souls in the group. And he stuck with us through thick and thin until the end of the trip. There were several others with whom we had some pleasant exchanges, but there were two captains from "way down South" who worked diligently to avoid any association with the only two Negroes on the plane. Weeks later these same two captains met us in an officers mess in London and greeted us like long-lost friends because we were the only people they had seen since their arrival who looked vaguely familiar to them.

Most of us had in a pocket a sealed envelope with secret orders and had been instructed as to when we could open the envelope. After about forty-five minutes over the ocean these envelopes began to appear in hands. No one opened them. We just fingered them. Finally, one fellow could wait no longer and said aloud, "I'm going to open this thing." He did and, after a pause which we hoped made the flight one hour long, we all tore open our secret orders. Some were surprised, some were pleased, some were indifferent. Campbell and I were shocked. In our bags we had lists of places and people to see in Paris, but our secret orders said London. We had received absolutely no information about London. "Oh, well, this is the Army—so what?"

By the time we arrived in Bermuda (we were traveling what was called the southern route), three hours and fifteen minutes later, one of the civilians had joined our threesome. The four of us had dinner together in the huge officers mess under the staring eyes of many of our fellow diners. We had broken all the rules; the fact that we were military did not make up for the fact that two white men and two Negro women were dining together. Some of these stares were very different in that there were lots of officers in this transient mess who had never seen WACs of any color, officer or enlisted, and some of them had never even heard of the corps.

The captain was very anxious to get a letter written to his wife, so we all went into the officers lounge and secured stationery. While he was writing his wife, Noel and I wrote our parents. I am sure that we broke all the rules. We put in our letters complete information as to where we were, where we were going, and how we were traveling, and on the outside of the envelope we put as the return address "AAF Air Field, Bermuda."

It had been just before sunset when we arrived in Bermuda and what could be seen was beautiful and lush, especially after the winter grays and browns of Washington. It was quite dark when we boarded the plane to continue our flight. We had hardly fastened our belts and prepared for take-off when the flight clerk appeared with his announcement. "The gas line to engine number 3 has a leak in it, and we will have another hour here before it is fixed." Brief and to the point. We had learned that only one of the nineteen passengers had done any flying before, so it was amazing how calmly this group of neophytes took that announcement. Almost immediately someone asked, "What will we do with this hour?" It was agreed that we would just wait in the plane because it was too dark to see anything on the island. Four of the men played cards during that hour, and the rest of us shared bits of information about ourselves.

When we had been out on this second leg of the trip about an hour, the flight clerk appeared again to announce that he had been "trying to figure how we can all get some sleep. I suppose the small ones will have to sleep on the seats and the large ones on the floor. There is a comforter for each person. It will be warm in here." Being one of the "large ones," I lay on the floor, and Noel was just above me on the seat. It was not long before most of the passengers were asleep.

I lay awake long after the others were asleep, contemplating my surroundings, circumstances, and feelings. The moon was full, and its light was reflected off the scattered clouds, which cast intermittent shadows on the ocean below. Occasionally, when I sat up, I could catch a glimpse of the shadow of a plane on the water, whether ours or some other I did not know. I thought a lot about faith as we moved at 425 miles per hour 10,000 feet above sea level. My traveling companions were sleeping soundly all around me, their faith obvious because I knew that their flying experience was as limited as mine. I breathed a prayer of gratitude, then slept.

We landed in the Azores Islands in the middle of the day with no idea of the exact time, for, as rookies, we refused to adjust our watches to the time zones, clinging to Eastern Standard Time as our link with home. As we taxied in to the depot for what seemed like ten miles, the only signs of human existence we saw were the large cultivated fields and occasionally a farmhouse with accompanying utility buildings. There were not a lot of people at the MAT depot, but there was a change of crews. Those who were stationed there had never seen Negro WACs before and had difficulty taking their eyes from us. As the passengers from our flight shared a meal, all except a sick captain, we were conscious of the unity of our group, as though we were one against the unknown. For the third time we paid 50 cents for our in-flight lunch, a couple of jam or bologna sandwiches, an apple, and a cup of lukewarm coffee; it was about as appetizing as K rations and was served by the flight clerk before we took off on the next leg of our trip.

Aboard, we taxied toward the take-off point for about twenty minutes when suddenly several of us noticed that we were seeing the same scenery one more time. The flight clerk appeared and announced, "There is a crack in engine number 4 so we are returning to the depot for repairs." As before, there was no apparent fear. I decided that everyone aboard must have felt as I did: thank goodness they found these things before we were off the ground. While the plane was being repaired, we were permitted to wander around the island—but that was not very far since we had no transportation.

About two hours out of the Azores, Noel said to me, "I'm pretty sure that we don't need the motion-sickness medicine. Shall we give some to the captain over there?" She nodded toward our green fellow passenger.

"Sure," I replied. "He hasn't eaten a bite since we left D.C."

When Noel offered the medicine, the poor man felt that nothing could settle his stomach, but he took the pill. Half an hour later he sat up straight. During the trip all those box lunches we paid for had piled up at the back of the plane because we had received a meal at each stop, and the captain, now cured, ate about six of the lunches at one sitting and missed no more meals.

About forty-five minutes from our destination the flight clerk made an announcement. "The captain has received a radio message that our destination airport is fogged in, and he has been directed to land at an emergency landing strip. Unfortunately, the emergency airport is fogged in, too." A small amount of panic set in, but we recalled how much we trusted our pilots and calmed down. Within a few minutes another radio message cleared our flight for landing at Prestwick, Scotland. It was 2:00 A.M., Scotland time. Since I had continued my refusal to change my watch, I had lost all track of time and date. It was here we were introduced to Red Cross coffee and doughnuts served to military personnel all over the ETO.

Because we were fresh from the States, we lined up for a cursory medical inspection, which turned out to be signing our names in a ledger on a desk in front of a corporal who did not raise his eyes from the book he was reading. Either the Army in Europe had utter confidence in the Medical Corps in the United States or it did not care what we brought in, for no one checked us.

Having women passengers on this flight created some problems for the billeting officer. After some discussion, along with the civilian woman we were sent some miles away to a Red Cross club for housing. En route to our sleeping accommodations, our civilian associate suddenly found us fun to be with and turned her charm toward us. All of her male companions had been sent to other housing. When we registered at the club, we were informed that the cost to us was four shillings per night. This was the first time that we had to give any thought to the currency of the realm, and we had none, only American money. There were several Army Air Corps officers sitting in front of a fireplace in the lounge who offered to change some money for us. Later, when I learned the exchange rate, I was sure that I had been cheated, but that night I had needed the shillings.

I may have been in colder weather at other times, but I suffered from the cold more that night than at any other time in my life. Noel and I concluded that this Red Cross building had not had any heat in it since it was built. Our room, Noel's and mine, was heated with a small gas grate that functioned only when fed coins (shillings), which we did all night. I think we managed to keep the temperature at about freezing. Before we went to bed, we had to find the woman in charge so we could ask for the location of the bathroom. We followed her instructions and found a room containing a bathtub and wash basin. That was not the room we were seeking. Three times we called the "house mother," and three times she directed us to the same room. Necessity forced us to explore the house on our own, and when we found a room with the letters "WC" on the door, we had found the room. From that point on we knew what question to ask. It was so cold that when we got in the small cots that were in our room, we slept in our clothing, including overcoats, but not shoes, and were still cold. We fed the heater every half hour, but we were stiff with cold when we got up at 6:30 A.M.

We had no breakfast before we returned to the airport, but we did have coffee and doughnuts there, before we boarded the plane (much smaller this time, a DC-3) for London. I had my first view of the English countryside, and it was truly beautiful. It was all snow covered, looking as if the scenery had been created by a landscape artist. This last phase of our trip overseas was very short, so it was not long before we began the descent. I thought that at last this flying was over. But not yet. It was very foggy and landing was difficult, since the landing had to be made at exactly the right angle. Because our approach was wrong the first time, we circled the field. It was wrong the second time. In fact, we circled the field seven times before landing. Each time the plane began the climb to circle, my stomach protested. One more time around and I am sure that I would have had the cheapest "drunk" on record. I made it, however, and walked out unaided.

We boarded a bus that conveyed us to the ATC office in London, thirty miles away. The ride lasted one hour, and we were fascinated by everything we saw, even as we tried to look like seasoned travelers. The only impressions I had about what England was like was that it was very foggy and that the English drove on the wrong side of the road. By the time we had landed and boarded the bus, the fog had burned off and the sun was shining on the snow-covered land, but the drivers *were* all on the wrong side of the road. While we were observing what was strange to us, we were being observed. We had forgotten how strange we seemed, to military as well as civilian personnel. Again we were among U.S. military personnel who could not believe Negro WAC officers were real. Salutes were slow in coming and, frequently, returned with great reluctance. The old, familiar problem was beginning all over again. For most of the military personnel we

WPCAE Form No. 42

S E C R E T

HEADQUARTERS
WASHINGTON NATIONAL AIRPORT ARMY AIR BASE
503d AAF BASE UNIT, ATC
PORT OF AERIAL EMBARKATION

Washington 25, D.C.

25 JANUARY   194 5 .

This is to certify that, in accordance with SO RESTRICTED ORDER ,AGO

par_____ , dated 20 JANUARY 1945   , CHARITY E. ADAMS
                                              (Name)
MAJ.   L-500001 WAC , is ordered to proceed to BRITISH ISLES, USA, SOS
(Rank)   (ASN)   (Destination)
                         LONDON, ENGLAND

Newell W. Truman
NEWELL W. FREEMAN
Major, Air Corps
Officer in Charge

S E C R E T

My orders to go to England

encountered, accepting any Negro officer in the U.S. Army was hard enough, but accepting Negro women officers was a real burden.

Having been safely delivered to the ATC Terminal in London, we were instructed to report to the Visitors' Bureau in Grosvenor Square. When we asked where it was and how to get there, we were handed two maps, one for each of us, and told to walk. "It's about three-quarters of a mile." I was still cold from the night we spent in Prestwick, I was hungry, and I was very tired from the long trip from the States. As tired as we were, that distance sounded like ten miles. I wanted to sit on the floor of the office and protest. We had with us our flight bags and field bags. Noel suggested that we leave the luggage at the ATC office until we had been assigned quarters.

We set out, mimeographed maps as guides, to find the Visitors' Bureau, and a funny thing happened to us on the way. Suddenly, our minority status disappeared. London was filled with representatives of all the Allies and neutrals, and every conceivable kind of uniform could be seen on the streets, worn by all races, colors, shapes, sizes, sexes, and religious persuasions. We realized that as we stared at the uniforms and the people, they stared at us. Finding our destination was not difficult, and the walk was highlighted by our observations of London and all the people we saw.

Maj. Margaret L. Philpot, WAC commander in England. *U.S. Army Signal Corps photograph*

My hunger and cold were gnawing at me, and my disposition, about which I had been proud all my life, had reached a point where it would have been rated vile. By the time we reached 47 Grosvenor Square, I was feeling "mighty low." A WAC sergeant came up to me and asked, "Are you looking for Major Philpot?"

"I'm not looking for anyone. Who is he?"

"Oh, it's not a he. She is the WAC staff director, in charge of all WACs in the United Kingdom, Ma'am."

"Since I am not looking for anyone else we might as well see her." The sergeant led us into the building, thus saving me from the experience of trying to find General Eisenhower, since we were told to "report to the Commanding General of the European Theater of Operations."

Major Philpot and I grew to be friends, but I am indebted to her because she ignored the mood I was in and forgave me for my cranky behavior. She arranged for us to have a hot meal and a bit of heat, and I was a different person within the hour.

28 January–20 March 1945

We were billeted in a hotel where we could have our meals, but, like thousands of military personnel in London, we took our lunch and dinner at an enormous military eating place. On our first day, because we did not know our way around, we took a "cabbie" to Grosvenor House where the military dining room was located. We had not learned to handle our money, so when we arrived, trusting soul that I was, I held out a handful of English coins, left over from the change received in Prestwick, and told the driver to take what we owed him. He turned my hand over into his, taking every coin. In a few days I had learned that he had taken about six times what was due. That was when I learned that the English were just like my fellow American citizens: take from the ignorant and they will never know the difference.

Hotel life should have been wonderful for unsophisticated young women, fresh from a racially segregated and discriminating country, but we were foreigners and rather uncertain about why we were there. Service was excellent, and once inside at the end of the day, one could hardly believe that we were in a war zone and, potentially, in danger. When we set our shoes out at night, we were relieved of a regular chore, for the shoes would be brightly shined next morning. It was during this period that we learned about the V-2 bombs, the second of the V bombs used by the Germans and being used when we were stationed in London. In a very short time we acted like everyone else in the city: it was safe as long as we could hear the motor in the bomb, for that meant that it was still moving across England; it was only when the motor stopped that we held our breath, knowing the bomb was on its way down. Only when we heard an explosion or enough time had passed did we exhale.

I think my greatest personal admiration for the English, especially Londoners, was at this time because they "carried on" in spite of the V-2 bombs. Each morning when we went out, the streets had been cleared of the damage from the bombs of the night before, and the destruction had been boarded up out of sight from the street.

We would have breakfast at our hotel before going to work. Breakfast was extremely well presented and quite tasty. It was several weeks before we learned that we were deceived by the powdered eggs and soybean sausage that accompanied the real toast. We enjoyed the food because it was almost like being home, and that made it easier for us as we started our work, which at this point consisted of finding out why we were in the ETO and what we would be doing. We found out that we would be part of the Postal Directory Service for the ETO. I was to be the commanding officer of our outfit, and the outfit would be part of the adjutant general's service.

We had arrived in London on Sunday, 28 January, when we checked in at the Visitors' Bureau and reported to WAC Headquarters. We were at war, and our assignments came without delay. The very next day we made our first trip to Birmingham and visited the King Edward School, where we were to be stationed. The trip provided us with some idea of the amount of work we had to do before the troops arrived. We were able to begin a list of needed supplies and the kind of space assignments to be made in our building. At the end of the day we returned to London, and that night we drew floor plans and tried to assign floor space for such areas as work space, barracks space, offices, recreational space, beauty parlor, and so forth, all in one building.

Four days later Noel and I were sent to Paris to report to the commanding general of the ETO, actually to his designee, the WAC director for the ETO. It was here that we received information about all the necessary courtesy calls we should make before we got down to serious work. One of the calls we had to make was to Brig. Gen. Benjamin O. Davis, Headquarters Staff Communications Zone, the only Negro general in the entire military of the United States at that time.

We were anxious to return to the United Kingdom and get on with the preparations for arrival of troops. We planned to leave Paris on Saturday, 3 February, but on Friday we received an invitation to dinner with Lt. Gen. John C. H. Lee, commanding general, Communications Zone, European Theater of Operations. The word "invitation" is read in the military as "is ordered to," so, of course, we remained in Paris for the dinner.

For strictly wartime female soldiers we were operating at a very high level. With all the "spit and polish" we could muster, Capt. Abbie Noel Campbell and Maj. Charity Edna Adams reported to General Lee's quarters

Brig. Gen. Benjamin O. Davis welcomes me and Capt. Abbie Noel Campbell to the European Theater of Operations, 2 February 1945. *U.S. Army photograph*

(actually, suites) in the Hôtel George V. To the well traveled just the name "Hôtel George Cinq" conveys it all; for others I will say only that it was *the* place, then and for many years after. There were twelve of us, including four WAC officers, for dinner. It was a great evening as we tried to relax and be socially proper as well as act according to military courtesy.

During the course of the dinner and all the pleasant conversation, General Lee turned to me and asked, "Adams, can your troops march?"

There was only one answer to that, so my reply was, "Yes, Sir, they are the best marching troops you will ever see."

As the words came out of my mouth, I realized that I was putting my first overseas duty efficiency report in jeopardy. Too late. I either had to prove my words or eat them later. (On the way back to our quarters, Noel, who was not as enamored of formations and marching as I was, wondered if I had not overstated the situation.)

General Lee then asked when our outfit would be in Birmingham. "They will arrive on the twelfth, Sir, and be in quarters on the thirteenth." "Good, I will be in Birmingham on the fifteenth to review the troops." From that moment I operated with two minds. One mind concentrated on:

1. meeting the troops and bringing them to our post
2. getting them assigned to quarters and to units
3. making sure the mess hall operated
4. having Special Service work at lifting morale
5. seeing that laundry facilities were in order
6. getting job assignments made
7. relieving fears of being overseas
8. getting officers assigned to quarters, units, and jobs
9. getting all personnel trained in our postal duties,

and on and on.

The list gives some indication of the things Captain Campbell and I had been working on since we found out what we would be doing.

The other mind concentrated on another series of questions, which I assigned to various officers for answers:

1. After the trip over on the *Ile de France,* zigzagging across the Atlantic Ocean, what would be the health status of the unit?
2. What would be the status of uniforms, and could necessary repairs be made in time?
3. What was the weather forecast for the fifteenth?
4. Where would we have the parade and troop review?
5. Would we be able to get the necessary permission from city authorities?
6. Could the troops march to the parade ground, or would they have to have transport?
7. How could we get a reviewing stand built?
8. Would the general and his party have a meal with us?

and on and on.

With all the moving around Noel and I had done, we still managed to prepare for and receive the troops whom I had committed to a review. On 10 February we went to London to receive final orders for our unit. The next evening we left by train for Glasgow, Scotland, to welcome the personnel arriving on the *Ile de France.* On this train trip we were going to see what it was like to travel first class. In our eagerness to travel in high style, we retired very early, barely taking time to appreciate our luxurious surroundings, each of us in our own private bedroom. The beds were made up with satin sheets, although they had been darned in many places. All materials were being used in the war effort, so the worn sheets could not be replaced. (I never did find out how satin fabric was used at the front.)

Just as I was finally getting sleepy in that cold, satin-covered bed on a moving train in a wintry English February, there was a brisk knock on the door. When I answered the knock, I was informed that I had to move to a second-class compartment because two "general" officers needed accommodations. Noel had been aroused just before the knock on my door. Oh well, at least we had found out what first-class accommodations were like; besides, it was too cold to sleep there. Second class was not bad for an overnight trip. We could stretch out, and with our clothes on, we would not be so cold.

We arrived in Glasgow in time to freshen up and get to the docks to meet the *Ile de France*. We could see the women on deck before they began to come down the gangplank. They had spent eleven days at sea on a zigzag course dodging German U-boats. The sight of two officers whom they knew, standing at dockside waiting to greet them, was like a breath of fresh air. Thanks to the seasickness, the salt-water spray, and the limited personal conveniences, the group was a very unhappy looking lot.

There were, of course, thousands of other military personnel on that ship, but I was concerned about the members of my unit, and they were the ones I saw. I have no doubt that the rest of the passengers looked very much the same as ours since, with few exceptions, crossing the ocean in a ship was a new experience for them. The Red Cross was there to greet the troops, and there were doughnuts and coffee in abundance.

The train to Birmingham was not far away, and we were aboard in a very short time. The women were tired, but there was real pleasure in being on land again. I was interested in hearing all the details of the trip to Glasgow, about all the hardships, like eating in shifts (in fact almost everything was done in shifts), the seasickness, all the adventures and misadventures. There was one group who promised that they would never go back home until a bridge was built over the Atlantic Ocean. After the ocean voyage they thought nothing could be wrong with a train trip.

General Davis was there to greet the troops when they arrived, and it was flattering to have him give the unit his attention.

We had carefully worked out assignments so that there would be little delay when we arrived in Birmingham. I was very anxious for the outfit to be settled in because of my having committed us to march in review in three days. Everyone was cooperative, and we got settled in a short time. The press was everywhere. The appearance of WACs on the scene, and Negro WACs at that, was news, so much so that we gave quick lessons in public relations.

The only credit I claimed for what happened was that I said we could do it and for thinking of and making the assignments for the many things that had to be done. Every officer joined in to make this parade a success, giving 200 percent of what I would have asked of them. I heard, after it was all over, that there had been some complaints that I had not allowed the women to get settled before I had them into some outside activity. But, after all, we were preparing a performance for our top commander—all the channels in between had to step aside for this one. And we did it. The parade was a tremendous success.

We got a site, the permits, marched the troops to the site in properly fitting uniforms, and waited for General Lee to show up for this "command performance."

I did have a few tense moments. I think that I must have been born with a "thing" for being on time, and military discipline had accentuated it (or maybe I was afraid of missing something), so at ten minutes before the designated hour I began to think that the general was not coming. At one minute before the hour General Lee and his entourage arrived. He was on time; I was early.

Following the successful parade of troops for General Lee, the unit settled in to be the postal directory service, and to live with the citizens of Birmingham.

We had not invited the citizens of Birmingham to the parade, but that made no difference; we were in their city, and they came out in great numbers to see us march. After the parade we had an opportunity to have our first meetings with them. We had arrived in the city with so many things to do in a very short time that we had not had time to react to the city and the citizens. That would come later, but we gave it a good start that day after the parade.

We noticed immediately how often the local citizens used the word "black." We were accustomed to the use of the word as an adjective, not as a racial designation. Of course, we had heard it when it was meant to be derogatory. (Twenty years later we were beginning to accept that designation, with pride and dignity.) Then, however, we called ourselves Negroes but never the feminine form, Negress, which we were beginning to hear.

King Edward School was heated by steam, and the building (practically everything connected with our unit was in this one building) was reasonably warm for February as long as we wore winter uniforms. The officers were billeted across the street from the school building, in two houses heated by fireplaces with small grates in each room. Until the weather warmed up, we were never quite warm while in quarters.

After we settled in the house where I lived, we attempted to improve the looks of the place according to our own tastes. Most of the house had been turned into bedrooms, but we did have a small entry hall–reception

Lt. Gen. John C. H. Lee reviewing my troops in Birmingham, 15 February 1945. *Sport and General Press Agency, Ltd.*

room. Most of our beautifying efforts were directed at the atrocious wallpaper. There were flowers and latticework and varied colors and shades all over. I suppose that the problem was not in the English housewife's taste as much as it was that we had now been in the military long enough to be adjusted to the monotony of institutional wall coloring. We scraped wallpaper for hours, for there were many stubborn multilayered places.

Company A, Capt. Mary F. Kearney, CO. *Sport and General Press Agency, Ltd.*

Though we tried wetting those spots, we did not succeed in getting all the layers off the wall.

When it was decided that we had done all we could to remove the paper, it was time to paint. We reached an agreement on colors and secured Kemtone and brushes. Everyone pitched in. We painted and painted and painted and painted, trying to cover the irremoveable paper and the strange color tones we had managed to uncover. It finally dawned on us that we should let the water-based Kemtone dry, and see what we had accomplished. Suffice it to say, we never did completely cover the old decorations; there were faded roses and shabby trellises on the wall until we moved.

On 31 March I left for Scotland one more time to meet the second contingent assigned to the 6888th Central Postal Directory. We returned to Birmingham on 1 April; the new officers and enlisted personnel were greeted by the earlier arrivals and many dignitaries, both male Army and WAC. The unit was now at its maximum strength of WAC personnel, thirty-one officers and almost nine hundred enlisted women.

In 1945 the U.S. Army's knowledge of women's needs was in the development stage. The basic needs such as food, shelter, and clothing were known, and these items could be provided for all. At the Training Center authorities had provided counseling services and recreational facilities;

Company B, 1st Lt. Dorothy Scott, CO. *Sport and General Press Agency, Ltd.*

those small but important services needed for morale, such as beauty salons, the women had to provide for themselves. As long as we were in the States, one could find such services in nearby cities. In Europe white women found the customary service, but Negro women used different makeup colors and hair treatments, whether at home or in beauty parlors, and could find no such service abroad.

Even before we left Fort Oglethorpe, the officers and I had discussed the need for beauty parlor equipment. How in the world could we keep morale up if the women did not feel that they could look their best? Inquiry supported our fears. There were no provisions for such equipment. In solving this problem I learned that if you ask the same question of enough people enough times, you can get the necessary information. Morale was a function of Special Services. Special Services needed equipment. Equipment was secured from the local market (in this case "local" meant England and France). On this basis we revised our Requisition for Special Services Supplies. We should not have been surprised to find that the French invented the marcel iron used for waving and curling the hair. With the support of Maj. Margaret Philpot, ETO WAC director, and others, we acquired the items we needed, including straightening combs, marcel irons, special gas burners, and customer chairs.

Company C, Capt. Vera A. Harrison, CO. *Sport and General Press Agency, Ltd.*

It was disappointing that the equipment did not arrive before the troops because they needed every kind of morale booster possible after their trip over. It was not long, however, before we had a complete beauty parlor. There were a few problems we had to solve with imagination and inventiveness. For example, the room for the beauty parlor was quite distant from a source of sufficient electrical power as well as from a gas line. Once the supply was connected, we had to have electrical outlets and gas burners properly distributed and installed in the room according to the placement of chairs. It is perhaps wiser not to detail the extent of our ingenuity.

While the unit was being organized at Fort Oglethorpe and we were lining up the personnel to go overseas, we made sure to include qualified beauticians, carried on the T/O as Special Services specialists. At last, everything was in order. That beauty salon was the busiest place on our little WAC post for several weeks, as the women who wanted to had at least one trip to the beauty parlor. I was certainly one of them.

Somehow the word got around, over the entire ETO, wherever women were stationed, that there was a place in Birmingham, in the United Kingdom, where Negro women could get their hair done "just like back home." After that, we were besieged by nurses and Red Cross workers who had

Company D, 1st Lt. Violet W. Hill, CO. *Sport and General Press Agency, Ltd.*

been in the ETO for long periods of time doing their own hair under the worst possible conditions. I do not know where all of them were stationed, but many of them used accumulated leave time to visit us, even from the continent, when they could be spared. At one point we had so many outsiders making appointments that a decision had to be made as to the priority of appointments. Members of the unit came first, but we tried to accommodate all comers. We were certain that no other Army outfit in Europe had the kind of recreational equipment we had.

I was the commanding officer of a unit yet to be formed. Noel was my executive officer and second in command. We were in those positions. We prepared the accommodations for the troops; we planned the assignments; we learned the job; and when the troops arrived, we put the unit in place according to our planned organization and schedule. All of this we did as a unit of the Headquarters, First Base Post Office. The only name our group had was "the Battalion." It was composed of the first contingent of Negro WACs.

The 6888th Central Postal Directory was organized into five companies, Headquarters Company, Company A, Company B, Company C, and Company D. The Headquarters Company was the administrative and service support unit for the 6888th; the other companies were the postal directory personnel. I was the ranking officer. I had been told that I was their CO, and I was working in that capacity. I kept waiting for orders from Com Z to make my position official. I began to wonder how long I could issue orders and be boss without those orders. I never questioned the validity of my information about my position, but, with almost eight hundred personalities to deal with, I speculated how long it might be before someone else did. I wanted orders, but no orders were issued. I decided to solve the problem.

On 2 March 1945 I issued General Order Number 1, which read:

> 1. Under the provision of paragraph 4, AR 600-20 and the authority contained in Com Z Ltr (Ag 322 OPGA) dtd 4 March 1945, Subject: "Organization Order" No. 147, the undersigned hereby assumes command of the 6888th Central Postal Directory.
>
> /s/ Charity E. Adams
Major WAC U. S. Army
Commanding.

On 12 March 1945 Maj. Charity Adams and Capt. Abbie N. Campbell received notice that they were "reld fr asgmt to 1st Base Post Office, are ssgned to % 6888th Central Postal Directory, Hq. European T of Opns" according to the orders from "Hq. UK base, ComZ, ETO."

The 6888th Central Postal Directory Battalion was responsible for the redirection of mail to U.S. personnel in the European Theater of Operations. The total number of U.S. personnel involved was estimated to be about seven million (only the War Department knew the exact number).

This number included people in the Army, Navy, Marine Corps, Air Corps, and Seabees, uniformed civilian specialists and technicians, non-uniformed specialists, congressmen and their aides on inspection trips, Red Cross workers, and every person involved in and with military and paramilitary activity in the ETO. Sometimes we thought there were assorted other persons whose business and classification remained undetermined.

The system worked as follows: Every piece of mail was subjected to attempted delivery at the address on the face of the envelope. If the mail was undelivered at that address, it was sent on to the directory service, where an address card was on file for all U.S. personnel in the ETO. The directory service checked the files for a new address, and the mail item was forwarded for attempted delivery again. Each time a piece of mail was handled, the date and initials of the handler were noted on the face of the envelope. Each piece of mail was "worked" for thirty days and, if undeliverable, was returned to sender.

In order for the system to work, there had to be an address card for each person. Initially this was not a problem, for everyone filled out an

A unit of the 6888th marching in Birmingham

address card when overseas duty began. Each time a person moved to a new area, it was his or her responsibility to send in a change-of-address card. We were in a wartime situation, which meant that most people, especially those at or near the front, moved frequently, sometimes sending two or three changes each week. In real combat situations there were designated personnel responsible for seeing that address changes were sent to the directory service. Whenever changes were delayed or not received at all, many items of mail were returned to the States.

With over seven million persons in the files, there were thousands of name duplications. At one point we knew we had more than 7,500 Robert Smiths. Had it not been for serial numbers, we would never have been able to distinguish one from the other. Robert X. Smith (A0000001) could thus be distinguished from Robert X. Smith (A0000021). There were, of course, tens of thousands of Roberts with other last names. Moreover, there were variations of first names, nicknames, that are used in the United States: Bob, Rob, Bobby, Robby, Bert, and so forth, just for Robert. Only someone who spoke our language knew where to look in the files for a Robert when one of the nicknames was used. This same problem applied to thousands of other given names.

The 6888th wasted no time in getting to the business of seeing that the

Commanding Officer

R E S T R I C T E D

HEADQUARTERS
6888th CENTRAL POSTAL DIRECTORY
APC 562   U. S. ARMY

GENERAL ORDER)
)   21 March 1945
NUMBER.......1)

    1. Under the provision of paragraph 4, AR 600-20 and the authority
contained in Com Z Ltr (AG 322 OPGA) dtd 4 March 1945, Subject: "Organization Order " No 147, the undersigned hereby assumes command of the
6888th Central Postal Directory.

                                            CHARITY E. ADAMS
                                        Major WAC U. S. ARMY
                                               Commanding

General Order No. 1, by which I assume command of the 6888th Central Postal
Directory

troops received their mail. All of the speeches and greetings we heard as
we got started reminded us that we were important to the success of the
war; morale could not be maintained without mail from home. We worked
three eight-hour shifts, seven days a week. When we began work in February 1945, there was a large backlog of mail to be moved. Great quantities of mail, six airplane hangars of Christmas packages especially, had
been returned to the United Kingdom from the continent during the Bat-

tle of the Bulge, which took place between mid-December 1944 and mid-January 1945, when German troops pushed a huge bulge in the Allied front. One of our first jobs was to get these packages to the troops.

As the women became immersed in the delivery of the mail to the men at the front, their appreciation for the importance of mail grew. The longer we were away from home, the more we understood what had become sort of a motto, "No mail, low morale." We knew how lifted we felt upon receipt of a letter from home. The 6888th (we called our unit the "Six Triple Eight") more than lived up to the motto. I quote from a booklet, *The WAC,* endorsed by Lt. Col. Anna W. Wilson, European Theater of Operations WAC staff director, written late in 1945: "The 6888th Central Postal Directory Bn., first Negro WACs to be sent overseas, were assigned to the First Post Office in February, 1945. The unit broke all records for redirecting mail. Each of the two [actually, there were three shifts before VE Day and two after] eight-hour shifts averaged more than 65,000 pieces of mail. Long-delayed letters and packages reached battle casualties who had been moving too frequently for mail to catch up with them."

The way packages were handled was truly marvelous. Some packages had been put together so poorly that it was easy to believe that they were never intended for delivery, or that the sender thought that APO meant "articles personally offered." After a few weeks on the job some of the women had developed great skill at putting packages back together based on how certain items fitted together in what was left of the original box. By the time we moved the unit to Rouen, we had a special "package restoration unit." This group could detect details that most of us would not see: item indentations, associated smells, color rub-off from one item to another, damage from moisture, different kinds of moisture, similarity of packing materials, date and locale of printing materials used for packing, all served as clues.

This redirection of mail continued without noticeable incident until one day I received a telephone call demanding the name of the person whose initials appeared on the face of an envelope that had been returned to the sender. The story was that a certain very high-ranking officer, and there were lots of them, had received word that a letter addressed to him had been returned. The letter had been from a lady friend. All I could say was that because we had no deliverable address for him, after thirty days the letter had to be returned. True, he was important enough to be well known and what unit he commanded, but units were moving faster than were the change-of-address cards. Besides, when one is working between four hundred and five hundred pieces of mail each day from thousands of file cards in front of you, who notices rank?

I investigated the matter as I had been directed to do. I found out whose initials were on the letter, but I refused to release the name, insisting that as commanding officer of the unit I was the responsible person and should be the defendant in the officer's call for a court-martial. We managed to imply to his aides that the publicity about the other lady and his persecution of the only Negro WAC battalion would make for unpleasant public relations. The case was terminated with a reprimand to me as CO.

Sometimes a negative is an inspiration for a positive. The Negro press (the *Pittsburgh Courier,* the *Afro-American,* the *Chicago Defender,* the *Cleveland Press,* the *New Amsterdam News,* and many more), which had lobbied the War Department to send Negro WACs to the ETO, was suddenly very critical of the 6888th. Not all Negro newspapers took up the cry, but a number of them were literally creating stories about our terrible performance when they had no idea what we were doing. At this same time we were receiving praise from our superiors and even from unit commanders in the field.

I saw the articles because several of the women working in the directory received them in their personal mail. There was strong resentment against the newspapers because the 6888th had been and was working at top efficiency. Actually, what the newspapers had done was to add to the cohesion of an already topnotch unit.

Not all of my duties were pleasant. Supervision of such a large group, doing work we had never done before and with limited military experience, meant that I was faced with many chores that I did not want to perform and was unsure how to perform. One of the first such chores was to remind the personnel about the penalties for the theft of governmental properties and from the U.S. mail. The handling of the warning about theft seemed simple enough to me. I made speeches that could have been summarized as follows: "I caution you about taking government property and stealing from the mail we handle. The penalties are severe and not distinguished by the amount stolen. The penalty is the same for stealing $10 as for stealing $10,000 or more. If you must steal, make it a large amount so that you can pay your legal fees, serve your time in a federal prison and still have enough left to make it worthwhile."

Censoring mail was a routine duty and was usually assigned to company officers. We had a PR officer in the 6888th who assisted in this chore; when I had the time, I would also assist. This was indeed a chore. Considering the amount of mail sent out by our unit, we had no doubts that women were the letter writers of the world. And it was boring, boring, boring. I understood the feelings the women had about officers reading their personal correspondence to loved ones, but the truth of the matter was that by the time a censor got to the fifth letter it had all been said, and what had seemed like a "goodie" in the first letter had lost its appeal. Once in a while we had to cut a few words from a letter, but even though we cut it out, the information deleted was not sensitive. The few times that we had to cut letters up to the extent that they had no meaning, I always felt they had been created just to keep the censors busy.

From the time the U.S. Army leased King Edward School there had been curiosity about what use the building would have. When renovations began and supplies began to arrive, the curious became less subtle. War in Europe had been going on for over five years when we arrived, and many of the comforts and conveniences had been sacrificed to the war. Petrol could not be used for such an unimportant action as driving out to watch the goings-on at King Edward School; the curious either walked or used public transit.

In February, when we were actually occupying the building, the pedestrain traffic really increased and remained quite heavy for weeks, until the citizens were accustomed to our presence. A number of people tried to get inside by pretending to represent one group or another, all unrelated to our activity, and a few tried to get in unseen. Standing instructins to the unit were that we would be courteous to the citizens of our host country at all times. Civilian officials came by to extend greetings to the commanding officer; military officers, U.S. and British, came with greetings. We became aware that a large number of American soldiers were stationed in the city. As I was receiving all these official greetings, I had expected that we would have large numbers of Negro soldiers to visit. An amazingly small number came.

The women began to visit the city as sightseers and were making friends as they met the people. Just when things seemed to be going well, we became aware that we had a morale problem on our hands. When the Women's Army Auxiliary Corps was formed, there were some people who believed the unsavory rumors about the organization. In civilian or military life, where there are large numbers of men and women thrown together, a few people will get together I am sure, but not "by order of the Commanding Officer." Some of the women had been on the receiving end of some very unkind remarks from American soldiers and, in a few cases, in letters from home.

The women were prepared to be friends to their brothers if they wanted friends. Most of us were very patriotic. The welfare of the country came first, even as we rejected our status as second-class citizens and sought legal redress. We held a firm belief that, by replacing a man behind the lines, we could help all men, fathers, brothers, husbands, and sweethearts, come home sooner. There were some who had responded to the call to adventure, and some, I suspect, hoped to find *the* man. Some of the women who had been out in the city away from the 6888th had encountered some Negro soldiers who said to them, "You all can just go back to the States; we get ours from white girls now."

After a few weeks, there were a number of requests for various women to visit the homes of the locals whom they had met and with whom they had become friendly. There was no problem with this. Meeting new people could be such fun, and I had several invitations myself. The women had been encouraged to visit in the community, and there had been no complaints from any of them about our curfew, for we all had heavy work schedules. Lieutenant Landry, my adjutant, called my attention to a peculiarity about the most recent invitations. They all requested that the women be allowed to remain at the home until 12:30 A.M.

When more requests began to come from prospective hostesses, I decided that it was time to find out why 12:30 A.M. was so important. I asked Sergeant Jones, my secretary, to let me talk to the next caller and to get the word out among the troops that we wanted to know why the sudden emphasis on 12:30 A.M. No one was asked, to my knowledge, to spend the night, only to stay until after midnight.

I soon learned that racial prejudice had reared its ugly head, reaching a new high. The people in the city had long grown accustomed to having American male personnel stationed in the area. When they asked the white soldiers why we had such an early curfew (I think it was 11:00 P.M.), they were told that all Negroes had tails that came out at midnight and that the CO insisted that they be in quarters before that time. Some of the good citizens of Birmingham wanted to see for themselves.

It was difficult to get the whole story. What they believed was that all Negroes had tails but, with the men, the very long tails would hang along the leg in the pants. However, with women in skirts, the tails would surely be visible since they were reputed to be three to four feet long. One of the ways we convinced our new acquaintances that this story was untrue, rather than telling them so, was to arrange for a few groups of us to be seen in public after the "witching hour" of midnight, wearing skirts.

Lots of stories were told about all sorts of things, and I was truly amazed at the ridiculous tales people would believe. One of the better tales was the one about the soldier who explained that his blackness was the result of special shots he took so that he could fight at night without being seen.

21 March–5 May 1945

We had been told that our assignment in Birmingham was temporary, which meant whenever I asked for equipment to improve our physical plant, the request was denied. To me "temporary" meant about two weeks, and when we did not move in that time, we were dug in for the duration. We all began to be more involved with our neighbors since we were located in what was primarily a residential area. Everyone was cordial, including housewives who found time to call during the day, and as we came to recognize them, we would stop for a chat when we met them on the street.

One day a woman, accompanied by her young daughter, came to call on me. We sat in my office and discussed various aspects of living in wartime conditions, especially the deprivation in material comforts and the absence of male family members. In a moment of compassion I invited the woman and her daughter to stay and have lunch with me. When she accepted my invitation, I apologized for the fact that "today's lunch meat is Spam," to which she replied, "You mean you all have to eat that, Ma'am? We thought that was something you Americans made only for the British to eat during the war." Her appreciation of Spam increased considerably.

As commanding officer of the largest U.S. Army unit in the area (which I was surprised to learn), I received a great many invitations: to call on the lord mayor, to attend or participate in various ceremonial functions, to have tea with ladies' groups. As a representative of our country, I accepted as many of these invitations as I could. When I could not accept, and it was proper to do so, I would have some other officer take my place. More important to me was maintaining the goodwill of the Birminghamites, in whose midst we lived, and repudiating many of the stories that had been told about the "coloureds."

Wartime conditions did nothing to lessen the importance of the Britons' traditional afternoon tea break, although some adjustments to time and circumstances had to be made. What really changed was the quality and quantity of what was served. The tea was weaker, smaller portions of milk were served, very little sugar and few sweet cakes were served, and the tea sandwich was developed to an art. In fact, it was in the tea sandwich that I first learned to eat watercress. To me, a sandwich had always meant meat between slices of bread even when there were other additives. A tea sandwich was made of two *very* thin slices of bread, spread with a *very* thin layer of butter (or butter substitute), with young tender watercress or cucumber for the filling. The sandwich was then cut into four triangular quarters. Actually, they were quite tasty, especially since we could anticipate the meat we would be served back at the Mess Hall.

During the course of attending ceremonial and civic functions, I met a young man, a civil engineer, whose job had kept him working for the city rather than off in the service. He took quite a fancy to me and, after struggling to overcome his English prejudice against "blacks," he asked me to accompany him to the theater. Before I could accept his invitation I, too, had a few personal and cultural adjustments to make. It was 1945, and I was a Negro from the United States, where racial discrimination was the custom; I had been raised in the southern part of the United States, where racial discrimination was the law; I was serving the Army of the United States in a segregated unit; and I was, and had frequently been, the victim of the prejudice of white people.

I remembered that the white soldiers in Birmingham had told lies about us, that even some Negro soldiers had insulted Negro WACs. I remembered that when I had been asked about how I felt about my WACs' going out with white men, I had replied (as it was easy to do hypothetically) that I had always thought of people as people, regardless of race. Ultimately, I did go out several times with my civil engineer friend, to the theater and civic functions.

One day he took me for tea at the home of friends of his. When we arrived and entered the house, I guessed immediately what was being prepared for "tea time." As it turned out, I was correct in my guess, but the result was far worse than I had anticipated. Becuase I was American, and Americans were known as coffee drinkers, the hostess had acquired some ground coffee and, without directions, had made coffee for me. The brew was impossible to describe and equally impossible to drink. I finally asked her how she had made the coffee. As I recall, what I asked was, "What did you do to this coffee?"

She replied, "I got the coffee started early this morning so that it would be ready by 'fourish.' I just put the coffee in water and brought it to a boil. Then I let it simmer. The problem was that in an hour or so the water was almost gone, so I added more water. I had to do that several times but I am sure that it is cooked by now."

She had not used all of her coffee, so I asked if I might show her how to make coffee. I did just that, and she found the brew quite palatable while I was learning to drink tea with milk.

As we were visited at our little post, we were invited to visit other units. I was especially impressed with my visits to Air Corps installations because they were located out in the beautiful countryside. Back home, one could ride for many miles and pass untended acreage with thick, jungle-like growth. All the land seem well cared for in the areas we traveled, grass-covered and mowed, with well-trimmed hedges between fields. One of the real surprises was the appearance of a large, grass-covered knoll in the middle of an otherwise flat, neatly mowed field. The real excitement was learning that the knoll was a camouflaged airplane hangar and that one of the grass-covered slopes leading to the crest of the knoll was actually two massive doors that opened for the planes to roll out and in. It had to be effective camouflage because at two hundred yards we could not detect the doors. On one occasion, when visiting one of the air bases, I found out what strafing was like. There was an air raid warning and all personnel dived for cover, in this case under tables and behind heavy doors and furniture. It seemed that whenever we forgot, there was something to remind us that we were there to win a war.

The 6888th Central Postal Directory Battalion was housed in what had once been a school building, a large hollow square with a courtyard in the center. The showers, in rows of stalls, were in the courtyard. The kitchen and dining areas were in a separate building in the rear.

The battalion offices, sleeping quarters for enlisted personnel, and all work and recreational spaces were in this one large building. Officers were quartered in houses across the street. Recreational space consisted of an office for the Special Services officer, some storage space, a beauty parlor, and a large multipurpose area that was called the gymtorium. Most of the week this area was used purely for recreational purposes.

At the end of the week the card tables and chairs, ping-pong tables, pool tables, and the like all disappeared, because on Saturday nights there were dances for the enlisted personnel and on Sunday mornings we had nondenominational Christian church services. The dances were easy; sometimes we used records, other times a Special Services instrumental group. There were thousands of available men for guests. But church services were another matter. Even without a chaplain we could have devotional services, and my request for an occasional visit from a chaplain was granted.

Then one day, to our surprise and, I think, pleasure, we were assigned a full-time chaplain, for which I had to find, without warning and in an all-female Army unit, quarters and an office. Even now, I recall that my suspicions came too late. How in the world did a military unit with fewer than a thousand members rate a full-time chaplain? One does try to have faith, even though there was trouble from the start.

I do not recall very well what the chaplain's services were like, except that they must have been satisfactory because attendance was great. When one is away from home and in a war zone, religious activities take on great importance; our services supported our hope that we would return safely to our loved ones. We did have a nice choir to sing for our services — that part has always been important to me.

For a CO who was proud of the job attendance rate, the small number on sick call, and the amount of work the unit was turning out, it was a real shock to begin to receive reports of women AWOL from the Postal Directory. Investigation revealed that our new chaplain was the culprit. He was directing certain young women not to report to work but to report to his office to help him and to be counseled, insisting to each that he had the authority to take them off the job.

It was my duty to "counsel" him to let the women alone, pointing out that I made the assignments in the 6888th. I tried to do this in a kindly manner since the chaplain was a minister in my own denomination and knew my father as a fellow minister. He stopped his meddling with job assignments but managed to be in trouble almost every day with his campaign against such sins as card playing, dancing, shooting pool, almost any recreational activity. I suspect that it was his plan to get back at me.

One weekend in mid-March, I followed my usual procedure. I checked the gymtorium late Saturday to be sure that it was set up for the dance and to be sure that everyone knew curfew time. About 8:00 A.M. the following Sunday morning, I met the chaplain in the gymtorium to be sure that it had been transformed into a chapel. The floor was clean, the chairs were neatly lined up in rows, the stage was set up as a pulpit with chairs for the choir on the side. Every bulb in the area was burning, including the lights over the stage.

Somehow, between 8:15 A.M. and 9:30 A.M. that morning, one light bulb burned out, right over the stage's pulpit area. The amount of light lost was hardly noticeable, but the darkened bulb was very visible. Services began right on time. I was seated on the right front row with several other officers, and there was a congregation of about 150 people. The opening of the service was routine. Then came the time for the invocation, one that I will never forget. The chaplain prayed with gusto:

"Dear Lord, we thank Thee for this gathering and for the blessings Thou hast bestowed on us. Bless us and guide us. Especially guide our commanding officer because she needs it. Keep us safe in these times of war and especially keep our commanding officer because she needs your help. Help us to perform our duties and especially help our commanding officer because she needs help. Lord, she made sure all the lights were burning for the dance last night and for the card party the night before. For all these sinful things our commanding officer made sure the lights were burning. But for Your service this morning, Lord, there is one bulb burnt out and she did not care, etc., etc., etc."

By this time there was a distinct buzz going through the audience, and if I had been white, I would have been beet red. The chaplain suddenly became aware of the buzz and concluded his prayer. There was a long pause before the choir rose and sang the hymn "Be Still, My Soul, the Lord Is on Thy Side." That was, and is, my favorite hymn, and hearing it calmed my anger sufficiently to sit until the end of the service, about forty minutes. I sensed that the chaplain did not preach the sermon he planned because it was a most disorganized discourse.

Immediately after the benediction I instructed my secretary to have the chaplain report to my office in five minutes. He took fifteen minutes to get there, and that did not help his case one bit. When he appeared in the office door, I said to him, "Don't bother to sit down, Chaplain, because you do not have much time. In exactly one hour my driver will pick you up at your quarters. She will drive you and your belongings to London and leave you at the office of the Chief of Chaplains. You do not need to remind me that today is Sunday. As soon as you leave your quarters, I will call the Housing Office in London. You are a support officer of this unit and you have done everything you could to undermine this organization. I don't care what you think of me but you will not put me down in front of my troops. I hope I never see you again. Good-bye."

(I did see him once more, three years later in downtown New York City. I recognized him because he was still in uniform with proper insignia. He did not recognize me because I was not in uniform.)

As the 6888th maintained its efficiency, we were inspected, visited, greeted, checked out, congratulated, called upon, supervised, and reviewed by every officer of any rank in the United Kingdom who could come up with an excuse to come to Birmingham. They wanted to see for themselves. In between were the bona fide inspections from our superiors.

On 20 March 1945 a general in the chain of command in which we operated decided to visit the 6888th. We made what we thought were all the right plans: for lunch, for inspection of the building and work areas, and for inspection of the troops. The plan worked well for most of the visit. We met the general and his entourage, toured the building, and then we had lunch. As we walked through the building, we encountered a number of women in bathrobes, en route to the showers, and the like. Each one stopped and stood at attention as the general's party passed. When the general wanted to enter certain rooms, I respectfully pointed out that the particular rooms were living quarters and that there were women asleep in the rooms. When we entered the work area, the chief postal officer reported to the general and explained the operations. My instructions had been that all people working at their files would continue unless the general addressed them. (We had received many inspections, and this was the usual system.)

We managed to get through the midday meal with protocol still in order. After lunch I was to have the troops lined up for inspection on the grounds behind the Mess Hall. We had planned our formation according to our interpretation of the instructions. Only off-duty personnel and headquarters personnel were to be in the formation, and that meant one-third of the unit. I presented the 6888th Central Postal Directory to the general, and the following conversation took place:

"Adams, where are the other personnel of this unit? It certainly does not look like a battalion to me."

"Yes, Sir, but we work three eight-hour shifts, so some of the women are working."

"Where are the others? I saw some women walking around."

"Sir, one shift would be on sleeping time now. The ones you saw—"

The general interrupted. "I wanted to review your troops. That means all of them."

"But, Sir, our instructions were—"

"I'll tell you what I am going to do, Major Adams. I'm going to send a white first lieutenant down here to show you how to run this unit."

Up to this point the conversation had seemed to be in normal volume, heard by the general's staff and my adjutant, who was with me as I presented the troops. That last statement seemed a scream, or maybe it seemed so because of the content. Anyway, I am sure it was loud enough to be heard by the officers and enlisted women I had lined up for the review.

There are times when the human mind must respond with the speed of the modern computer, based on its data bank of information on human behavior. I am not sure exactly which word or combination of words, "white," "first lieutenant," or "white first lieutenant," triggered my reaction. I realized in a fraction of a second that I would no longer be able to command if I did not make the proper response to the general. What I said was, "Over my dead body, Sir."

He sputtered and finally said, "You'll hear from me, Adams." He saluted to indicate my dismissal from his presence and walked to his limousine.

As I watched the general's limousine slowly disappear from view, it dawned on me that I was in trouble. The work day was finally over, and in my office were assembled my executive officer, my adjutant, my secretary, and one company commander who was a close personal friend from college days. There were two topics of discussion: what had the general meant by "you'll hear from me" and what possible defense did I have for speaking to a general as I had. We sat up very late that night, going over the same material over and over again. Just before midnight there was a telephone call for Lieutenant Landry, my adjutant, from a member of the general's staff advising (warning) her that he had received instructions to draw up court-martial charges against me. During the next three days my defense was the major concern of all the headquarters personnel. There was never any question about whether I had to respond to the general's remark; the question was why had I not just "requested another chance" or some other less startling remark than "Over my dead body."

After much deliberation someone, probably Sergeant Jones, who handled the filing, remembered some letters from SHAEF that cautioned unit commanders about using language that stressed racial segregation so that our allies would not suspect disharmony among American troops. These letters did nothing to ease discrimination. My own "war council" helped me to decide to put these letters to an unintended use. I would draw up court-martial charges against the general on the grounds that he had disobeyed a directive from SHAEF Headquarters. That was stretching a memorandum into a directive, but I had nothing to lose and everything to gain.

In order to forward my charges against the general, I needed supporting evidence. The best that we could come up with was sworn statements from personnel who had heard the verbal exchange. All of our efforts were quietly and privately moved forward. After all, we had a job to do, and this was certainly not the time to slow down. On the evening of the third day of all our frenzied activity, Lieutenant Landry received another call from the general's staff member. He had decided to drop his charges against me, not because he felt that his charges would not hold up, but because I had more rank (time in grade) than any other WAC officer in the ETO, and it would be too expensive to bring officers from the States who were my senior, as required by court-martial regulations. This may have been a "cop-out," but I was not a fool; I did not pursue my charges against the general.

I was, of course, very relieved that the general had dropped his charges against me. I had not really felt that I could win, but I knew that I would have kept my self-respect. I was sure that I would never have to face that man again. Was I wrong! Three days after the 6888th moved to Rouen, France, from Birmingham, England, shortly after VE Day, I found in the routine correspondence from Com Z a notice that General X had been relieved of duty in the United Kingdom and assigned to Com Z in Normandy, headquarters in Brussels, Belgium. That was the same unit to which we were assigned. Three days after I found out that the general and I were again in the same unit, he came to visit the 6888th.

His manner was altogether different on this visit. His main concern was that we keep up the good work we had done in the United Kingdom. He was very pleasant, and you can be assured that I was. It was as if we had never met before that day. We saw each other twice more during our overseas assignment. After things settled down from VE Day celebrations, the general sent his personal plane to bring me to Brussels for a conference.

The American Red Cross was much involved with providing recreation for U.S. military personnel. In Birmingham there was a large and active club for enlisted personnel where the staff was at least receptive if not cordial to Negro troops. Apparently the social activities were successful, under controlled racial tension, with both Negro and white male soldiers in attendance. Suddenly there were female Negro soldiers in the city and at the Red Cross Club. As far as I know there was never any real "incident" at the club to cause the Red Cross staff to decide that Negro WACs would not be happy in an integrated situation and to look around for a site for another Red Cross club just for Negroes.

In the meantime, back at King Edward School, the 6888th had plenty of recreational space but limited equipment. I had sent in the necessary requisitions for supplies and equipment, but we were scheduled for transfer to the Continent, so there was no rush to fill our requisition. We did receive a number of items from units stationed in the area, both donated and liberated. We were managing.

One afternoon, soon after the Red Cross decided on the need for a segregated club, I got up from my desk and just happened to look out of a window and saw, to my surprise, an Army trailer backed up to a door on the front of our building. I called to Lieutenant Landry to go down and find out why the trailer was there. She came back in a few minutes and reported that the trailer was loaded with recreational equipment sent by the Red Cross and that it was being unloaded into our gymtorium. I hope that I did not scream when I said, "Go get Carter. I want to see her *now.*"

When Captain Carter, our Special Services officer, came into my office, I said, "Put every item back on that truck. If our girls are not good enough to visit their club, then their equipment is not good enough for them to use."

"But, Major Adams," Captain Carter wanted to explain.

"No 'buts,' Captain, we'll do without. Send every piece of the equipment back to the Red Cross. Don't even keep a deck of cards or a pack of ping-pong balls." We sent it all back and survived without that equipment. It was a difficult decision to make, and even more difficult for Captain Carter to carry out my decision. I was concerned that our recreational facility was deliberately being turned into a segregated club, and Captain Carter was true to her main concern, providing recreation for the troops.

The experience should have been a warning of things to come, but one hopes for the best.

English trains, with varying classes of accommodations, were extremely efficient, and during the war all Allied personnel in uniform rode free. For members of the 6888th, a weekend pass was enhanced by free transportation. In London there were WAC recreation hotels, one for enlisted personnel, the other for women officers and women Red Cross staff members. These hotels were the preferred and approved overnight accommodations. At one's own expense one could spend the night in a hotel if there was a vacancy. All of us in the 6888th used the two approved hotels for women.

On my frequent trips to London, I had come to know many of the Red Cross staff members, especially those in the operations office. In fact, I had several dates with one member of the staff. He was white, and perhaps that black-white combination on dates may have been the reason for what happened next. I received a call from Red Cross Headquarters asking me to "please" come into the city next day if at all possible. It was possible, and I went.

At the Red Cross office I was presented with a piece of news that was supposed to excite me. It made me angry. The director said, "We realize that your colored girls would be happier if they had a hotel all to themselves so we have leased a hotel from the British government, and we are in the process of renovating and furnishing it now."

"Did the white girls complain?" I asked.

"Oh, no, we just know that your girls would rather have a place of their own."

"More important to me, I have not had one single complaint from my 'colored girls.' My advice is to leave well enough alone."

"Oh, please," the director persisted. "Won't you let us take you out to see it?"

We climbed into a vehicle and went to the hotel. Later, I summed up my reaction to the hotel to my officers as follows. "It will make a lovely R&R hotel, but it is as far off the beaten path as it could be and still be a nice place and in the city, and it is the most blatant segregation and discrimination I have ever encountered."

Warning the Red Cross director, one more time, that this was a shameful waste of volunteer contributions, I returned to Birmingham. Over the next several weeks we watched and waited and planned. Finally, the call came. The hotel was ready, and would I please come see it before the women arrived? The next morning I was off to London again. I did have a vehicle and chauffeur assigned to me for official business, so I could make these one-day trips into London, as well as to other military locations on short notice. When I arrived in London, I was rushed out to the hotel for my "colored girls." For war times, the hotel was quite nicely furnished, the kitchen was complete and stocked, supplies adequate, and staff sufficient. Everyone was beaming and waiting to know what I thought of it. I toured the entire place, room by room, before I made my comment.

"I am sorry that you have gone to so much expense and trouble. I advised you that the Negro WACs had had no problems with the white WACs, so this hotel is not necessary. I promise you that, as God is my witness, as long as I am commanding officer of the 6888th Central Postal Directory Battalion, not one member of that unit will ever spend one night here."

Back in Birmingham I prepared to put our plan in operation. The following morning for the first and only time I shut down the eight-hour shifts and had every member of the unit (the only ones excused were the ones in the hospital) assemble in the gymtorium, and I laid out the strategy. All this took place after the unit was at full strength, so there was not enough room for nearly a thousand people to be seated. I had prepared my remarks carefully.

"Since we have been here, those of you who have had passes to London have stayed at the WAC hotel for enlisted women. Not one of you has ever complained about sharing a hotel with white WACs. Whether white WACs have complained about you is not my problem. Several weeks ago I was informed that the Red Cross was going to prepare a separate hotel for members of the 6888th because that organization feels that you would be happier in a segregated building. They described it as your own private hotel.

"Yesterday I visited the hotel. It is very nice, but it is very segregated. What it does is to create a segregated hotel when we already have an integrated situation, which is working. Yesterday as I stood in that hotel, I promised that not one of you would spend a night in that hotel. I cannot force you to support me, short of not granting any overnight passes. I will not do that, but I do ask your support.

"We have worked out several options that we hope you will use. First, since transportation is free, you can take your pass to London by going in the morning and returning here in the evening to your regular sleeping quarters. For this, we will make adjustments in curfew hours based on the train schedule. Second, if you want to stay overnight in London, you may go to any hotel and pay your own bills. Third, if you want to stay overnight in London and you want approval of the family with whom you want to stay, you'll get approval with a minimum of trouble."

I am very proud of my service as CO of the 6888th, but one of the proudest times was when the women of that unit supported me in this action. I have never deluded myself that this support came out of love for me. What we had was a large group of adult Negro women who had been victimized, in one way or another, by racial bias. This was one opportunity to stand together for a common cause. If even one member of 6888th spent a night in that hotel, the Red Cross kept it from me.

Near the end of April, I was in Paris preparing for our move to Rouen. I was sitting at a table at the WAC officers' hotel sidewalk restaurant when a Red Cross director assigned to duty on the Continent came up to me and said, "I heard that we [the Red Cross] had quite a bit of trouble with you in the U.K."

"Oh, no," I replied. "I had lots of trouble with you." I was assured then that I would have no trouble in France. That was when I increased my contribution to the Red Cross just in case I had trouble again. I thought I could put up a better fight from inside the organization.

Not all of my visits to this Paris hotel were as intense and business related as the one recounted above. One evening as a group of us were having dinner in the hotel dining room, an officer from another table came over and told me that a civilian woman at her table wanted to have a word with me. When I asked what she wanted, I was told that the woman had definite vibrations that led straight to me. When I asked who she was, I was told that she was a fortune teller whom many people had found to be quite "good." I had never had contact with such a person before, so it did not take too much for my friends to get me to agree to the conversation. The woman asked if I would join her at an unoccupied table, which I did.

The woman asked to look at the palm of my right hand. She stared at it for quite a long time, and I thought I heard a low rumbling human sound as she looked. Then she said that "something was not as she expected." I had no answer to that. After a pause she asked to see my left palm. When I extended that hand, she bent over and exclaimed, "That's it! That's it! That's where the vibrations came from!"

"That's what?" I asked.

"The lines. See those lines. See the star, it's so unusual. I don't know its full meaning but I know it's special. I'll find out, and the next time you are in Paris I'll tell you what it means. Look at your hand; see the star!"

I looked, and I saw what she called a star. What she saw was five points moving out from a center. What I saw was two lines crossing and a fifth line coming from the point of intersection.

As far as I was concerned the matter was closed because I did not plan to notify her of my presence in Paris. Besides, I had always felt that I did not want any predictions of the future. If the prediction was bad, I did not want to know, and if it was good, I wanted to be surprised.

About five weeks later, after I had forgotten all about the palmist, I was in Paris again, and some of my acquaintances asked if I had seen the woman again. I gave a negative reply. I was informed that she was calling the WAC hotel about every third day to find out if I had arrived. She must have called that afternoon, for shortly after I had finished my dinner in the dining room of the hotel, the palmist showed up and asked to speak to me. This is what she had to say to me:

"As I told you, that star in your hand is special; it is very rare. It means that you can be successful in many fields. In fields that require communications you can do extremely well. Every palmist hopes to see such a star in their career." That was pleasant to hear, but it did not influence my behavior on my assignment in the ETO.

When one is close enough to the ugliness of war, there is a small tinge of guilt associated with any moment when the war action seems beautiful. Such a moment happened to me late one Sunday afternoon in front of the WAC R&R hotel in Paris. It was just after 4:00 P.M. as I stepped out to the sidewalk in the bright afternoon sun (a rare day for April, all clear and bright) and glanced up at the sky. What I saw seemed to be highly polished silver balls soaring over the city. After a few minutes I realized that I was looking at planes that did not seem to disappear. Each was being replaced in my sight by another, over and over again. There were thousands of planes in the sky. When I looked toward other sections of the vast overhead, I noticed that as the hundreds of planes from one direction completed their pass over Paris, other hundreds from another direction came over the city, all going to the east. I was witnessing a rendezvous of Allied planes on a bombing mission. The assembly of air power, coming in from many different airfields, took over an hour, and for that time I forgot why I was in Paris, lost in the beauty of the flight.

Although we were busy with our part of the war effort, we were aware of the efforts made to keep up the morale of the civilian population. King George VI and Queen Elizabeth were greatly involved in this part of British life. Occasionally, when the queen was visiting, small groups of WAC officers would be invited to be present and to be presented. There was a great deal of discussion about whether military personnel should salute or bow. The decision was that we should bow. In the few presentations about which I can report the reality was that the uniformed WAC officers saluted. The queen was gracious; she accepted the salutes with a nod and a very slight wave of her hand.

After only a few weeks we had realized that having all activity in one building had its disadvantages. Our non-coms were reliable and efficient, the kind every unit hoped for, but there was no place for them to relax from the intensity of everyday operations. We needed a noncommissioned officers club.

Next to our quadrangular building was a large open field that we used for formations and reviews. I visualized our NCO club on part of that field. On a trip to Litchfield to visit an enlisted woman in the 33rd Station Hospital, I saw the kind of building I needed. Back at the 6888th, I addressed a request to the U.K. supply officer for one Quonset hut. In spite of all the channels through which my request had to pass, it was back in seven days. The last endorsement read "Request denied." Two more times I sent in my request for one Quonset hut. Each time, my letter, with all the endorsements up the chain of command and down, came back "Request denied." The fourth letter of request somehow became a request for two Quonset huts. "Request denied."

The fifth request, for two huts, was evidently the charm. Three days after the letter left the 6888th, I received a telephone call from a colonel in U.K. Supply Office who demanded, "Adams, don't you know what 'request denied' means?"

"Yes, Sir, but there are no regulations prohibiting new requests."

"Don't tell me about regulations! What the hell do you want with Quonset huts? You are moving to the Continent in a few days."

"Yes, Sir," I answered. "They told me that in February and we are still here and March is almost gone. Besides, Sir, Quonset huts can be broken down and moved to a new site, if and when we do move."

"Well, let me think about this," the colonel replied. "How are you women going to put up a Quonset hut?"

"Sir, if I get the huts, I'll find a way to put them up." I was not sure, but I thought the colonel had softened a bit.

On 3 April two Quonset huts arrived at the 6888th. That was not all. With the huts came Lieutenant Kelly and a platoon from the Corps of Engineers. The "engineers" were Negro soldiers who were laborers just because they were Negro soldiers. Second Lieutenant Kelly was in command, and he was white. In 1945 that was the way things were. What was different was that this platoon of engineers and their CO were attached to the 6888th for duty, and this white officer had a Negro commander.

When Lieutenant Kelly and his engineers reported, I informed them that the construction job was already overdue even though the huts had just arrived. The message must have been loud and clear, for in a very short time the first hut was up, and the non-coms spent all their free time getting the place ready for opening and use. We had no funds to invest in this project, but everyone was being paid regularly and made contributions to the cause. We were again surprised how much equipment the GIs could come up with, just as they had done when we returned the Red Cross supplies. There was a gala opening to which the officers were invited. We all put in appearances but did not stay; this was the NCO club.

The next step was an officers lounge, and that required more time to get done. Although it was desired, it was not pressing since we did have quarters in houses with some very small social space. Besides, we officers did not have as many gallant young men liberating and furnishing equipment for us. But we made it, and on 22 April we opened the officers lounge.

We were scheduled to move to the continent, and, now that we were comfortable, we did. We used our lounge for less than a month.

Part of our equipment when we moved into the King Edward School was a telephone system with numerous in-house extensions and sufficient outside lines for business and social use. It was probably almost "state of the art" for wartime 1945. There was a large switchboard with many tubes that had to be plugged in to make connections and unplugged when calls were completed. This kind of system sometimes required that the operator open a switch to listen for the completion or continuation of calls.

As we settled in and associations were formed, friends made, the number of telephone calls to the outside from the 6888th increased. There were eventually complaints that the operators were listening in on personal calls. I found this difficult to believe, but on the other hand I also thought that the telephone operators had about the dullest jobs in the unit. Maybe they listened from boredom. I really did not know what the jobs were like, but because I always felt that I should know about any job to which I assigned others, I decided to work the night shift for a couple of nights. The worst, I felt, in the middle of the night would be a few in-house calls. I had forgotten that with the directory working three eight-hour shifts there were a few people up and about, engaging in regular and routine activities twenty-four hours a day. Working on that switchboard for two nights was the dullest job in the world, after censoring the mail. If we had been civilians I would have felt, as boss, that telephone operators were underpaid.

Meanwhile, the operators of the 6888th were developing very friendly relations with other operators in other units, in Birmingham, in London, and other English cities. We never tried, and were not sure it was permitted, to make transatlantic telephone calls, but my operators knew all the proper procedures and personnel to handle overseas calls to the United States since such calls were directed through the Birmingham exchange as one step to the seat of the government to London. We had all of this wonderful telephone equipment in King Edward School, but in the houses where the officers lived, there was one telephone in each house, on the wall in the entry hall.

After midnight on the evening of 12 April the telephone in our house rang and rang. I did not get up because everyone in the house was a junior officer. Besides, who would call the CO at this ungodly hour? Then there was a knock on the door, and a voice said, "Major Adams, the chief operator is on the telephone and says that she must speak to you." I had not realized until then how vivid my imagination could be, as I tried to think of what could have happened.

"Major Adams," the operator said. "I just got a call from one of the Birmingham overseas operators with whom I have a telephone friendship. She is in the process of putting through a call to the prime minister at

10 Downing Street, but she paused long enough to signal that the president just died. President Roosevelt is dead."

I think I just hung up the receiver without a word. I was in shock. Not because I was a political creature, but rather I was instantly concerned about what the mood and policies of the government would be in relation to Negro military personnel. My concern was shared later, when it was announced that the president was dead. The main reaction of Negro troops in the ETO was to wonder whether we would get home again or, at best, whether we would have to remain in Europe until all white personnel were safely home.

Roosevelt had been perceived as the diplomat, the statesman, the champion of little people, the savior of the economy of the United States, even indirectly a friend of Negroes, for when the economy was going well, the economic life, if not the societal life, of the Negro population improved accordingly. Almost immediately after the death of Franklin D. Roosevelt, Harry S Truman was sworn in as the new president. Truman was reputed to be a product of the infamous Pendergast machine of the midwestern United States. I did not know what that meant, but my reading of the political news had not led me to anticipate great good. I would later develop great admiration for President Truman.

On 11 April I had received orders to go to Paris but, on 12 April those orders had been revoked, so that I was at my post at the 6888th when President Roosevelt's death was announced (this was several hours after I had received off-the-record word of the death). What I did not know was that it was the responsibility of the ranking officer of the U.S. Army to represent the United States at memorial services for the commander in chief. Suddenly, race was not important, and I was *it*. The importance of the American involvement in the European part of World War II was clearly brought home to us at this point.

Birmingham was a very large city, which meant that there were many memorial services for President Roosevelt. I was invited, along with the 6888th, to participate in about thirty services. By asking volunteers and making a few assignments, we managed to be represented at most of the services. I personally attended five services, all of which were the important civic and military services. Fortunately, all the services were short. A hymn, a prayer, and a few remarks and it was all over. At the 6888th we had a memorial formation with virtually the same format. The difference for the 6888th was that we each felt we had suffered a personal loss and had a concern for the future.

The memorial pauses were brief, and the war efforts continued. My orders to proceed to Paris were reissued, and I took off for the Continent to begin preparations for our long-anticipated move. The next few days were filled with hectic jeep rides between Paris and Rouen. I had the luxury of flying back and forth between London and Paris on my trips, but most of the other travel was in military vehicles, jeeps or C&R cars. On 16 April I flew to Paris; on the seventeenth I went to Rouen and returned; on the eighteenth it was back to Rouen to spend the night; I then returned to Paris on the nineteenth.

In Rouen, where I was to move the 6888th, the situation did not look promising. It looked impossible, but it had to work. I sent for several officers and enlisted women to work with the people who were to put the place in order. I met them in Paris, and this time we flew "toward" Rouen, landing at an unfinished airfield, and finished the trip in a weapons carrier. I left the new arrivals with the preparations and returned to England.

By Tuesday, 1 May, I had gotten out the invitations to a party I was giving for the officers of the 6888th, to celebrate our having an officers club. The party, on the following Saturday night, was quite a success. I think that it was at this party that I realized how immersed my life was in Army protocol. The affair was a success, but it seemed a little too polite, too stiff. There was not a lot of "rank" between officers in the 6888th, certainly not as much as there was between me and the colonels and generals who were my supervisors. But it came to me that I did not really relax in the presence of my commanding officer, and I did put the final word on efficiency reports. As soon as I could gracefully do so as hostess, I left the party. It is my understanding that the fun then began.

6 May–31 July 1945

I received orders, dated 5 May 1945, for another trip to Rouen, this time by rail transportation, on or about 6 May. As it turned out, I left for Rouen on 7 May to go by "boat-train" to Paris and on to Rouen. This was a great experience: by train from Birmingham to London, by train to the point of embarkation for the boat trip across the English Channel to Calais, by train to Paris.

Passengers boarded the ship for the trip about ten in the evening. I went to bed immediately so that I would be well rested when we docked next morning, but mostly I wanted to be asleep before the ship left the English dockside. I slept quite well, awakening several times during the night, recognizing that the rocking of the boat was par for the crossing of the channel. We all dressed and packed, prepared to disembark in Calais, only to discover that we had not left England. The English Channel had lived up to its reputation as the roughest body of water on earth, and this roughness had prevented our crossing during the night. As daylight increased, the rage of the channel calmed somewhat, and we crossed.

On the French side we left the boat and took our places on the Paris train. Except from the air, this was the first time I had seen the French countryside. It was May, and the crops were in full green, interspersed with almost-covered scars of the war. There had been several months for the land to recover, and flowers had been planted in abundance. The weather was not yet really warm, but warm enough for spring growth.

The route to Paris took us through a countryside where the citizens had worked hard to regain some normalcy. The train passed, without stopping, through many villages and towns, but many people were on hand at the various local railroad depots to wave and cheer. I remember thinking that it was strange for people to come to the station just to wave at people on a train, regardless of who might be en route to Paris. On the other hand, the French were very patriotic and, at that time, grateful for the U.S. entry into the war as well as for the liberation of France from Nazi control.

When we arrived in the villages on the edge of Paris, the crowds seemed larger and livelier. In Paris itself the streets were crammed with people, and as we left the train we stepped into an almost solid mass of people, obviously celebrating. It was hard to believe that it was VE Day, anxiously anticipated for weeks, and we had made that long train ride unaware of it. That's when the fun began.

From the moment we stepped off the train, everyone in U.S. military uniform was subjected to the victory hysteria of the French. We were kissed on the cheek, sometimes on the lips, offered drinks, asked for souvenirs, and if you had none, something was taken: your cap, insignia, epaulettes, even the braid on the sleeves. All the time this was happening to me, I was just trying to get to the billeting office or the transportation office, or even the military police. When I lost one shoestring as a souvenir, I began to be desperate. With great difficulty I made it to the billeting office.

If my uniform jacket had not had an inside breast pocket like the uniform for men (I had had it tailored), I am sure I would not have been able to produce identification at the office. As it was, I presented myself in some disarray, almost a comical figure, to the billeting officer. He was a first lieutenant, and my papers listed me as a major. He had some difficulty controlling his laughter at my appearance. In recognition of the serious celebrating in the city, he decided to assign me to the nearest hotel to which he could provide transportation.

The hotel? It turned out to be the Men's Transit Hotel, used primarily for male officers on temporary duty in Paris. Fortunately, the hotel had a dining room where I had dinner that night. I did not dare venture out of the building that evening. I had to be very careful in my use of the "facilities" by knocking on every door I entered, even to the room to which I was assigned. After all, this was a hotel for men, and none of them would know that a woman had been quartered there. Besides, in the early days of women in the Army, acceptance took separate paths. Some combined common courtesy and military courtesy; some felt that if women invaded their territory, they had to be treated like one of the boys; and the last group, not the largest number by any means, felt obligated to be disrespectful to Negroes under all circumstances.

My room was in the front of the building, and I sat that evening in the darkened hotel room. The only light came in from the dim lights in the street, where the VE Day celebration continued. A U.S. Army captain drove up to our hotel and parked. When he entered the building, his vehicle became expendable. I watched as it was disassembled for souvenirs, right down to the chassis, at which point one man somehow started the motor without the key and drove it away as his souvenir.

Sometime during the evening my flight bag arrived from the train station, and I realized that I had survived VE Day in Paris. On VE Day plus one, for the first time, I was anxious to get to Rouen.

At our new post in Rouen, I surveyed the situation. Great quantities of supplies were being brought in. We would again be a separate and self-sufficient unit. This time we had a small enclosed post said to have been built for Napoleon's troops. I believed it, because everything seemed to be built for durability. On entering the gate, one had a great view of the entire post. We used the building as follows, starting on the right, going counter-clockwise: First was a small two-story building that housed the battalion headquarters on the first floor and the medical facility on the second floor. Next was a large two-story building that housed the supply office and storage, as well as the motor pool. The next building housed the mess hall, kitchen, and recreational space on two floors (behind this building were several small buildings that were eventually used for storage, laundry, and other unspecified activities). Next was the largest building, a four-story brick building in which was located the Postal Directory work area on the ground floor; enlisted personnel were quartered on the other three floors. The last operations building was a small one-story building that housed the main laundry facility. (With more than nine hundred women, we needed lots of laundry space.) This was followed by two houses, Officers Quarters 1 and Officers Quarters 2, and then back to the gate.

With the fighting ended in the ETO, there was considerable pressure to move the Postal Directory unit closer to the majority of troops so that mail delivery could help maintain morale. As we prepared to move the entire unit from the United Kingdom to Normandy, we kept putting in requisitions for needed supplies and equipment, and the requisitions were filled with unusual speed. Those of us who were in Rouen preparing for the arrival of the 6888th were living in a hotel in downtown Rouen in reasonable comfort.

One of the unusual aspects of our preparations was the assignment of three hundred POWs to do the repairs and heavy labor. Prior modifications of this post for Napoleon's troops had been modest at best. Hence, a great deal of modernization was needed: windows sealed, doors repaired, showers installed, interior painted, beds set up. . . . Beds set up? Forty-eight hours before the 6888th was to arrive in Rouen from Birmingham, the beds, the army beds, could not be located. They were to have been shipped by rail from the south of France but, apparently, had been put on a siding someplace. Twenty-four hours of telephone calls still did not get us any assurance that the beds were en route.

By telephone it was ascertained that the 6888th was packed and ready to move, and there were no beds. Someone suggested that we requisition canvas cots. The problem with that was that the plans called for bunk beds in the barracks, and using canvas cots would require more space than we had. I think that it was one of the POWs who suggested that we get the canvas cots and that we double-deck them. We were all a bit slow understanding this concept. Our vision was of how difficult and uncomfortable just a plain canvas cot would be, but to be in the upper deck of double-decked canvas cots — impossible. Once it was decided that the job was possible, our next task was deciding how to do it. Using two-by-fours, the POWs built frames in which the cots rested securely when opened and placed in the proper supports. In about eighteen hours enough frames had been built and put in place to provide sleeping places for everyone.

There was much surprise, some displeasure, and quite a bit of discomfort associated with those double-decked canvas cots, probably the only ones in the U.S. Army during World War II. Once we were settled in, word got around about the suffering of the women — and on the Continent there were plenty of GIs to hear about the suffering. Early one morning there was delivered to our post exactly the number of mattresses needed for all the canvas cots. Now I really understood what was meant by "liberated" supplies. They were reputed to be surplus from the quartermaster depot. Months later when we moved to Paris, I had quite a bit of trouble getting rid of those mattresses. I was unable to turn them in to the depot because there was no memorandum receipt, the official documentation to show that the mattresses had been issued to the 6888th. We had to use some GI ingenuity to re-create the surplus at the depot.

About a week after we moved, as I was walking across our little Army post, a non-com said to me, "Major, there are 725 enlisted men for each enlisted woman and thirty-one male officers for each female officer."

"I guess you mean in the ETO, eh?"

"No, Ma'am, I mean outside our gates."

I really had given little thought to the ratio of men to women, and the figure given me was certainly not accurate by actual count — but it could have been. There were uniformed Negro soldiers as far as one could see when I looked out of the gate. It looked worse when I surveyed the crowd from the second floor of one of the officers quarters.

We had been on the Continent only a few days, but word of our arrival had spread with the speed of sound, and a great many men suddenly found that they had business in Rouen, all appearing at our gate. We had assigned a few women to be our security unit, and, with the help of MPs in Rouen, we were able to keep the people outside the gates. The city police were insistent that we get rid of the crowd but neglected to tell us how to do it.

This was all taking place shortly after VE Day, when many troops were being moved back from the front. At times it appeared that all troops were being routed back through Rouen, especially when we noticed that the horde of visitors now had a number of white soldiers in the group. In general, we had very positive feelings about the men who wanted to visit. Many had been away from home for several years, and just the sight of an American woman, regardless of race, was important, a connection with "back home."

There were many GIs who had legitimate reason to visit the 6888th. The problem was to separate those who had reasons to visit from those who just wanted to visit. There were husbands, fathers, fiances, boyfriends, brothers, uncles, cousins, classmates, and family friends of members of our unit. Then there were claimants, those who claimed mostly to be cousins and a few uncles, relatives who possibly had been heard of but not well known or not seen for a long time. I tried to be understanding, for I had an uncle who was a chaplain with Allied forces moving north from North Africa. I felt that he might show up any day, and he did. Also, almost immediately, I had encountered a classmate and friend stationed in the area, so I was aware of the possibilities of chance. In fact, there were three occasions when young men managed to get inside the gate claiming to be my cousin. Two of them struck out unequivocally. The third young man did better. We had the same last name, some similarities of background, but if one already has lots of cousins, one doesn't hastily accept another.

It was, of course, sort of pleasant to have all the attention from the men. To tell the truth, it was very pleasant. After all, we had not been out of the States very long, less than six months, and we were still aware of the shortage of young men back home unless there was a military installation nearby.

This state of social euphoria could not and did not last very long, about two weeks. I felt it before then, but I had learned that a good CO suffers inconveniences so that the troops would have the convenience. We did have a job to do, so to cut down on the socializing, we specified the time and the number of male visitors to our limited grounds. After about two weeks we made a rule that only those who came to visit a person by name would be allowed on the grounds. After all, in two weeks all who were interested would surely have met one person whose name they would remember.

Our various regulations helped, but not enough. One day, in my office, I received a committee of non-coms, representing all five companies in the battalion, and essentially what they said was, "Get rid of the men! We need some female time." Quite a discussion followed, and I did understand. There was no time to do personal laundry and hang it out to dry; there was no time to wash hair and put it in rollers to dry; and on and on—all because there were always men around the place. The result of this discussion was an agreement and a new rule. No men on the post on Monday except the German POWs, who worked for the 6888th, with their guards, and those men who came on official business. It worked.

Social visitors were not the only ones who came. Not everyone, but almost everyone, with the rank or title qualifying them to make an inspection tour of the 6888th, found time to do so, regardless of race, creed, or color, ours or theirs. For weeks I spent half my days receiving strange officers who wanted to see "how you are getting along," "if you need anything," "if civilian authorities are treating you well," and so forth. I had been raised to be courteous to everyone, and I was for those first few weeks, but I was getting behind in my work. Lieutenant Landry, Sergeant Jones, and I discussed the problem and decided on various strategies to discourage long visits and to discourage visitors' insistence on seeing the CO. None of these worked.

Then, one day as I sat at my desk, I put my hands on top of my head and leaned back, which caused me to slide forward on the chair seat. Suddenly I had my solution to time-consuming visitors. There was a chair in front of my desk that attracted almost all visitors when I invited them to be seated. We studied the chairs in the office very carefully and put the best-looking one in the favored spot. Before we put the chair in place, however, I had the front legs cut down one-fourth of an inch. It was amazing how difficult it was to sit at attention when the front legs of the straight hardwood chair were lower than the back legs. We did use that special chair with discretion, being careful to move it when general officers and genuine supervisors came to visit.

Among other agreements the U.S. government had with Allied governments was the provision of jobs for civilians. As a result, the 6888th was assigned two hundred civilian workers to "help" in our postal service. We already had a large number of POWs attached who took care of maintenance and the handling of large and heavy mail bags, so the only jobs available for French citizens were the Postal Directory Service.

We were all absolutely delighted to work with them. I think we felt, subconsciously, that some of the much-read-about and much-admired French characteristics would rub off on or be absorbed by us: sense of style, strong independence, fierce patriotism, appreciation for music and the arts, and the like. But the post office wasn't the best environment for cultural exchange. The language barrier and the different names and spellings even for words with similar meanings, made postal work a great challenge for the French civilians. Pronunciation of the alphabet was even very different. Moreover, who but an American would know the diminutives and variables of an American name? But the French worked at learning, and we worked at teaching. It is important to note that we were all appreciative of the suffering France had endured under Nazi occupation, so we were eager to be as helpful as possible.

Part of the agreement was that we would feed our French workers one meal each day, at noon. The U.S. Army noon meal was a banquet compared to the sparse meal of the civilian diet. This created a problem: this noon meal was ingested by a system not adjusted to the content and quantity of food, which was more than the digestive system could handle. About an hour after lunch they would begin to pass out, one by one, sometimes as many as twenty after a single meal. In a short time our mess officer, a trained dietician, suggested a solution to this problem. Use the same ration and serve two meals each work day, at noon and at the end of the work day. This system bent the rules a bit, but our unit was better served and appreciated.

Our relationship with the citizens of Rouen was unique. We represented the U.S. government, which was white in their minds, but we were black. There was much curiosity about us, and they were very friendly, sometimes in a meddling and nosy way. There was a certain amount of resentment about our everyday existence, which seemed to have luxuries that had been stripped from them by the war. In the minds of the officers, the only things that seemed luxurious were having French maids to take care of our quarters and buying French perfume, both of which we paid for out of our personal pockets. The other side of that was that the maids cleaned the quarters quite well, but they searched all wastebaskets for items that could still be used, and they used our fine perfumes, adding water to the bottles to maintain the content level. However, they were superior at polishing our shoes.

One night in Officers Quarters 2, where the first floor was our officers club, we were entertaining some friends when someone noticed smoke coming from the ceiling over the fireplace. We investigated and called the Rouen fire department when it became obvious that there was fire in the wall of the second floor. They arrived, not with haste, at about 12:15 A.M. The firemen studied the situation, discussed it, and finally decided that they would have to chop away the hearth and mantel to get to the source of the smoke.

True, it was summer and the days were warm, but the nights were frequently cool, and sometimes we required a small fire to take the chill off. However, this particular fireplace had not been used for at least twenty-four hours, so whatever the source of the smoke was, it had been smoldering for some time. The firemen brought axes, hammers, crowbars, shovels, and brooms. They examined the fireplace for a few more minutes before

Major Adams

RESTRICTED

HEADQUARTERS
6888th CENTRAL POSTAL DIRECTORY
APO 562   U. S. ARMY

SPECIAL ORDERS)
:
NO.........18)   30 May 1945

    1. Announcement is hereby made of the change of designation of Headquarters Company, 6888th Central Postal Directory to Headquarters and Headquarters Detachment. (EDCMR 31 May 45)

    2. The following named WAC Officers are asgd to Co indicated: (EDCMR 31 May 45)

Hq Det,

2nd LT	FRANCIS S FLATTS	L-201378	CO
2nd LT	JULIA A RICH	L-310863	Ex O

Co "A"

1st LT	BERNICE G HENDERSON	L-501504	CO
2nd LT	AUBREY A STOKES	L-1000267	Ex O

Co "B"

1st LT	VASHTI B TONKINS	L-508032	CO
2nd LT	BERTIE M EDWARDS	L-204945	Ex O

Co "C"

CAPT	VERA A HARRISON	L-500024	CO
2nd LT	LILLIAN V DUNCAN	L-402584	Ex O

Co "D"

1st LT	ELLA B TATUM	L-800726	CO
2nd LT	GUSSYE D STEWART	L-1000500	Ex O

    3. The following named WAC Officers are asgd to Hq & Hqs Det 6888th CPD for Adm & dy as indicated: (EDCMR 31 May 45)

Major	CHARITY E ADAMS	L-500001	Battalion CO
Capt	ABBIE N CAMPBELL	L-402518	Battalion Ex O
Capt	MILDRED E CARTER	L-115021	Spec Serv O
Capt	MARY M KEARNEY	L-125005	Chief of Mail

RESTRICTED

-1-

One set of organizational orders issued under my command of the 6888th Central Postal Directory

they began wildly hacking at the mantel and its surrounding wall. We, the officers who lived in this house and I, remained on the scene but far enough away to allow the firemen to work.

Suddenly, as if by some signal unheard by any of us, the firemen stopped working and began gathering up their tools. With desperate effort, using

R E S T R I C T E D

(Hqs, 6888th CPD, APO 562, Special Order No 18, par 3 dtd 30 May 45 Cont'd)

1st Lt	MARGARET E BARNES	L-500995	PRO O
1st Lt	DORIS N CABLE	L-500022	Postal O
1st Lt	WILLA G CHERRY	L-600718	Postal O
1st Lt	MILDRED V DUPEE	L-500418	Postal O
1st Lt	FANNIE A GRIFFIN	L-200109	Postal O
1st Lt	VIOLET W HILL	L-600015	Postal O
1st Lt	CATHERINE G LANDRY	L-303726	Bn Adj
1st Lt	DOROTHY H SCOTT	L-600432	Postal O
1st Lt	BLANCHE L SCOTT	L-303576	Personnel O
1st Lt	CORRIE S SHERARD	L-402006	Mess O
1st Lt	JULIA H WILLIAMS	L-402781	Bn Supply O
2nd Lt	ALICE E EDWARDS	L-900401	Ass't Bn Supply O
2nd Lt	VIVIAN N ELZIE	L-304676	Ass't Mess O
2nd Lt	MERCEDEES A JORDAN	L-200271	Transportation O
2nd Lt	ELFREDA S LE BEAU	L-801480	PX O
2nd Lt	CALONIA V POWELL	L-801525	Postal O

4. 2nd LT HAZEL E CRADDOCK, L-702372 is reld of dy as Postal O and asgd to Hq & Hq Det for Adm and dy as Post Utilities O.

By order of Major ADAMS:

CATHERINE G. LANDRY
1st Lt, WAC
Adjutant

OFFICIAL:

Catherine H. Landry

CATHERINE G. LANDRY
1st Lt, WAC
Adjutant

R E S T R I C T E D

-2-

long ignored high school and college French added to what we had picked up in the short time we had been there, we struggled to find out what was going on. It was 1:55 A.M. and we learned that this crew would go off duty at 2:00 A.M. — which they did, at 1:59 A.M. Promptly at 2:00 A.M. the next crew stomped up the steps and finished the job. I have always wondered if the first crew would have departed so punctually if we had seen flames rather than smoke.

In spite of their curiosity about us, the citizens of the area were very cordial, and we came to know quite a number of people in the immediate community. We also met other military personnel who had been in the area much longer than we, and, as time permitted, we enjoyed visiting other towns and villages in the area. We especially liked the villages where we could get a good meal and buy items to take home. There were all sorts of festivals in the villages now that the fighting was over. For me, these trips afforded an opportunity to let down a little from the posture of a commanding officer. I had learned that one could not party as one of the gang at night and then be in charge the next day.

When the 6888th moved to Rouen, in May, the routine of censoring mail took a change for the worse for me. I received a highly confidential visit from an Army Intelligence officer, which made life very unpleasant for me. I was given instructions to personally censor the mail of several of my officers. One in particular was to have all mail censored. Why? It seems she made contact with French civilians immediately upon arrival in the city. These particular civilians had been and were still under surveillance for Communist associations, and this officer had friends and one in-law who had Communist associates in New York City. I had two problems with this assignment. First, it meant that I had to share this confidential information with at least two other officers, and second, knowing this second lieutenant, I had no doubt that she could make friends within an hour of her arrival anywhere. I managed the censoring without mishap, but at no time did I find anything to report. In all honesty, I found nothing suspicious in the letters; perhaps I was too naive.

The chore that was the most difficult for me came in a directive for unit commanders to be alert to homosexual activity. Those of us who came from highly protective backgrounds barely knew what the directive was about and had no idea what to watch for. But we were not stupid, and when there were as many women together as there were in WAC units, attention was always directed at relationships that seemed extra close. When this directive first came to me, I thought long and hard about it. I remembered the childish accusations of misunderstood relationships we heard about in college and in the public arena of work. When I had exhausted my thinking and the discussions with my closest associates, I called the next echelon to ask for guidance in following the directive. The response had two parts: one, the concern should be directed toward those homosexual activities that negatively influenced the performance of the unit, and two, it was suggested that the CO make surprise inspections during the hours when troops were in bed. We had rather an open communication system, so I felt that, had there been any such problem, one of the officers would have heard of it. Besides, we worked hard all day, and I was not about to do a bed check without the company commander, and I was certainly not going to wake up a company commander to accompany me. I cannot swear to the kind of social activity that took place with all the members of the 6888th, but I will swear that the efficient performance of the unit was not impaired.

There was one situation that required our collective tact. Our civilian workers, mostly women, resented working at the same facility where German POWs were working. Pointing out that the Germans were prisoners while the French were free citizens helped establish an acceptable, if not pleasant, atmosphere.

Among the POWs there seemed to be a craftsman in whatever area we needed one. Name the craft, and it was represented; we had carpenters, plumbers, electricians, painters, mechanics. The unit operated very smoothly with such skills available. All we had to do was to indicate what we wanted the result to be; there was no need even to give detailed instructions.

Post exchange services were based on the number of personnel to be served. Even though we were a fairly large unit, most supplies still had to be rationed, one item per person. Such items as cigarettes and soap, however, were in sufficient supply. Small units, with personnel numbering from thirty-five to one hundred, had more difficulty getting supplies.

Other officers complained to our post exchange officer about the difficulties of serving very small units, especially when they tried to purchase from our exchange. It occurred to the head of our post exchange that ours would be better supplied if we became the service unit for all the small units in our area. After Lieutenant LeBeau had signed up two or three units, word began to get around, and we were besieged with requests to join. We accepted as many as we felt we could handle, considering the personnel and space we could assign to the exchange. This meant that the nature of our requisitions changed. Also, we received many more of the items that were rationed one per x number of people, items such as razor blades and shaving cream, which were rationed at one for each seventeen people. Alcoholic beverages were also sold through the post exchange, with a larger ration for officers than for enlisted personnel. Since we were serving so many other units, we handled quite a large ration of liquor, actually more than we could use, and occasionally, to the amazement of some of our male friends, the post exchange requested reduced liquor rations. Some of the products sold through the exchange were manufactured in Allied countries and were not at all what we were accustomed to, especially toilet soap, which was gritty and coarse and produced absolutely no lather.

Cigarettes were in great supply, at least one carton per person per week. They were also very inexpensive. Not nearly everyone in the 6888th smoked, but all the cigarettes were bought. I was later to find out that cigarettes were not always used for smoking, but rather as a medium of exchange.

When the 6888th moved from Birmingham to Rouen, the mess officer had reported, properly, to the quartermaster depot for food rations based on the number and category of people to be fed. In our unit we needed rations for the noon meal for POWs and their guards as well as for civilian workers. The 6888th, itself, was composed entirely of women, and it is interesting to note that the supply depot assumed that the unit was a hospital unit and issued rations accordingly: fresh meats, vegetables, and dairy products. It was almost like being stationed back home.

I tried very hard to refrain from using my position to obtain services and supplies that were unavailable to everyone else. The good, fresh fried chicken was the pressure point for me, and I did use my position to get extra portions. Whenever I planned to entertain in the evening of a chicken day, I would get word to the mess officer that I would appreciate her sending some of the leftover chicken over to my quarters. The chicken was usually accompanied by fresh rolls and carrot and celery sticks. My own small group in Quarters 1 became very popular as hostesses. I later found out that while I was using my authority, there was fried chicken all over the place, in both officers quarters.

For almost three months we ate well. Then there was a drastic change. Someone from the inspector general's office, on a routine inspection trip through the Normandy sector, wanted to know where there was a medical unit with over a thousand nurses. We were *it,* and there was not a nurse on the premises. The 6888th was not in trouble since no one had claimed that we were a hospital unit; it had been a masculine assumption based on our outfit being all female. The nature of our food service changed overnight when we were taken off hospital rations. Sooner than we thought possible, our food supplies came from large olive-drab cans.

It was now late summer, and vegetables were being harvested in our area. Our mess officer had already learned her way around the countryside, sometimes on the recreational trips we shared. While the rest of us were learning about local customs and joining in festival activities, she was learning what the farmers planted, what they had to trade, and what they wanted to trade. As we switched to powdered eggs (they *can* be prepared in a tasty manner) and other preserved foods, including meats, the complaints began to trickle in. Hospital rations were certainly better than C rations. There was a partial solution to the problem.

Damaged goods removed from the post exchange inventory because they had been damaged in transit or through fair wear and tear were desirable and useful to many farmers and their families. I suddenly began to receive information about the increased number of damaged cartons of cigarettes and bar soap being received. Using the damaged goods as barter, our people could scour the countryside and return with all kinds of fresh vegetables for our mess: carrots, cabbages, beans, beets, and peas. What a difference that made—all of us were enjoying foods we had never liked before. I was very pleased with the way our mess hall supplies were handled. I did worry a bit that the surplus items, some of which I paid for to ensure that we had fresh food, were used strictly to barter for food and not for French antiques and designer items. But I just worried. I had enough problems; no need to look for more.

During this period I developed my recreational addiction: playing ping-pong. I had engaged in a few polite pitter-patter games, but this was the summer in which I developed some real defensive skill at the table. Lieutenant Landry was my teacher and coach, and when I was finally able to beat her, I began to take on all the good players I could find. I was really quite good at the game, and that was the problem. I wanted to play all the time, even when there were visitors waiting to see me. This was the only athletic talent I ever had had, and I used it every minute I could. I even kept one general waiting once while I played five games to win a match. However, eventually duty won, and I was forced to reduce my playing time.

I was very proud of the Six Triple Eight. My personal pride was because I was the commanding officer of this terrific outfit. There were many women in the corps who could have been the CO, but I was the fortunate one to hold the position. My feeling of personal achievement was only a minute part of my pride in the unit. The women of the 6888th had ventured into a service area where they were not really wanted; they had assumed jobs that had normally been assigned to men; they had been and were performing in a valiant and praiseworthy manner; they had survived racial prejudice and discrimination with dignity. They were proud and had every right to be.

After VE Day many of the reporters and correspondents disappeared from the ETO, especially less glamorous areas such as Normandy. Presumably, most of the big names had moved on to the Pacific, where the fighting was still hot and heavy. However, there were still a number of them around asking questions. I recall an interview with a Chicago correspondent whose approach was to express sympathy for Negroes and how he had always felt they were mistreated. He expounded this idea more than he interviewed. As a matter of fact, the only question he really asked was long and leading: "Haven't you considered remaining in Europe after the war since Europeans do not have as strong anti-Negro feelings as whites do in the States?" He never understood the answers he received from the personnel in the 6888th:

"I am an American and I can, at least, seek legal redress in the States."

"My family is in the States."

"I am not so sure that we would be any better treated in France if we stayed after the war."

"They are only nice to us because the United States entered the war and saved their country."

"I haven't lost anything in Europe."

"The English are more prejudiced than other Europeans."

"Who do you think started slavery in the United States?"

And so forth.

Of course, there were a few women who were intrigued by the idea of being in Europe. It was not until after I had allowed this correspondent to interview many people that we realized what he wanted. He needed a headline story, and he was looking for a denunciation of the United States by Negro troops.

All this time, men were returning from the front in great numbers, a lot of them still, apparently, routing themselves to come by the 6888th. The number of men who visited the unit fluctuated but never became small. We had great security on the nearby streets outside our small post. At our gate and inside we had our own security system, the WAC MPs. Once or twice things got a bit out of hand, and we had to call the regular military police. Some men were overly insistent that they be allowed into our compound.

I requested that our WAC MPs be armed either with rifles or sidearms after proper training, but the request was denied. There was no time to engage in my repeated-request technique. As luck would have it, a young British soldier whom I had met while still in Birmingham appeared in my office. He had been a member of a paratrooper unit involved in the Battle of the Bulge, and his training had included some forms of the martial arts, possibly needed for his action as a paratrooper. He offered to teach our MPs jujitsu, which he claimed would serve them as well, if not better, than firearms.

We set up a schedule of classes for the women and trained our own MPs to handle the men at the gate. It worked. I saw them in action several times, and I would not have dared to challenge them. The WAC MP whom we thought to be the most effective was the shortest member of the group, just barely over five feet. Maybe it was just the sight of this small woman tackling a six-foot, three-inch man weighing nearly two hundred pounds made us think that.

Several weeks after we set up shop in Rouen, one of the company commanders reported the first and only case of a woman's being AWOL from the 6888th, as far as I know. An investigation was begun, but before very much progress had been made the young woman had returned. The company CO was rather insistent about a court-martial, but I was just as determined to avoid that if possible. The young woman claimed that she had just had to get away from so many women, that she just wanted to get away for a few hours. Following up her statement, we visited the hotel where she claimed to have spent two nights alone, never leaving the room. Statements from the housekeeper and the desk clerk verified her story. As far as we were able to ascertain, her story was true. Her CO was not happy about my decision to have her give company punishment to this errant soldier. The truth was that I understood about wanting to get away from so many women for a few hours. I could, as battalion CO, get away whenever I wanted. There were, however, grave assurances to the entire unit that any further behavior like this would not be treated with such leniency.

Special Delivery was the name of our weekly mimeographed newspaper. It was used primarily for announcements, accolades, and editorial uplift. There were also many personal and social tidbits about members of the unit. In the 25 June 1945 issue the 6888th announced the beginning of our United Negro College Fund drive. The following quotation is one paragraph from the front-page editorial appeal:

> In America there are 32 outstanding Negro Colleges and Universities. For some time a drive has been under way to raise money for the maintenance of current operating expenses and the urgent needs of these colleges. The contribution which we could make here would not only put this organization on record as backing the Negro college fund drive, but would be definite evidence of the fact that we as Americans realize the importance of education. This is our chance to make the future more promising for Negro youth. We can help provide adequate facilities to expedite and fulfill these needs. Money is what we're asking of you.

We set an ambitious goal of $10,000 to be raised in two weeks. The final total was $4,503.70.

A few sample headlines from *Special Delivery* are quoted below:

4225 QM ENTERTAINS WACS
At Picturesque Chateau Mont Blanc

WACS ATTEND CONCERT IN PARIS
HONORING DEAD NEGRO GI'S

1st NEGRO WAC TO WED ON FOREIGN SOIL

BATTALION SOFTBALL TEAM WINS
SENSATIONAL 7–0 SHUTOUT GAME
OVER PARIS SIGNAL CORPS WACS

The medical facilities in Rouen were not as available to us as the facilities in Birmingham had been, so the 6888th had its first medical officer assigned for duty. He was Capt. Thomas Campbell, the brother of Capt. A. Noel Campbell, my executive officer. I never did find out how that was managed since having siblings in the same unit was so unlike Army personnel assignments. Tom had plenty to do. With the work load lessening, there was more time for personal concerns. When he was not needed for medical service, he was invaluable as a counselor. One day, to our surprise, we were assigned another medical officer, a Lieutenant Johnson, whose civilian specialty had been obstetrics and gynecology. He had just returned from the front, where for three years he had worked only on fresh combat injuries. As soon as he arrived on the post, he asked for a private conference with me, at which time he expressed his concern about practicing his specialty after his years at the front. We agreed that he would restrict his practice to simple cuts, bruises, and colds until he was able to refresh his skills. Our agreement worked out rather well. His specialty, fortunately, was not in great demand.

We made every effort to address the concerns of the troops. Many of their problems surfaced as the pressure of their jobs abated. My personal effort was to hold one night each week open so that anyone could, without appointment, talk to the unit commander. These evenings proved very valuable to me as well as the women who came to talk to me. They knew that someone heard and shared their concerns, while I learned the feelings of the women.

One important realization for me was that in the ETO we performed as if the war were over simply because European hostilities had ended. When the 6888th celebrated the Fourth of July with a day off from work, it seemed to be the appropriate time to address the continued fighting in the Pacific Theater of Operations. I asked the unit PR officer to create a system for keeping personnel informed of the war status in the PTO. What she, Lieutenant Barnes, came up with was a series of briefings about the Pacific and our own "situation map" on which she tried to keep up with the activities about which we heard. There were no feelings of horror when we heard about the atomic bombs falling on Japan. After all, we were members of the Allied military. We heard very little about the historic battles that became famous. What narrow worlds we lived in!

As part of the Allied forces we celebrated VJ Day and thought all the "proper" ugly things about the conquered enemy. It was shortly after this time that we women found that our prewar enemy in our own military was not dead; it had just been quietly sleeping while we shared another common enemy. Racial discrimination had never even rested, but now the male ego was awake and active, and discrimination based on gender again appeared.

However routine our activities were for women, it was new to the men to have to make adjustments for and give consideration to female soldiers. As long as we did the job well and we did not interfere with or challenge the maleness of the military, things would go along with surface smoothness.

When Negro women were involved, the situation became slightly more tense. The problems could be summarized as follows:

The presence of women in the Army was resented by many because, traditionally, the military was male.

The resentment was doubled by the service of Negro women because the laws, customs, and mores of the World War II era denigrated and discriminated against Negroes.

Negro males had been systematically degraded and mistreated in the civilian world, and the presence of successfully performing Negro women on the scene increased their resentment.

The efforts of the women to be supportive of the men was mistaken for competition and patronage.

We lived with these attitudes with dignity. I knew that it was my duty to look out for and protect every member of the 6888th, and I did just that, often assuming the role of the "bad guy" in their eyes. I worked long hours and participated in every activity where my presence could serve the cause. I survived in a state of pleasant belligerency. I had no chip on my shoulder; I kept it slightly below the shoulder.

There were lots of invitations for the women to visit other units for social activities. When the times, the places, and numbers were right, we made arrangements for the visits. Even the officers had lots of invitations, and we took advantage of them when we could.

I spent a great deal of time visiting various installations, generally to complete plans for an activity involving members of the 6888th. The Army had assigned a limousine, with chauffeur, for my use. The limousine was a fine French vehicle, but the chauffeur was too much and too old. He was a very nice man, seventy-eight years of age and the sole support of two small grandchildren whose parents had been killed in a bombing raid. At one time he may have been a good driver, but that time was long before we met him. We called him "Papa," and because of the language difference I have always thought that we misunderstood him, that he was actually caring for his great-grandchildren.

Whenever I left the post in my car with Papa driving, I spent a great part of the trip in prayer. Papa's peak driving days had to have been when automobiles were uncommon—certainly he was unprepared for the traffic congestion made up of all kinds of drivable civilian vehicles and the thousands of military vehicles used by Allied personnel. Even when they had no particular place to go, French drivers always seemed to be in a hurry. The ones I knew tried to pass every other vehicle on the road. We amateur psychologists associated this reaction with the war's being over in Europe. Passing other vehicles expressed victory and pride.

The French drivers' habits might have worked except that the drivers of many U.S. military vehicles had a little game they played against French drivers. The game was called "Squeeze," and the rules were simple. Whenever two or more military vehicles were traveling together, or just on the same highway, the drivers would leave large spaces between vehicles and drive at reasonable speeds. When a speeding French driver would pull out of the line to pass, the military drivers would increase their speed and close up any space available for pulling back into the line of traffic. As oncoming traffic approached, the French driver was caught in an accident-threatening situation, causing all approaching traffic to come to a screeching halt.

I never heard of any French citizens' actually being hurt as a result of the game, but it did make riding in my French limousine very scary. I finally had to give up the limousine when I was traveling outside Rouen. I turned it over to our motor pool to make it available to officers for local transportation. In exchange, one of the jeeps, with driver, was assigned to me.

My new driver was a very attractive young woman, and a very good driver. Officers were not permitted to drive military vehicles, without approved exceptions, so my driver and I traveled many miles together. Even this transportation mode became a problem. When I had occasion to visit a large Army installation that involved having a meal with the CO and/or other officers, I would have my meal in an officers mess while my driver would be required to have her meal in a mess hall that could, when needed, serve several thousands of enlisted men at one sitting. We never stayed overnight away from our post, so we had no need to be concerned about sleeping accommodations, but I was very worried about my driver. I accidently found out that she was skipping meals to avoid eating in the mess halls. She had never complained to me.

A conversation with the captain of the local MP detachment provided me with information and forms needed to request exception to the regulation forbidding officers to drive military vehicles. I filled out the proper form and sent it to the "Commanding General, Hq Normandy Base Section, Com Z, ETO, [etc.,] attention Provost Marshall," dated 24 June 1945. In less than ten days I had the approval. I continued to use the driver on many occasions when I was not visiting large Army installations.

The jeep, as a military vehicle, may have seen spectacular combat service, but it was highly valued far behind the lines. There was one fad in which I was happy to engage. Using plywood and the skill of German POWs, we turned many jeeps into sedans, beautifully enclosed according to many varying designs. Riding in a closed jeep was a bit claustrophobic, but it was wonderful in bad weather and for showing off to other unit commanders.

Hostilities were over, but there were still a few land mines and unexploded shells in the area. We occasionally heard of GIs' being injured by the explosion of land mines, and once, when riding with a group of friends, we came upon the scene of such a tragedy. It was not pleasant to see, and we were thankful that no members of the 6888th had been involved in such accidents. We did have several women injured in a C&R vehicle accident. They received the best of care and soon returned to duty.

The 6888th did have one real tragedy. On an authorized social trip to another military installation, three women from our unit were killed in a vehicle accident. I do believe that the most difficult job I have ever had was writing the letters to the families of Mary Bankston, Mary Barlow, and Delores Brown. I was gratified that the notes I received in response were so understanding of the fact that the women had died in the service of their country. In one case, the deceased was referred to as a heroine.

We were able to arrange for two funeral services, one service for the two women who were Protestants and one for the woman who was Catholic. The hospital where they had been taken following the accident had two chapels that were used for the services. I was able to attend both services. The only difficulty had been in the purchase of caskets. As Americans we had not experienced, or even heard about, getting caskets by the deceased's size. This was handled by selecting three women, of the same approximate sizes as the dead women, who were willing to go to the casket maker and be measured for caskets.

1 August–27 December 1945

☆　☆　☆　☆　☆　☆　☆　☆　☆　☆　☆　☆

From the time the 6888th was formed, its members were participators. Before the unit broke up we had had our own band, several competition-winning WAC shows, and teams in many sports: tennis, softball, volley-ball, and the like. As the work load decreased, the need for organized recreation increased, and we became involved in all sorts of activities that required travel.

Members of the outfit were going in all directions. As often as I could, I would be present to show my support of our varied activities. Consequently, I spent a great deal of time driving through various parts of Allied territory in my jeep along with my assigned driver, Pvt. Romay Johnson, and, usually, accompanied by one or two officers from the 6888th. Once, when four of us were on orders to go by government vehicle, on or about 21 August 1945, "to Namur, Belgium, for the purpose of attendance at WAC Championship Softball Tournament," we were also on orders to travel to Rheims, France, on or about 22 August 1945. The women who were involved in the tournament, fifteen players, the coach, the reporter, and two drivers, all in two large vehicles, left before I did with my small group in the jeep. We made it to Namur, but not before we had taken a wrong turn and were stopped at the German border, where we were turned around with new directions to follow. The softball tournament was over when we arrived, but the team had evidence of our support. We were on time for the games in Rheims.

Among other trips I made, was one at the behest of my CO, whose head-quarters was in Brussels. He sent his personal plane to Rouen to pick me up. The plane was a single-engined two-seater and, although I had learned to accept flying even in small planes when I was making my bimonthly trips between London and Paris, flying in this plane was almost more than I could handle. The pilot was very young, probably one of the more recent ninety-day wonders turned out in flight training, and I was convinced that he was reincarnated from one of the original stunt fliers.

In the course of our conversation, this young pilot asked if I had visited Germany. I told him that the closest I had been to German soil was when we had been stopped at the German border as we tried to get to Belgium. He decided to deviate from our direct route and take me over Germany. Just flying over a small portion of that country would have sufficed for me, but the pilot decided to have some fun. First, we buzzed a few farms where farmers were working. This was followed by a few dives and pull-ups, followed by a couple of rollovers (these are my terms) in which I definitely felt the pull of gravity against the seat belts holding me in the plane. I persuaded "Red" (he had brilliant red hair) to stop his acrobatics and take me to Brussels. As I left the airport in Brussels, he said, "See you on the return flight." I returned his salute and thought to myself, "Like heck you will."

I reported to my CO, and we discussed the project he had in mind. As men returned from the front, it was recognized that thousands of young Negro men who had been drafted into the service before receiving job training would return home with no skills and therefore with no eligibility for worthwhile employment. I was amazed at this sudden concern for Negro soldiers. The general wanted to discuss the possibility of setting up a clerical school to train some of the unskilled men who were scheduled to return home. He and I agreed that we would do just that in Rouen since I had many very able clerical workers whose time was not being fully used. After working out certain details as to supplies, location, and teachers, I was ready to return to Rouen.

"How was your flight up, Adams?" asked the general.

"It was safe, Sir, since I got here without injury," I replied, "but I found it a bit rough."

"Were you airsick?"

"Well," I began, knowing that to tell him the details of my flight would get that young pilot in trouble, "a bit, Sir. If it is not too inconvenient, I would rather return to Rouen by motor vehicle." I was sure that he thought my hesitation had more to it than I expressed. Nevertheless, he did send me back to my station in his limousine. Since the general himself was not riding in the vehicle, his flag was removed from the front of the car. I wondered what kind of reaction the driver and I would have received if they had forgotten to remove it.

The general was the same one who had threatened me with court-martial in the United Kingdom. Since that time we had developed a good working relationship on the Continent. One day, several weeks after we had conferred on the training of Negro soldiers, he showed up unannounced at the 6888th to say good-bye to me. I could not believe what he had to say. We had fought each other fairly and settled our differences.

He spoke tersely. "Adams, I've received my orders to return to the States. Otherwise, I would not be here. It's not easy for me to say what I've come to say. Working with you has been quite an education for me, especially about Negroes." He had finally learned how to pronounce the word. I waited as he continued. "The only Negroes I have ever known personally were those who were in the servant capacity or my subordinates in the Army. It's been a long time since anyone challenged me, black or white, but you took me on. You outsmarted me and I am proud that I know you. I would not have told you this if I thought I would ever see you again." And I never did see him again. About ten years later, I just happened to read a small, three-quarter-inch filler at the bottom of a column in a newspaper announcing his passing.

The social events for all members of the 6888th continued to increase, so a great deal of time was spent arranging transportation and escorts so that everyone would be able to attend the affair of her choice. I had learned that I should not ask anyone to do anything that I would not or could not do myself, so I took my turn being one of the escorts to the various affairs. Sometimes this duty turned out to be great fun, and I met lots of interesting people.

One thing that we officer escorts always noticed was that although we made sure the women arrived at the dances on time, usually held in a gym facility, very few of the men would arrive on time. I thought that perhaps I did not understand the etiquette of arriving at a dance. The only reason I inquired about why the majority of the men arrived so late was that I thought arriving fashionably late was a female characteristic and definitely not military. I got quite an answer. It seemed that the men had arrived and were waiting outside the dance hall. Every few minutes one of them would step into the hall for a short time, then go outside and report whether it was time to enter. Since these affairs involved very few, if any, personal relationships, they were purely occasions for some "heavy" dancing. Apparently, the barometer for entering time was "when the place begins to smell like a good basketball game, the place is really rocking."

As I traveled around from installation to installation, I tried to observe the speed limit set for military vehicles. All such vehicles were reputed to have governors on them to prevent speeding, but I doubted that any of those governors were still operative. I had no idea what the status of my jeep was. However, on one occasion I was going along a highway leading from Rouen at a rather nice clip when I was stopped by an MP for, of all things, speeding. In fact, I do not think I was stopped for speeding because the first question he asked was, "Ma'am, do you have permission to drive this military vehicle?"

He was extremely polite and pleasant, but his face said, "I've got me one this time." I smiled as I handed him my permission to drive that military vehicle. That's when he reverted to the speeding charge.

"Ma'am, may I inquire as to where you are going in such a great hurry?"

"Isn't the Army Hospital at Camp [I named a nearby camp]?" I answered, without telling a lie.

"Why, of course, Ma'am. Just follow us and we'll give you an escort."

Well, I was going to that camp; I just had not planned to go to the hospital. But I did.

People should be rewarded for doing good jobs, especially when the performance is above and beyond the call of duty. As soon as we were settled in at the directory in Birmingham after overcoming many obstacles, and once the women were performing the Herculean task of moving the backlog of letters and packages, I began my quest for an allotment of officer grades and non-com ratings. My requests were denied several times; each denial was followed by another request. The promotions were finally granted in mid-summer. By the time we received these, I had already prepared my next request for allotments.

Our job remained the same, to get the mail to all American personnel. As troops moved back, from one locale to another, including the staging area for movement home, the directory process became quite hectic. Sometimes letters and packages had so many canceled addresses that a space for a new address was created by pasting on a new front. We had broken records, and the 6888th received praise for the work done. We were determined to maintain our high level of performance. To do this, at one point with troops moving so rapidly, we had to find new ways to see that the mail followed each addressee. We made arrangements to send mail by the French railway system. Disaster! In the late summer, we found that the most effective delivery system was courier service, direct to the camps and staging areas.

Late in the summer the 6888th began to be affected by the point system. The women who had been among the first to join the corps began to accumulate enough points to be eligible to return to the States and to be discharged from the service. Some members of the unit were anxious to go home and took advantage of the chance to go. Most of those eligible to go chose to remain with the unit on the first round. As I watched the first group leave, I realized that these departure scenes would occur every month. Our time in the service had been short, but the effort and energy and performance of the unit had been long. The 6888th was "peeling off," getting smaller every day. I suppose it was a touch of nostalgia for what had been that caused my sudden desire to have the troops in formation and execute a bit of close order drill. My rationalization was that we had to maintain discipline, especially with the lighter work load. It was not a compulsory formation, strictly volunteer, but each afternoon I was out with a drill group—and we did execute some fancy steps.

In September we heard the first rumors about the 6888th moving to Paris. When I inquired about such a move, I received a typical bureaucratic reply: "The matter is under consideration."

During the summer months we had a series of reunions and some weddings. My marriage counseling sessions had made me very unpopular because all of my efforts were directed at preventing the marriages. I understood the call of romance, but I feared that romance might be made up of homesickness, loneliness, too much female companionship, and loving the idea of being in love. I always assumed that the young men were fine and upstanding citizens. I had no way of knowing otherwise. After VE Day I was not much easier in my approach. The war was not yet over, and who could predict what might happen? What I said in these counseling sessions seemed cold and uncaring, but I said what I did because I did care.

"You've known this man for a very short time [sometimes less than a month]. You think that you know him and maybe you do. But we are still at war and he is a soldier. If he survives the European situation, he may be sent to the Pacific Theater. If he should come back to you, when the war is over, with both legs gone, are you prepared to spend the rest of your life with someone, and taking care of someone, with whom you have spent one night?" There was more, but if they persisted after my conference with them, I approved the request for permission to marry.

There were marriages with less traumatic concerns. Several women whose longtime boy friends were in the ETO were married when the men found their way to the 6888th. We had beautiful weddings, religious ceremonies and civil rites as required by French law, with both the bride and groom in uniform, the bride carrying the proper bouquet. There were reunions with longtime friends, and new friends were made.

I suppose that many of us who were single and unspoken for sometimes felt a tinge of jealousy when we saw the marriages and reunions. The man whom I later married visited me in Rouen because we already knew each other. Our permanent relationship had not developed. However, I knew several men with whom I spent some social time. There was one man of whom I was very fond. I am sure that I was a good CO, but I had learned that skill as I moved along. What I was not was socially sophisticated, so I was extremely cautious in all aspects of social behavior. My friend moved too fast and, after a very short time, asked me to marry him. I ducked that question as long as I could, and when I finally had to give an answer, I said that I would have to wait until we were civilians

With the 6888th's two Captain Campbells: our medical officer, Capt. Thomas Campbell, and his sister, Capt. Abbie Noel Campbell, my executive officer

before I could answer. He asked why, and I answered, "I want to see you in civilian clothes. I want to be sure you don't wear a zoot suit." I must admit that he never came back to see me again. The last I heard about him was that he had married a Scandinavian woman. She probably had never heard of a zoot suit.

At last I received a telephone call informing me that the unit would move to Paris. Before the written orders arrived, followed almost immediately by revocation, I realized that we had a few problems that had to be solved. All of the GI furniture, except the mattresses that I mentioned earlier, could be turned in at a quartermaster warehouse, but there were some other items that had been "liberated" for our use. I had been on the using side of several such pieces. One piece of furniture had been with me for a very short time. Soon after we moved to Rouen, someone had provided me with a coffee table for the small (and I do mean small) living room connected with my bedroom. Several weeks later a gentleman had appeared at our post headquarters in search of some items of furni-

Myself and one of the 6888th's trucks

ture that had been removed from his home while the house was unoccupied. He wanted especially to recover a Duncan Phyfe coffee table. I
understood, for who would not want to recover such a piece, even though
I was not familiar with how the furniture looked.

I readily agreed that we should look in the two officers quarters because
the barracks would certainly not have a coffee table. I could not imagine

where the table could be since the living room of Officers Quarters 2 was actually our officers club and was almost filled by a ping-pong table. Except for bedrooms, the only other place would be my very small living room. The upshot of this search was that I, the CO, "Miss Good Girl," the nothing-will-interfere-with-my-job idealist, had that coffee table in my very small living room. I happily relinquished the table. It had been useful, but (this is heresy) it was ugly.

What I did have that was sheer beauty, and which I could have easily gotten off my hands, was the ultramodern desk in my office. The desk was large, very large, six feet by four feet. The front had a twelve-inch overhang; the sides had eight-inch overhangs with shelves underneath. What separated that desk from later modern models was that it was oval. Several of our visiting senior officers had taken special interest in the desk. A few had asked where I got it. Some had asked how. The strongest action taken was when two very senior officers requisitioned the "transfer" of that desk from the office of the CO of the 6888th to their offices. Since the desk was not listed as GI property, it could not be transferred, especially as the desk was listed on our records as being on loan as long as the 6888th was stationed in Rouen. To avoid playing favorites, I left it to the Normandy base quarter-master to dispose of the desk when we closed down "Napoleon's post."

The orders finally arrived and were not recalled. The 6888th was moving to Paris. We would do the same job and be closer to the center of activity. There was the usual hustle and bustle of preparing to move, packing both personnel and unit property. The pressure of moving even included the last-minute purchase of souvenirs from the Rouen area.

Rouen is about seventy miles northwest of Paris, and before we moved, I had made the round-trip many times. I knew all the turns, gradual and sharp, as well as those sections of the road with reverse slopes (outside banks). I had even learned some landmarks that kept me on the right road and signaled how much farther I had to go. I sometimes thought my jeep could travel the route without guidance.

While the preparations to move were going on, we were actually operating two units, the 6888th in Rouen and the advance unit in Paris getting ready for the arrival of the rest of us. Some of the women had gone home on points, and many were just waiting to accumulate enough points, so the outfit was not as large as it had been but was still large enough to operate as a battalion.

This move took place in October, when the weather was unpredictable. We organized quite a convoy based upon our observations, our needs, and the information found in Army manuals. Every other time we had moved, we had received great assistance from various higher headquarters. I usually went ahead and was at the destination to greet the unit upon its arrival; this time, however, I was present and leading.

The convoy lined up. First, battalion headquarters personnel and equipment, followed by the medical officer (Lieutenant Johnson had returned to the States; Captain Campbell remained) and his supplies and equipment. After this were the companies with personnel and equipment. Altogether, we were more than thirty-five vehicles strong, made up of jeeps and 6 × 6 trucks, with my jeep at the head of this column. At least, this is how we began the move. I have no idea in what order we arrived.

Late in the afternoon we set out for Paris, only seventy miles away. On my many trips from Rouen I had always allowed myself three hours to report wherever it was I had to report—two hours on the highway, forty-five minutes for Paris traffic, and fifteen minutes for reporting.

At that time of year darkness came suddenly. For a few minutes we saw a red sunset; then, as if a curtain had been dropped, the light was gone. With our long convoy, traveling at reduced speed in order to stay together, we were hardly out of Rouen when darkness fell. The worst thing that could happen happened. With darkness and dropping temperatures, all of Normandy became enshrouded in a fog that continued to thicken. The rate of travel was getting slower and slower as the sky darkened.

By midnight we were literally traveling at a snail's pace, what with the darkness, the fog, and the length of our convoy. Even the low lights, normally used as fog lights, created too much reflection on the dense fog. Visibility was about one foot. We were long past village lights. Even the farm families had retired for the night. The only lights around were the blurred headlights of our own vehicles. We moved along even more slowly than if we had been walking. Every now and then, as driver, I would feel the front wheel start off the edge of the road surface. At the pace we were moving, it was easy to pull back onto the road.

Suddenly, we saw the faint glow of a yellow light swinging from side to side. We came to a halt immediately, knowing that any light that could be seen had to be very close. We moved forward cautiously. One of the non-coms in the jeep with me jumped out as we stopped again. She hailed the moving light since she was unable to see the person swinging the light. The response was that it was Sergeant "Somebody" from a convoy ahead of us that had halted because of problems.

At this point, I got out and joined my sergeant and called, "Where is your commanding officer?"

"He's up front, Ma'am."

"Then I'll go up and speak to him." I moved forward and came into the range of his lantern light. He looked at my face first and then my shoulders, then came to attention as much as was possible holding a lantern at shoulder height.

"Oh, no, Ma'am," he said. "You just wait. He'll come back here."

It was cold and damp, and I climbed back into my vehicle to wait. Many drivers and escort officers from our many vehicles came forward to see what was holding up a move that was already about five hours late. We waited. When I saw the light of several flashlights approaching us, I got out and waited beside the jeep. A young white second lieutenant appeared out of the fog and stepped very close to me. He had obviously been told that I was a major, and Negro, and had made up his mind.

He saluted smartly and said, "Major, I am so glad you are here and can take charge."

I returned his salute and answered, "Wait a minute, Lieutenant, what do you mean by take charge? I have my own outfit here."

"Well, Ma'am [his white-to-black politeness made me very suspicious], we seem to have become one unit since my outfit is halted here on the road and yours cannot get by in the fog. I guess we have to travel together, and you are the senior officer present." His speech was not convincing.

"Why have you stopped, Lieutenant? You would have to move slowly in this fog but you could continue."

"Ma'am," the politeness continued, "we have a real problem. We are moving a piano with us. There are several of the men in the back of the truck with the piano and, as we were making that turn back there, the piano fell over on one of the men. I am worried about whether we can move him or even whether we can continue our trip."

I asked Captain Campbell, our medical officer, to look at the man. He went forward with the lieutenant as the rest of us climbed back into the vehicles out of the cold. When the captain returned, he reported that the young soldier apparently had a broken back and had to be taken to a hospital immediately. In all that pea soup? We had decisions to make.

It did not take very long. The situation explained itself. I was the senior officer in a very large group of Army personnel made up of at least two units (it was possibly more since our units blocked the highway and could have been joined by others) headed for Paris. I had a medical officer who insisted that a wounded soldier needed immediate transport to a hospital, and I was responsible for Captain Campbell. The word passed up and down the line of vehicles in no time at all. So with over a thousand GIs, female and male, watching or listening, and a few hundred guides along the front part of the convoy holding flashlights, torches, or cigarette lighters to show me where to drive, I pulled into the lead position of all the vehicles. I had hoped (how unmilitary of me) that the vehicles from the 6888th would be allowed to fall in behind their CO. I found out later that it did not happen as I hoped, but rather became sort of a game as to which vehicle would get in the line next. I have no inkling of how that ended, or even of how many vehicles followed.

We set out for Paris and had driven only a few miles when the fog thickened to the "thick enough to cut with a knife" stage. We could no longer depend on what could be seen through the windshields to guide us. We needed a person hanging out of each side of the jeep trying to see the edge of the road. Finally, the density of the fog forced us to a halt. We began to worry about the injured soldier because the only reason we were moving in this fog was to guide the truck to the hospital. One of the non-coms who had been hanging out to see suggested that the two of them would do better if they sat on the front fenders with flashlights. They would be able to watch for the edge of the road. I kept my place at the wheel because I was sure no one wanted to replace me in this mess. Besides, all authorized drivers were driving our other vehicles.

We knew we had arrived at the outskirts of Paris when we saw more lights, although they were dim and we were unable to distinguish their source. In the city our first effort was to locate our position on a map in relation to the hospital that was our destination. The streetlights looked like small dull yellow bug lights and were no help at all for seeing street signs, which were located above the ground floor on corner buildings. These signs were too high for us to see when we got out of the jeep equipped with the six-volt battery flashlights. In desperation, and after consultation, I drove the front wheels of the jeep over the curb toward the "cornermost" building where the street signs were located. With the front of the vehicle elevated and the lights on the high beam, we were just able to make out the names of the streets. Using that system, we arrived at the hospital just before dawn. The services of Captain Campbell were not available to us for several hours while he assisted with the care of the injured white soldier who had suddenly become our responsibility.

For weeks our entire unit was concerned about our young injured soldier, and we announced daily reports on his progress. After we were assured that he would be all right, we all became interested in other things.

Once settled in Paris, we occupied three different sites. The enlisted personnel were quartered in one large hotel, the Bohy Lafayette Hotel, which was within walking distance of Montmartre and Sacre Coeur, the Place de L'Opéra, and the Folies Bergère; the officers were located in the small Hôtel États-Unis; and our primary work area was in a large warehouse type building. Since we had to provide transportation to and from the work site for both officers and enlisted personnel, our drivers had to have a blitz course on the routes of Paris.

After the move was completed, it did not take long to catch up on the backlog of work. After that, what we wanted most to do was to catch up on Paris. Traveling abroad was not as routine and casually accepted as it would become. For most of us, Europe had been only a dream, with Paris as the star of the dream.

On Sundays and after work hours, we had time to see and be part of the French capital. We took in the shows, the shops, and the scenes. We learned how to get around on public transportation, the Métro subway system and buses, and, occasionally, dared to use a taxi, although we were frightened by the way they were driven. As we observed the people, it was interesting to note that the French did not observe us. It seemed that many citizens felt that if we, U.S. military personnel, had to be there, we should be invisible. On the walls of buildings, where GIs had scribbled "Kilroy was here," was also scribbled "Yankee, go home!"

Being a Negro citizen of the United States, I had been on the receiving end of the arrogant, though artificial, superiority of our citizen majority. We sensed that many French resented the "you owe us; we saved your country" attitude expressed by many American personnel. As long as we spent our money to shop and to enjoy the culture and atmosphere of the city, the people did not care whether we were Negro or white. On an earlier trip to Paris, Noel and I had found time to go to the Folies Bergère. We found it as dazzling and extravagant as reputed. My major memories of the show were, first, how the usher who seated us said in a firm voice, "You will teeeep, pleeese" and, second, how the GIs in attendance had more applause for the excellent acrobatic acts than they did for the girlie acts.

Continental culture was very different for all of us, but perhaps less so for those who had lived in the metropolitan areas. We were fascinated by such things as the handling of food items, especially the lack of wrapping for the bread; the open, uncovered, unrefrigerated display of meat; and the use of a shopping bag to contain fresh vegetables and fruits in place of individual paper packages for each type. The most shocking thing we saw in Paris was probably the most practical—the "comfort station."

There were many things I had noted about the French but, until we moved to Paris and my schedule permitted me to converse with them, had not appreciated. They were proud and patriotic. Occupation and victimization by the Nazis could not dampen these characteristics. What I had not recognized was the evidence of defiance expressed by the citizens. Fashionable female dressing, in 1945, included a pompadour style of dressing the hair high over the forehead by drawing long hair forward and over a roller or newspaper or frames, sometimes as high as six to eight inches. Also in style were very high heels or platform soles, sometimes with ankle straps. These styles were associated with height, a statement of defiance.

There was a style of Parisian female dress, other than hair and shoe styles, that had an incidental relationship to the property of the 6888th. As cold weather settled in during November, there was a noticeable increase in requests for bedding, which we attributed to the need for blankets to ward off the damp coldness of hotel living. When the demand for additional sheets took place, an investigation was in order. We soon found out what was happening. A few of the women had found a great market for woolen Army blankets and tough cotton sheets. Even when they were charged for the loss of a blanket, they still realized a profit.

Talk about high style! It was absolutely amazing how beautiful a coat, made from a dyed U.S. Army blanket, could be. (I think the dye used must have been the best in the world.) I never found out how the sheets were used, but I have no doubt that I would have been impressed. Add to the above various slightly altered parts of the U.S. military uniform—jackets, shirts, overcoat, slacks, caps—and there was a whole school of fashion that I called "avant-garde militaire."

My ultimate indulgence in French culture was a trip to a beauty salon. I knew that there would be no problem regarding my hair since the French had invented most of the equipment used by Negroes, and I was very happily anticipating beautifully manicured nails. The product of my trip was that my hair was cut so short that it barely showed around the edge of my cap and, in order to get my nails pointed, the manicurist filed them so far down on the sides that I contracted a fungus infection under the nails.

In Paris we were assigned a new group of civilians who worked primarily in the package section. It was then that our package reconstruction unit was tested to the limit because of theft. From a war-deprived populace, we had some workers who had developed skills of survival, and one of the skills was the ability to filch small packages without being noticed. They stole from packages that had popped open in transit, and even from those that seemed about to pop open. The items taken were usually sweets like chewing gum and candy, although razor blades and other hard-to-get items were on the list.

With less work there was more time for inspectors to visit the directory. Because of the number of thefts from packages, we were required to set up a search detail to recover stolen items. This search was not limited to handbags, lunch boxes, and outer garments. The unit had to do body searches to find items that were taped onto or inserted into parts of the body. The search unit, as well as the rest of us, were very unhappy about performing this duty because we considered it degrading and undignified. On the other hand, these small thefts were affecting the efficiency and success rate of the package reassembly unit. Recalling the indignities to which we had been subjected, we performed these searches with great reluctance.

One of the changes involved in our move to Paris was that we no longer had cooks who were members of the 6888th. We had a hotel staff of cooks, as well as other hotel staff. The rations were basically the same except that food was prepared *à la français,* to which we quickly became adjusted. The only staple food our new cooks had problems with was cornmeal, absolutely unknown to them. When informed that meal was used, generally, for the same purpose as flour, the cooks found that the only recipe that worked for them was a cake recipe. When the cornbread cake was first served with a meal it was a real surprise, but we just saved it for dessert.

We had no trouble adjusting to hotel living. Besides being less primitive than our little post in Rouen, it put us closer to the action and the people. In a very short time some of the women developed acquaintances and were invited to participate in or observe family rituals. The pageantry of French weddings and funerals could be seen by all of us. I was personally impressed by what I saw of family relationships; the parents out with their children walking, playing in parks, and attending public concerts.

The Hôtel États-Unis, where my officers and I lived, was three buildings from a busy intersection where there was a small, but very busy bistro. Whenever we passed during the day, we would see fathers with their sons beside them sitting at the bar. With our typical American misinformation about the French and wine drinking, we were concerned about what we saw. Our inquiries relieved our concern. The young sons were not drinking wine but rather a wine diluted with water designed to teach young people respect and the technique of wine drinking.

Living in hotels away from the work site necessitated special transportation arrangements. The drivers picked up all personnel, officers and enlisted, at their quarters and dropped them off at the proper workplace, directory personnel to the postal site and administrative personnel to battalion headquarters, which was located in the hotel where the enlisted personnel were housed. As CO I had my own transportation, which I used generally during business hours but only in the line of duty. At the end of the work day the vehicles were used to return the personnel to their quarters. There were late-running shuttles to pick up those who were unable to finish up by the end of the regular work day. After that, there was to be no further use of our vehicles. During off-duty hours, we were to use public transport or furnish our own in some way. Besides, I was very concerned that the drivers also be free after work to enjoy Paris.

After a few weeks in Paris I noticed that several of our drivers were reporting in later than I thought they should have. I credited their delay to the city's unbelievable traffic. Then I received a direct complaint from several drivers about having to work quite late and then be expected to make the early shift. Further inquiry revealed that some officers were ordering the drivers to take them to various places after hours and to pick them up after the trip to return to quarters. I issued a new and stronger directive, including a punitive notation, about the use of military vehicles. I knew who the offenders were and noted that they stopped the unauthorized use of the vehicles. This was the strongest action I had had to take against any of the officers in the battalion, and it resulted in what I considered the ultimate compliment.

In the hotel where the officers of the 6888th lived, my room was on the sixth floor. Other officers lived directly beneath me on floors three, four, and five. The ventilation grilles for the bathrooms on all the floors opened into a common open-air shaft. As a matter of fact, the officers could converse with one another via the air shaft.

The evening of the day on which I had issued a new directive restricting the use of unit vehicles, I was soaking in the bathtub, right under the air vent, when I became aware that two of my officers were talking, one very loudly as if near her bathroom air vent and the other in an indistinct mumble as if in the bedroom near the window.

"Whatever got into Big Ma [my nickname in the 6888th, used under the assumption that I did not know it] today? She was mad as hell."

I was as still as a mouse trying to hear the reply and, more importantly, trying not to disclose my presence in my bathroom. I heard a mumble and understood only a few words that made no sense. Then came the compliment from an officer several floors below.

"Well, I'll say this for Big Ma. She doesn't play favorites. I think she would arrest her mother if she broke the law." Their conversation made my day, for these two officers had been the worst offenders with the unit vehicles.

The unit grew smaller, and the day soon came when there was no way to justify my rank as part of the T/O. I was told that I would be assigned to WAC Headquarters in the Pentagon. That was not appealing to me. I remembered two thirty-day stints of TD in the Pentagon. I had enough points, so I decided to go home and get on with my life.

Since the day I had been sworn into the WAAC, every moment had been a challenge. The problems of racial harmony, black acceptance, and opportunity were still unsolved, but these were problems I could still work to help solve as a civilian. Besides, I was beginning to feel that the racial situation was worse in civilian life. Civilians in the United States had not shared the nonracial commonality of danger, fear, and patriotism.

I do not recall that I ever gave any serious thought to making a career in the Army, although I had surprised myself at how well I had taken to regulation and regimentation. There was some concern by a couple of family members about my voluntarily giving up a job that afforded me rank, status, sure compensation, and recognition.

Based on my ASR of forty-six points, I requested release from ETO duty and return to the United States for release from active duty. My request was granted and, along with Capt. Noel Campbell, other officers, and many enlisted personnel of the 6888th, was transferred to the States. After completing the required health, equipment, and record checks, we were put on orders to go home.

The matter of racial identity, though obviously visible, was not to be left behind administratively. Even though we had become accustomed to, but never pleased by, separate quarters, separate units, separate social facilities, and separate orders, we had never before received separate orders that had further racial designation: an asterisk for "colored troops." The double asterisks indicated the "in charge" person for various groups bound for specific destinations. Along with all these orders was an order that designated me as "Group Commander" for the "colored troops" until arrival in the United States.

I was not at all pleased with the extra effort to stress racial identification, but I was going home. I certainly did not mind being in charge of the Negro WACs, for I had been their CO for their European tour of duty. It did not work out that way. The first change came as we were about to board. There were some Negro nurses going home, and they were added to the list of my group. No problem there. We all boarded the ship, and that was when trouble began.

The ship, which thousands of us boarded, was a troop transport ship, converted from a former German royal yacht. As a yacht, the small ship had been designed to accommodate forty people, and it afforded all the royal amenities that the kaiser might require. As a troop ship, the only amenity was one bunk bed for each of the six thousand military people aboard.

As I recall, we were to leave port at midnight, and it seemed that we were all settled in by 10:00 P.M. Noel and I, and several other members of the 6888th, totaling eighteen people, were safely and tightly housed in a cabin with double-decked bunks, one deck up from the main deck. We had received all our instructions about meal shifts, recreation time, and the location of various facilities. The one surprise I had, just before I turned in for the night, was that the captain of the ship had, by reason of my seniority in grade, put me in charge of all women on the ship. I did not know what that involved, so I did not bother to find out who my additional charges were. In this case, all women on the ship included some six hundred nurses, all white, en route home from the ETO.

About ten o'clock one of the enlisted women from the 6888th came up to our cabin to tell me that there was a real argument going on down below next to their quarters. I said that as long as they (the 6888th members) were not involved, it was none of our business. After an hour another enlisted woman came up to report that we would probably not set out for home that night. It seemed that there was a problem among the nurses that might delay our trip.

After all, I was in charge, so after consultation with Noel and some speculation as to what the problem might be (we guessed right), I went down to take care of the problem among the nurses. I had never been in this part of this ship, nor any other ship. I had entered what had been the hold, the cargo area, which had been renovated to a troop carrier by the addition of stairways and proper doorways. The area I entered was very large and, to my surprise, was filled with triple-decked bunks that seemed to reach too high for anyone to use as sleeping space. This area was also filled with irate white women whose personal belongings were hanging from bunks and anything else that would accommodate a strap or a hook.

When I appeared in the doorway of the nurses' quarters, it became absolutely silent in a matter of seconds. I was fairly certain that I knew what the problem was, but since no one had told me specifically what it was, I decided I would have to ask.

Before I could say one word, even of greeting, a woman, apparently the spokeswoman for the group, yelled at me, "What the hell are you doing in here?"

The question did not ease my annoyance at having to get out of bed to see what their problem was.

"I understand that there is a problem and that you nurses do not want to go home on this ship."

"That's not the problem. We want to go home but not under the command of a colored woman." I suppose that was the greatest putdown that she could manage.

My disposition was being shot to pieces. I had not and have never been a coward, but I was getting emotional. I could usually rise to the occasion and release my emotions later. This was one time when I had to work hard to maintain control. After three and one-half years I was leaving the service facing the same kind of prejudice I had encountered when I entered.

I answered. "I am sorry you feel that way, but I did not put myself in charge."

"We have our own white major here; she should be in charge of all the women on this ship. We insist that she be put in charge."

"As I understand it," I replied, "I am the senior female officer on board this vessel. I have been given an assignment which I intend to carry out. I intend to return to the States on this ship, so I am not getting off. If you cannot go home under my command, I suggest you pack your belongings and disembark quickly. Those who really want to go home should stay aboard." I looked at my watch. "It is now twenty minutes to twelve midnight, and we sail at midnight. You have twenty minutes to get off. I don't care whether you go home or not, but if you go, you go under my command." That last comment was caused by sheer anger.

I turned to make a dramatic exit from the area and came face to face with the ship's captain, who had apparently been standing in the door while I made my last speech.

He stepped into the room and said, "Major Adams is absolutely right.

Regulations state that the senior officer will be in command. She is the senior female officer, very senior. Those who wish to disembark now have seventeen minutes to do so." The captain and I left together.

We sailed on time. The next morning, I found out that I had more duties than I had thought. The very first thing the captain asked of me involved the nurses. He told me that we would have seasickness that we could never even anticipate (I had felt a bit queasy myself before I got out of bed). He asked that I establish a duty roster of the nurses to take care of the sick. I knew just how popular I would be with the nurses, so I decided to use a more tactful approach. I asked for a meeting with the nurse major and asked her to handle the duty roster. It worked. Amazingly, by the time we reached the United States, we were on generally polite terms, in some cases even friendly.

My first night out on the troop ship *George Washington* was not very restful. The ship rolled from side to side. I was excited about going home, and I had difficulty calming down from my confrontation with the nurses. The ship was small and reacted very easily to the movement and moods of the Atlantic Ocean. The higher up on the various decks, the more one felt the roll of the ship. The number of cases of seasickness was very large, although we suspected that some of it was due in part to hangovers from the celebrations before boarding the ship. Most of the seasickness abated after about five days, although some people were sick during the entire trip.

About the fourth day out we sailed through a snowstorm. It was fascinating to watch a heavy snowfall land on the water and disappear. I would stand on deck until I was chilled, just to watch the storm. This was followed by a raging sea with strong winds and high waves. The *George Washington* rocked and rolled in the storm. A new round of seasickness started. At times the ship rolled over so far that we feared it would capsize. During the storm the rudder was loosened from the ship, and we floundered without steering power for forty-eight hours before it could be reattached. After the storm was over and all was back to normal, some of us found out that the ship had actually listed five degrees beyond the capsize point and had been righted by the waves and wind.

Almost from the moment the ship left Le Havre, there had been dice (crap) games going on in many parts of the ship, wherever there was a corridor wide enough and two men to play. I did not understand the game but I came to recognize the importance of certain terms such as "snake eyes," "your point," and "side bet." The games were interesting to watch because there were large sums of money at risk. Many men had been moving from place to place so frequently that their pay had accumulated, amounting to considerable sums when they were paid. The fascinating thing about these games was the honor involved, or the fear, for as the ship rolled from side to side, the money would slide on the heavily waxed floors in the direction of the ship's list, back and forth. When the ship tilted more than normal and the piles of money kept sliding, the onlookers pushed back so that not one dollar was touched by one observer. The gambling was serious business, and some players seemed to be playing for a stake in their futures. The few times I watched these games I always had a feeling that, though the players seemed not to watch or care where the money was sliding, should a hand reach out and touch a pile of the money the owner would draw back a stump.

On the morning of the twelfth day, as we were approaching New York harbor, most of the passengers rushed to get a glimpse of the Statue of Liberty. The Lady meant different things to different people: leaving the violence of war behind, seeing loved ones, renewing old friendships, love of country, victory, patriotism, even a return to bigotry. But for a few minutes most of us were joined in tilting a small ship, without discord, in order to see a statue that meant we were home.

We landed, disembarked, and were transported to Camp Shanks for debriefing and reassignment to various separation centers. We spent several days at Camp Shanks, and we filled every day with adjusting to being back in the States. Twelve nights on a rolling ship had created physical changes in our bodies, so we needed time to adjust to land. I had spent so much time walking with one knee slightly bent to keep my balance aboard ship that I had a small difficulty walking the first two days on land. The first two nights at Camp Shanks I slept very little because my balance system was geared to the roll of the ship but my bed was absolutely still.

Before I left for Fort Bragg, North Carolina, my separation center, and Noel to hers, we spent a day and a half with Noel's sister and her family. We ate great meals, posed for lots of pictures (Noel's brother-in-law was a photographer), and spent hours talking about our adventures.

I did not get home for Christmas, but I did get there shortly after. The orders relieving me from active duty were issued, effective 26 March 1946. My promotion to lieutenant colonel was effective 26 December 1945. I had reached the highest rank possible in the WAC. By law, in 1945, there could be only one full colonel, and that rank was held by the WAC director. Even as I was leaving the service there was the satisfaction that I was one Negro WAC who had made it.

Fort Bragg was about 150 miles from my hometown, Columbia, South Carolina. When I was sure that I could go, I called my father, who drove up, accompanied by my sister, to pick me up and take me home. By the time they arrived, a small hitch in my departure had taken place. During my final physical examination before release, the doctor was concerned that my pulse rate was rather high, eighty-eight beats a minute. I did my best to persuade him that my normal pulse rate was higher than average. I did not appreciate that his actions were for my own good, considering

The National Council of Negro Women, Inc.

Presents This Scroll of Honor to

Charity Edna Adams

*Lieutenant Colonel in the Women's Army Corps,
who gave distinguished service as commanding
officer of a battalion in the European theatre of
operations in the world war against fascism*

Washington, D. C.
March 15, 1946

Mary McLeod Bethune
Founder-President

The scroll of honor presented to me by the National Council of Negro Women
upon my discharge from the service

the possibility that I might have acquired a heart condition "in the line of duty." My most desperate plea was that "the Army took me with that pulse rate, I can't see why they can't let me go home with the same rate." The examining doctor put in a long-distance call to the Medical Records Office in the Pentagon to check on what I had said. The response to the call took two and one-half hours, during which time I visited with my father and sister.

The answer finally came. It had been determined at the time of my entry in the WAAC that although "the pulse rate was a little above average it was within normal ranges." At last I was going home to visit family. I was not in command of, in charge of, or responsible for anything or anyone except me.

After

For the next few weeks I indulged myself in the comforts of home and relationships with members of my family, immediate and extended. After that, I began responding to the many invitations directed to me, some to speak and some to just visit. Many of the invitations were from church groups that expressed pride in my accomplishments, and they felt that by telling my story I would provide motivation for young Negroes looking forward to the future. I had given little thought to this aspect of my life, but I now had to face it; there is no pleasure in achievement if it is not shared.

I began a round of speaking engagements and social visits. My military experiences had been interesting, at times exciting, but, more importantly, I had developed a strong sense of responsibility and personal dignity. These were the things I talked about as I related my story to interested audiences. In February I made my first trip to Florida with my parents. We spent the night in Tampa at the home of an aunt. What was memorable about this trip was that I felt the cold second only to Prestwick, Scotland. The homes had been built for semitropical weather and my visit was made during the worst cold spell on record.

Later that month I went to Tuskegee, Alabama, to visit Noel and her family. I had to change trains in Atlanta and, aboard the second train, I prepared to settle down for the trip by putting my suitcase in the overhead luggage rack. As I raised the suitcase, a young Negro corporal moved forward to help me put the bag on the rack. As he reached me, he happened to notice my rank. (I wore my uniform until my discharge the following month.) Instead of helping me, he walked right past as if he had not seen me but I heard him say, softly, "If she's strong enough to hold up those silver oak leaves, I guess she's strong enough to put her suitcase up on that rack." Acceptance of women in the military had not yet been accomplished.

My Army career was almost over. I had decided to return to Ohio State University and complete the work for my master's degree, which I had begun before I joined the corps. En route to Columbus, Ohio, to return to graduate school, I stopped in Washington, D.C., where I met with the noted Negro educator, Mary McLeod Bethune. That evening at a meeting of the National Council of Negro Women she presented me with the organization's award for distinguished service.

On 26 March 1946 it was over. The Army behind me. I was, however, not just a civilian again; I was a veteran of service to my country.

I returned to school as I had planned, but my apprehension grew. I was afraid that educational techniques might have developed beyond my ability to catch up after four years away. All of my self-confidence was suddenly dissipated. I selected courses closely related to the areas in which I still had some security remaining. I took copious notes from the lectures but did not dare participate in class discussions.

Two weeks after the beginning of that first quarter back, the professor of my philosophy of education class asked me to remain after class for a minute.

"Miss Adams," he said, "I remember you as a very active participant in other classes you had with me. You have not said a word this quarter."

"Well, Sir," military courtesy still present as I replied, "I have been away from the world of education for almost four years and I am sure that things have changed so much that any comments I have would not be relative."

"Nothing has changed. While you were away fighting to save democracy, we kept education just as it was."

How right he was. In a short time it was almost as if I could finish a sentence I had begun in 1942. The greatest problem I encountered was a professor who objected to a master's degree's being granted in only three academic quarters. With three other students to whom he had also given unacceptable grades, I found a solution to the problem through formal appeal.

Several weeks before summer graduation in 1946, I was visited by the president of Southern University. After three days of discussion, I was persuaded to sign a contract as dean of women at his college. I doubt that he was halfway back to New Orleans before I had second thoughts.

I suddenly remembered a moment in Rouen when, exhausted and discouraged, I had whispered a prayer: "Lord, if you let me do a good job as CO of this group of women, I promise that I will never again take a job which involves only women." Immediately I sent a telegram, followed by a letter, requesting release from the contract I had so recently signed. I cited the real reason for my request and was understood.

The job I did take was with the Veterans Administration in Cleveland as registration officer. I was one of the people who reviewed requests for educational benefits under the GI bill and decided whether the veteran was eligible and how much he or she would receive. The pay was good but the work was definitely not challenging. As much as possible, I used this job as an opportunity to lessen my appearance of independence and become the dependent and helpless person that everyone expected. One morning I looked up from the papers on my desk and saw a large spider hanging from its web, right over my desk. I rolled up a newspaper, stood on my desk chair, and prepared to smite the spider when it occurred to me that a "lady" would never be able to do what I was about to do. As a supervisor, my desk was rather isolated, and my actions had not drawn any attention. I climbed down from my chair, sat down, and uttered my best scream, a combination of a shriek and hysterical laughter, which drew immediate response.

One smart-aleck asked, "Who killed the spiders when you were in the Army, Colonel?"

"We did not have spiders in the Army. I am sorry to say that we had lots of jerks, and I knew how to handle them."

When I had returned to graduate school earlier that year, I had wished that I had been a better student. I had always been an honor student but never a scholar. The lack of challenge in my job turned my thoughts to the field of education. I had left teaching once, but despite all the negatives, it was more stimulating. After a year at the VA I began to look around the job market and to listen to bidders for my services.

The one talent I absolutely lacked, which had caused my much embarrassment, was musical ability. When I was asked to be the manager of a music school, I felt challenged. I had learned to run a section of the Army postal section, why not management of a music school? Subconsciously, I must have thought keeping the Miller Academy of Fine Arts in order would compensate for my lack of talent. As it turned out, my lack was my greatest asset on the new job. In all its affairs outside of the musical training, I kept the Academy running, unaffected by any sour notes, verbal and instrumental debates, and teacher-pupil differences. There was nothing I could do about any of those things.

In the service I had developed a strong sense of accountability, so when the owner of the music school began to override my decisions regarding reimbursement for his personal expenses (one Monday morning I discovered the operating funds almost depleted by the purchase of a Cadillac convertible), I knew that it was time for me to move along.

I returned to the field of education, serving as dean of Student Personnel Services at Tennessee A&I College (now University) and Georgia State College (now Savannah State College). At both colleges my special concern was for freshman students, who, having spent those years all the way through high school in protected situations, were suddenly thrust into independence. I remembered my own freshman year in college and tried to keep my door open, to be a resource for the young and uncertain.

After a year and a half at Georgia State College, on 24 August 1949, I was married. My husband was a medical student at the University of Zurich, in Switzerland. After a brief honeymoon and all the required Swiss permits, we moved to Zurich for the completion of his medical training. To survive in the German-speaking section of Switzerland, I had to learn the language, so I enrolled in the Minerva Institute (an educational institution above our high school level and more closely related to the American junior or technical college) for the senior year, with all classes conducted in high German.

After ten months it was determined that my skill in the German language was sufficient to enable me to enroll in the university. For the next two years I took courses at the University of Zurich and, during the second year, at the Jungian Institute of Analytical Psychology.

By the time my husband finished his training and it was time for us to return to the States, I was expecting our first child. He returned home by ship, accompanied by our belongings, while I flew home by Swissair, accompanied by, I found out later, a sterile delivery kit — just in case.

After my second child was born, I began to be involved in community affairs. I have served, and am serving, on committees, task forces, and boards, encompassing the areas of human and social services, education, civic affairs, and, in recent years, corporate business. From each area I have increased my knowledge of the state of our society and hope that, along the way, I have made some valuable contributions.

The trailblazing by the women who served in the military during World War II has been virtually ignored and forgotten. That is why I have written my story. In truth, I have accomplished much since my military service. I have opened a few doors, broken a few barriers, and, I hope, smoothed the way to some degree for the next generation. The problems that were my concern during my service, and to which I have devoted my energies, are still with us — but I keep trying.

Index

One Woman's Army was composed into type on a Compugraphic digital phototypesetter in ten point Times Roman with two points of spacing between the lines. Time Roman was also selected for display. The book was designed by Jim Billingsley, typeset by Metricomp, Inc., printed offset by Thomson-Shore, Inc., and bound by John H. Dekker & Sons. The paper on which the book is printed is designed for an effective life of at least three hundred years.

TEXAS A&M UNIVERSITY PRESS : COLLEGE STATION